11
ARISA

Contents

ARISA

Secret King's Room

The story so far

Tsubasa and Arisa are twin sisters living apart. They finally reunited after three years, but then Arisa jumped out her bedroom window right in front of Tsubasa, and went into a coma.

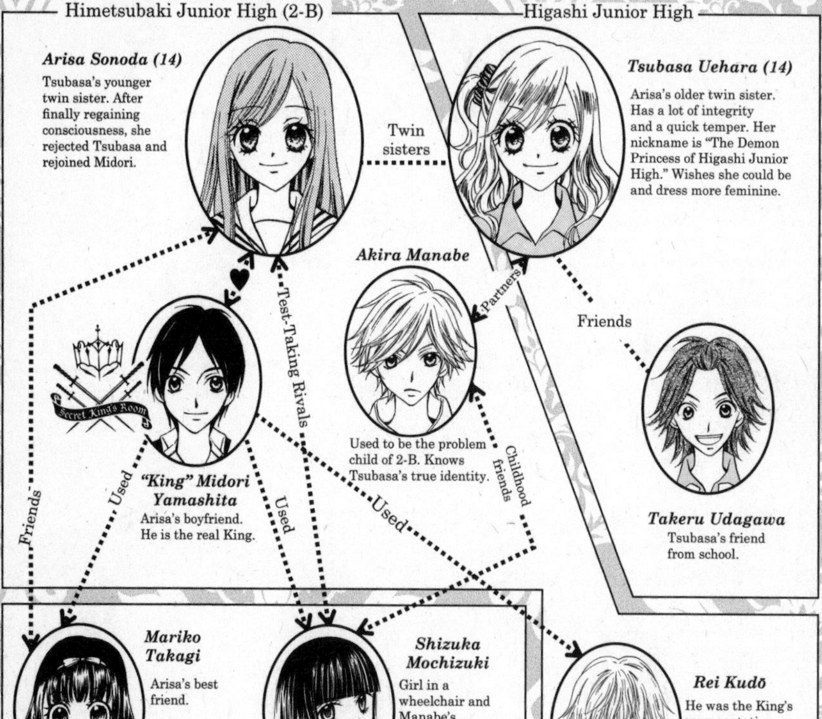

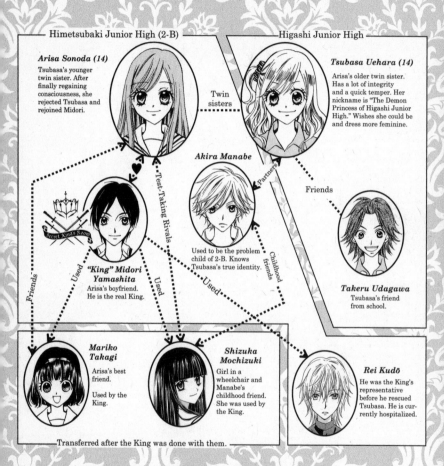

Himetsubaki Junior High (2-B)
Higashi Junior High
Arisa Sonoda (14)
Tsubasa's younger twin sister. After finally regaining consciousness, she rejected Tsubasa and rejoined Midori.
Twin sisters
Tsubasa Uehara (14)
Arisa's older twin sister. Has a lot of integrity and a quick temper. Her nickname is "The Demon Princess of Higashi Junior High." Wishes she could be and dress more feminine.
Akira Manabe
Partners
Friends
Test-Taking Rivals
Secret King's Room
Used to be the problem child of 2-B. Knows Tsubasa's true identity.
Childhood friends
"King" Midori Yamashita
Arisa's boyfriend. He is the real King.
Friends
Used
Used
Used
Takeru Udagawa
Tsubasa's friend from school.
Mariko Takagi
Arisa's best friend.
Used by the King.
Shizuka Mochizuki
Girl in a wheelchair and Manabe's childhood friend. She was used by the King.
Rei Kudō
He was the King's representative before he rescued Tsubasa. He is currently hospitalized.
Transferred after the King was done with them.

In order to discover the secrets Arisa was hiding, Tsubasa pretended to be her and attended Himetsubaki Junior High. Upon learning that someone known on the Internet as the "King" ruled class 2-B, she began digging for his secrets. Despite falling for Midori's trap and getting locked in a room with explosives, she discovered that the King is Arisa's boyfriend, Midori Yamashita. Kudō managed to save her, but all that awaited Tsubasa after her close encounter with death was Arisa's cold shoulder! Arisa chose to stay with Midori even after finding out his true identity!!

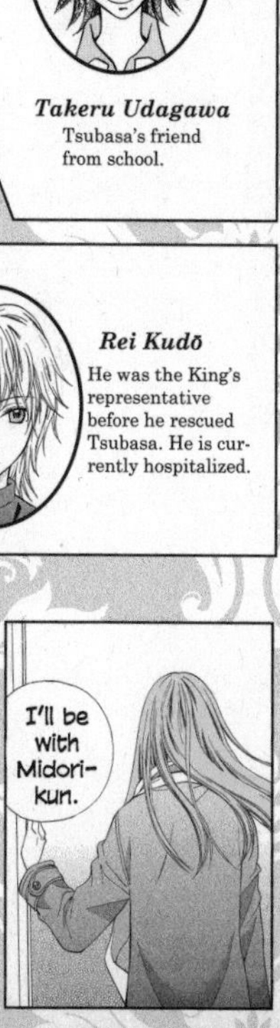

I'll be with Midori-kun.

ARISA

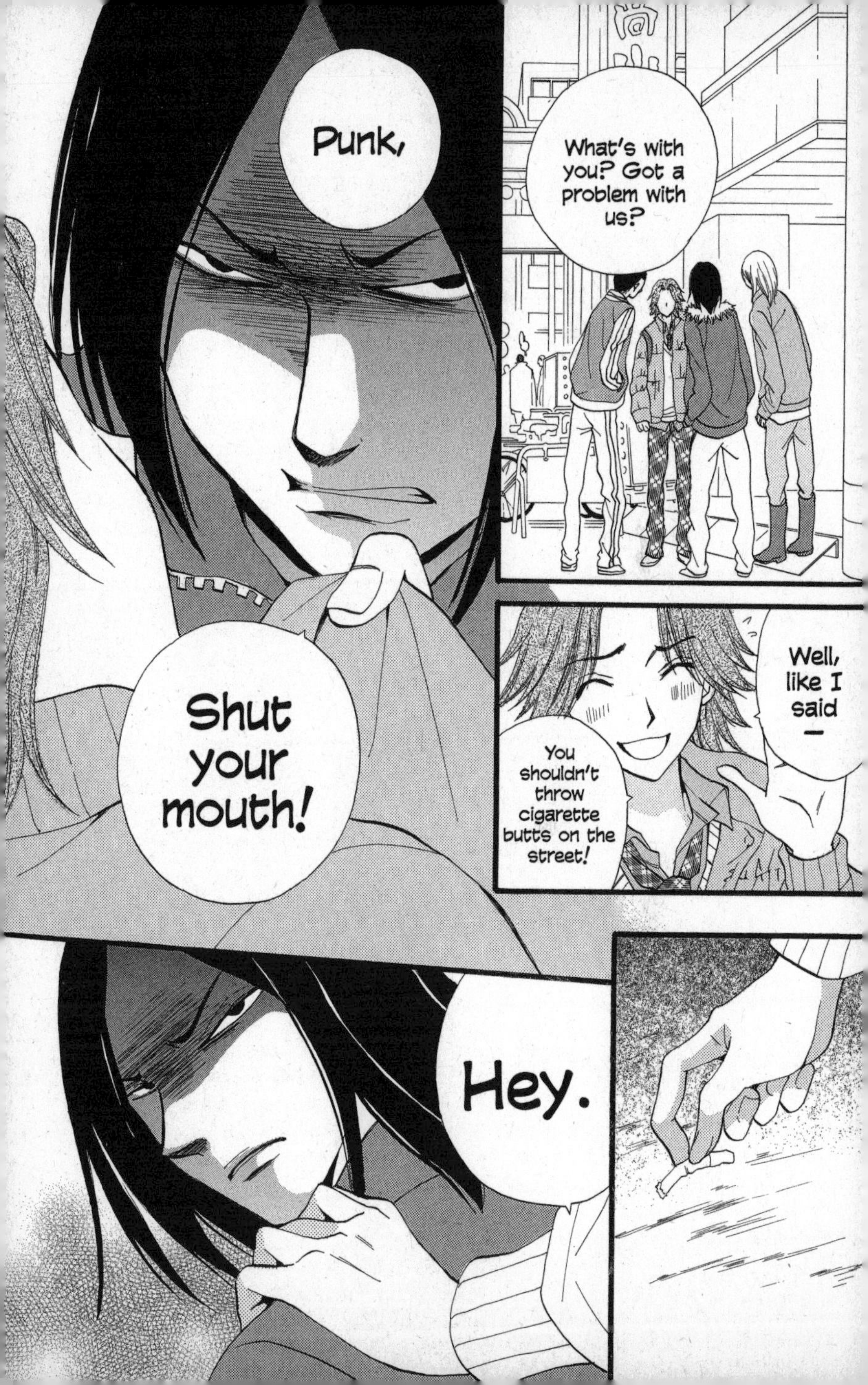
What's with you? Got a problem with us?
Well, like I said —
You shouldn't throw cigarette butts on the street!
Punk,
Shut your mouth!
Hey.

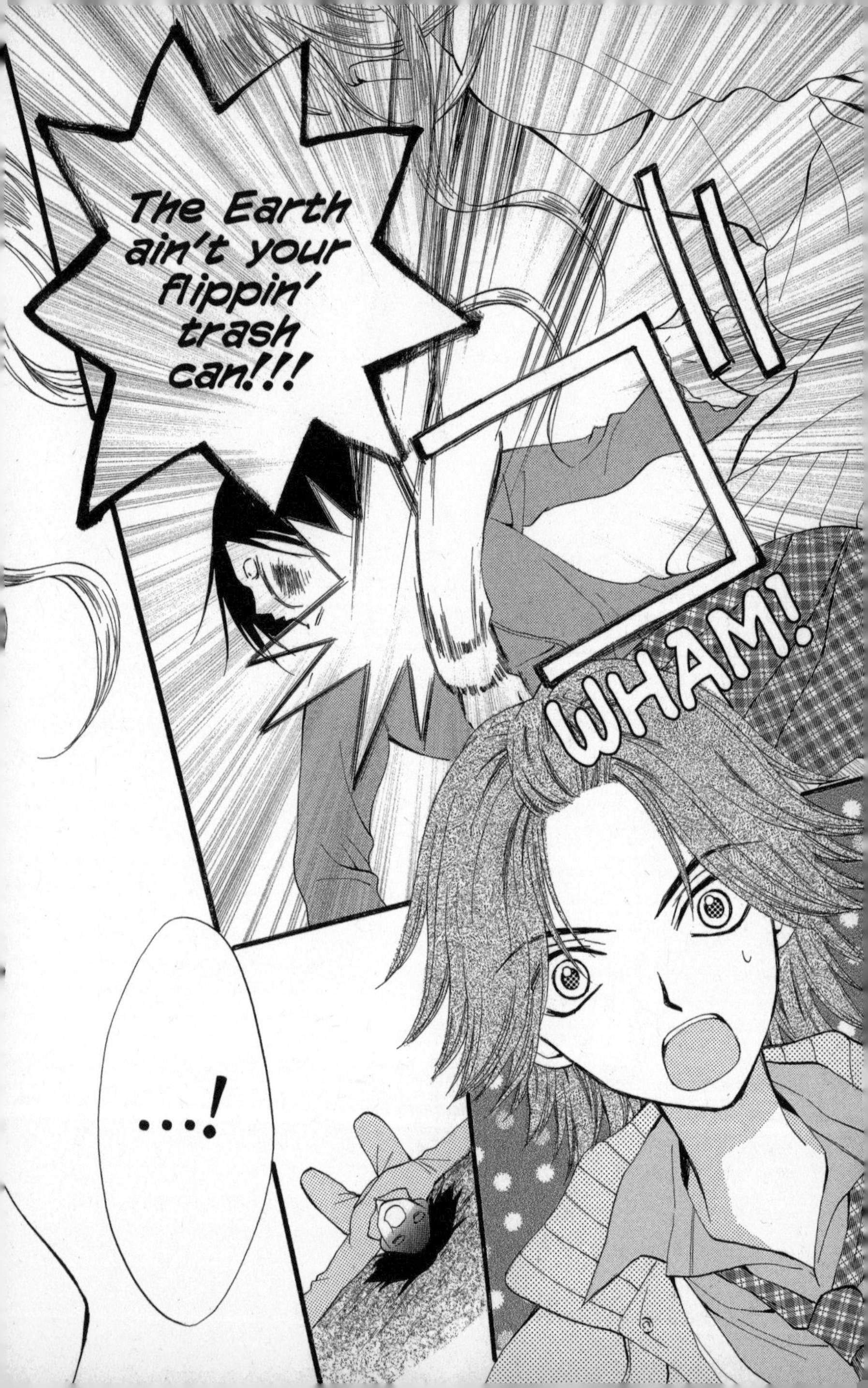
The Earth ain't your flippin' trash can!!!
WHAM!
...!

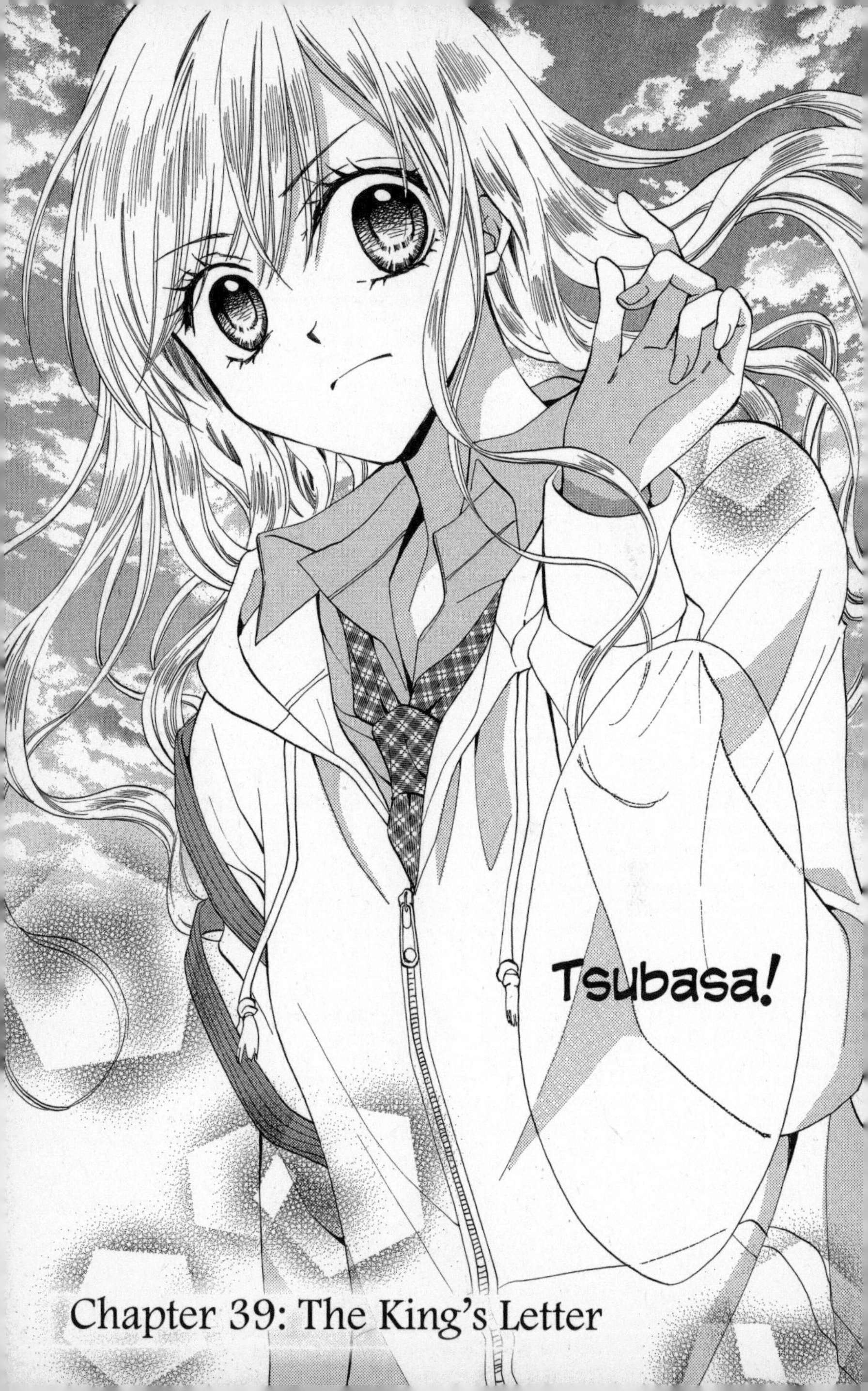
Tsubasa!

Chapter 39: The King's Letter

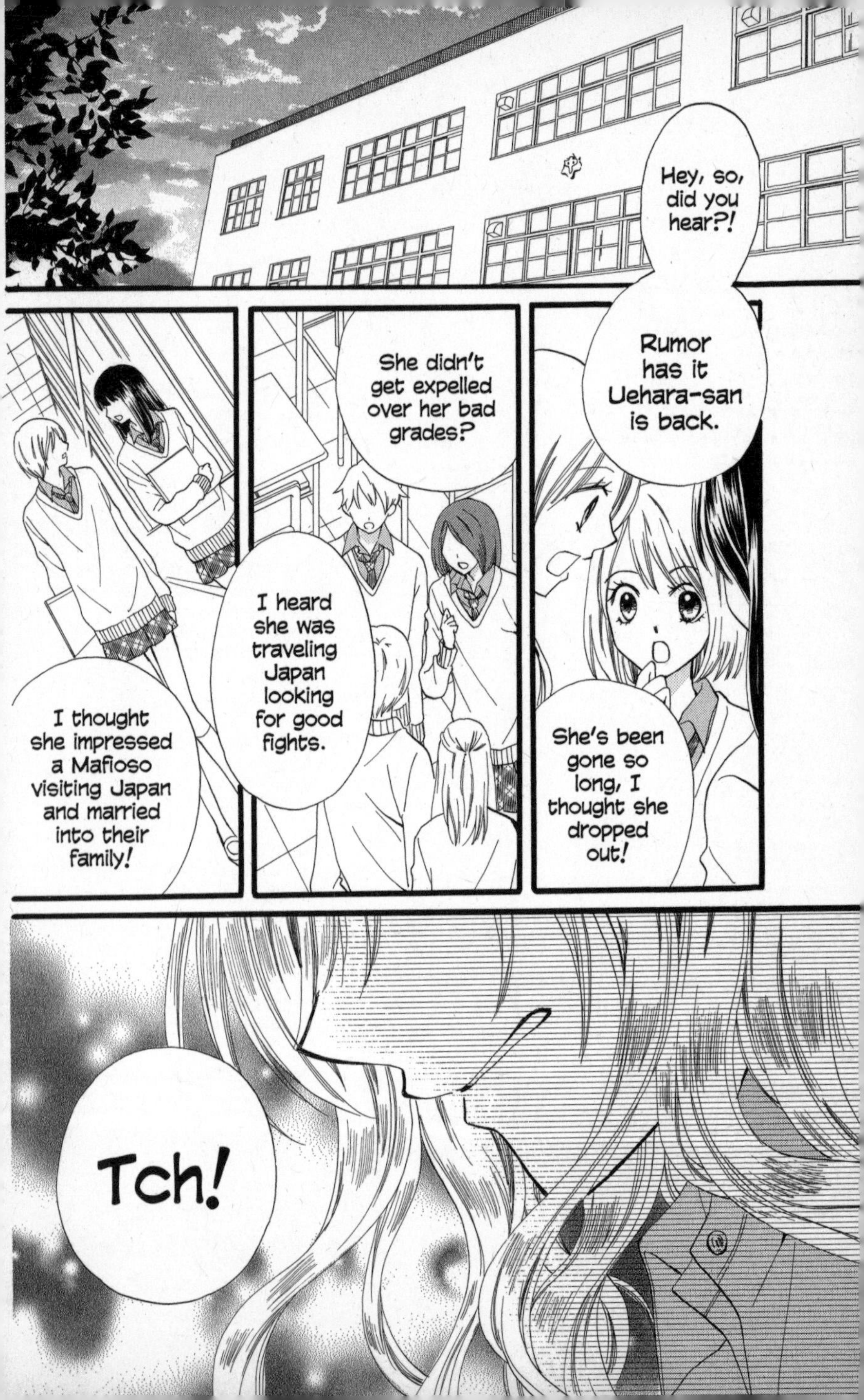
Hey, so, did you hear?!
Rumor has it Uehara-san is back.
She's been gone so long, I thought she dropped out!
She didn't get expelled over her bad grades?
I heard she was traveling Japan looking for good fights.
I thought she impressed a Mafioso visiting Japan and married into their family!
Tch!

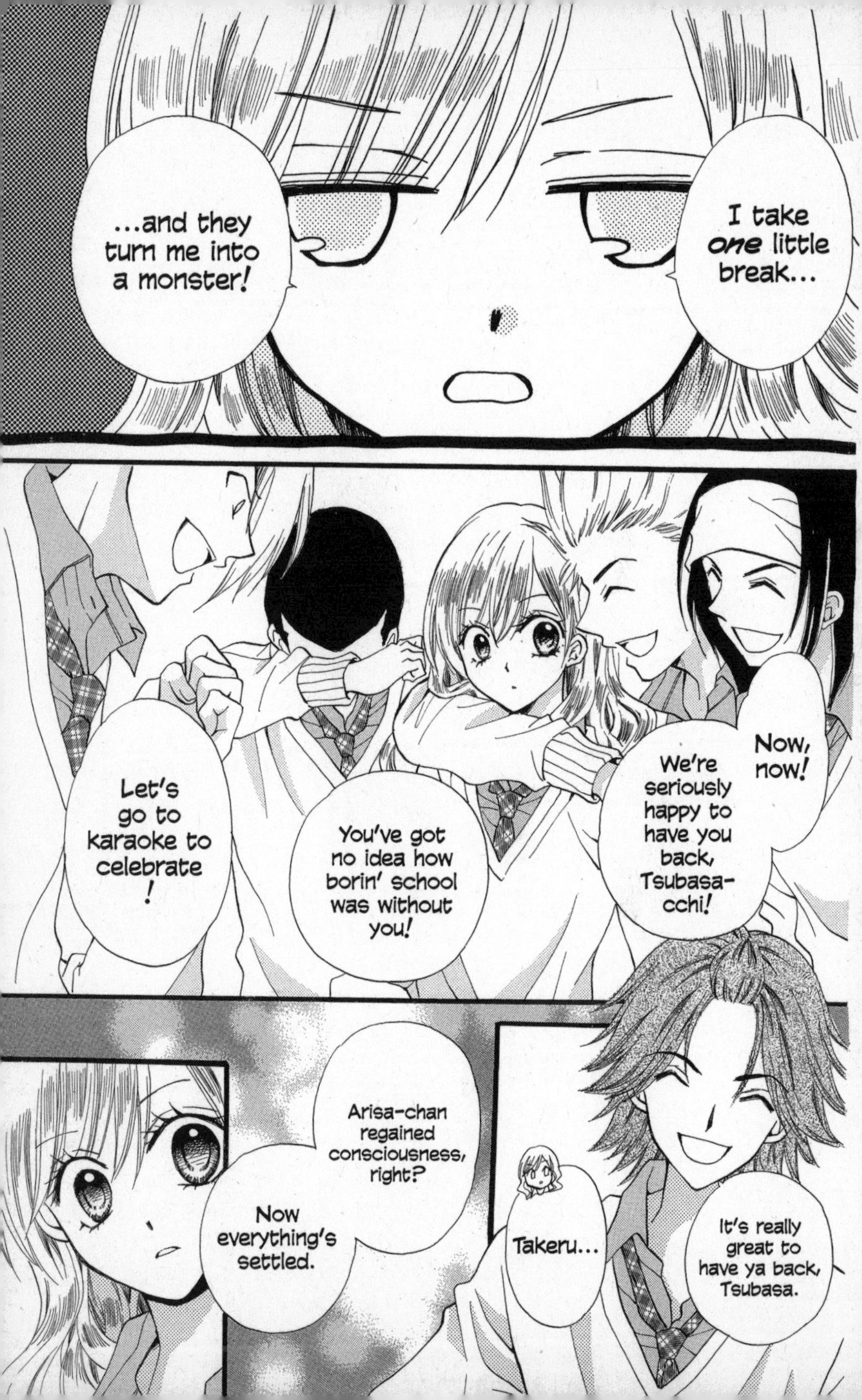
I take *one* little break...
...and they turn me into a monster!
Now, now!
We're seriously happy to have you back, Tsubasa-cchi!
You've got no idea how borin' school was without you!
Let's go to karaoke to celebrate!
It's really great to have ya back, Tsubasa.
Takeru...
Arisa-chan regained consciousness, right?
Now everything's settled.

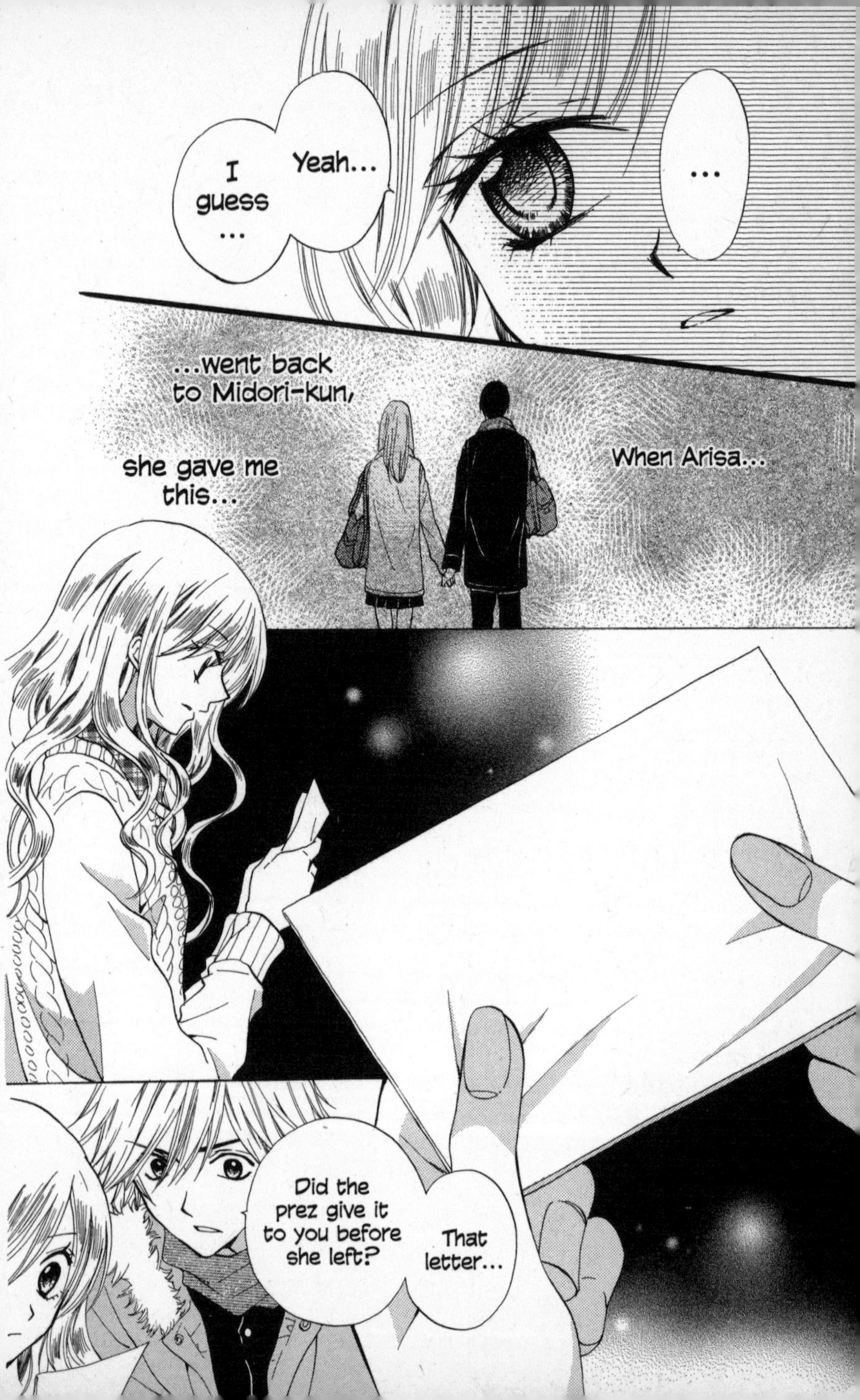
...
Yeah... I guess...
When Arisa...
...went back to Midori-kun,
she gave me this...
That letter...
Did the prez give it to you before she left?

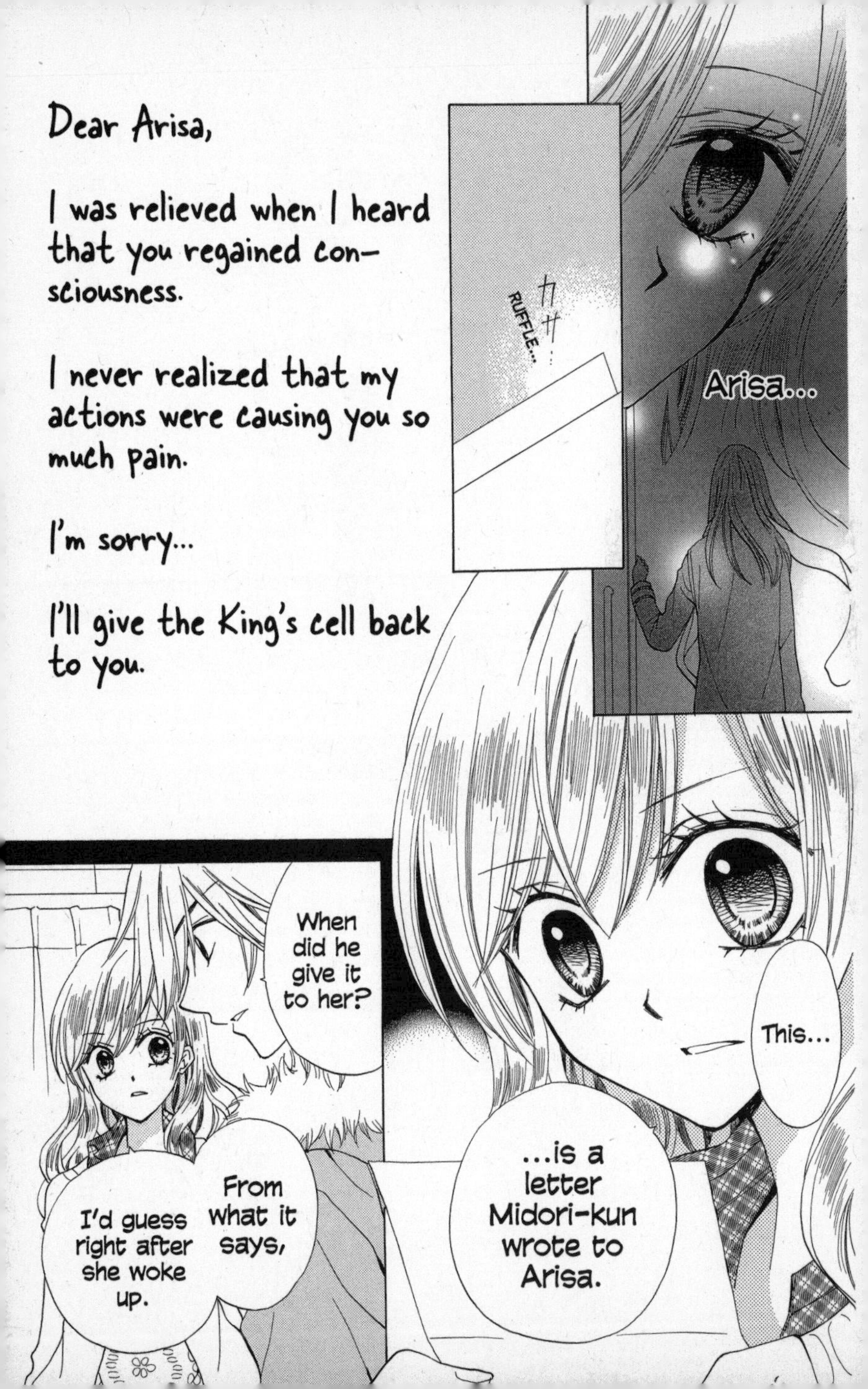
Arisa...
カサ…
RUFFLE...
Dear Arisa,
I was relieved when I heard that you regained consciousness.
I never realized that my actions were causing you so much pain.
I'm sorry...
I'll give the King's cell back to you.
This...
...is a letter Midori-kun wrote to Arisa.
When did he give it to her?
From what it says,
I'd guess right after she woke up.

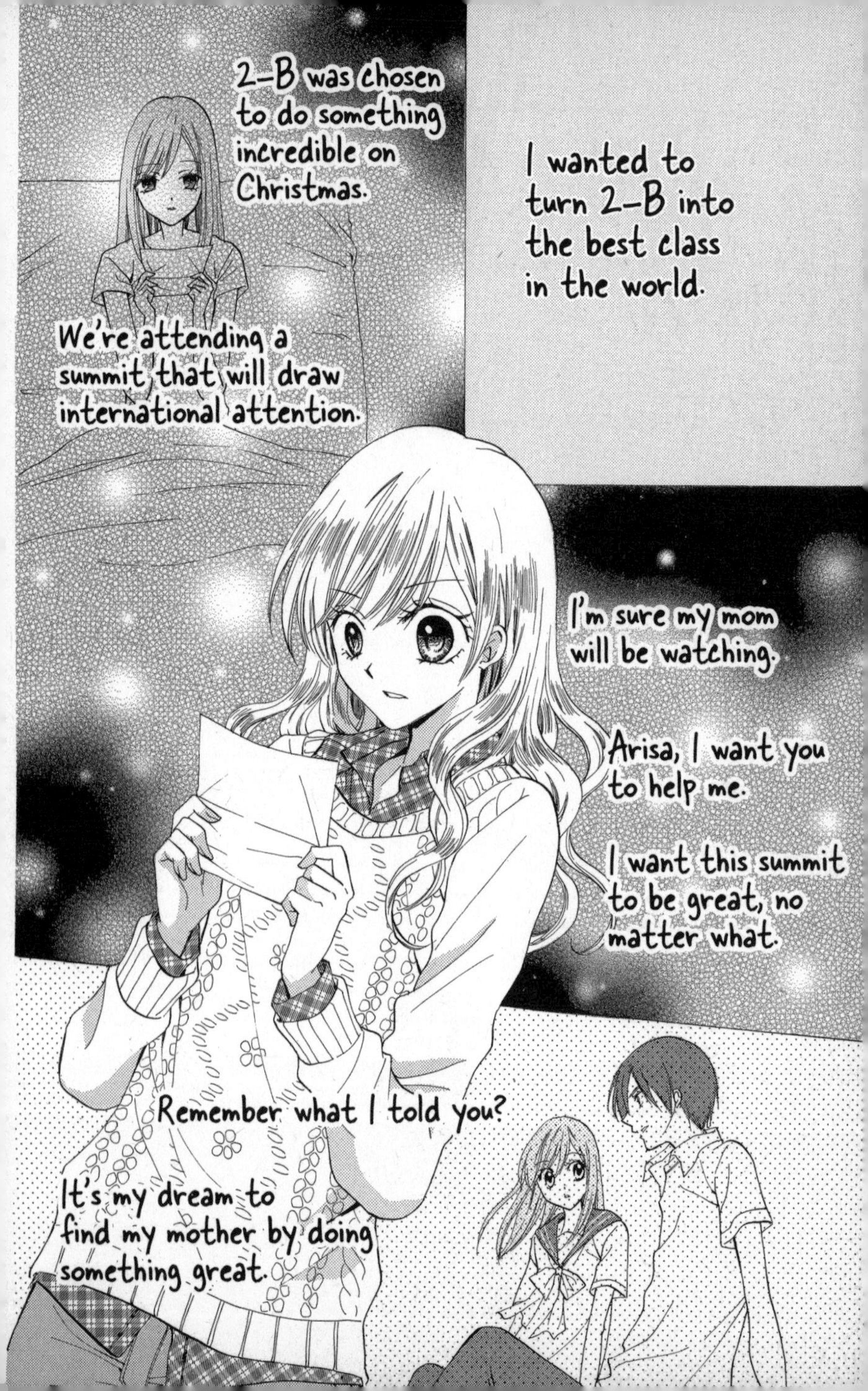
I wanted to turn 2-B into the best class in the world.
2-B was chosen to do something incredible on Christmas.
We're attending a summit that will draw international attention.
I'm sure my mom will be watching.
Arisa, I want you to help me.
I want this summit to be great, no matter what.
Remember what I told you?
It's my dream to find my mother by doing something great.

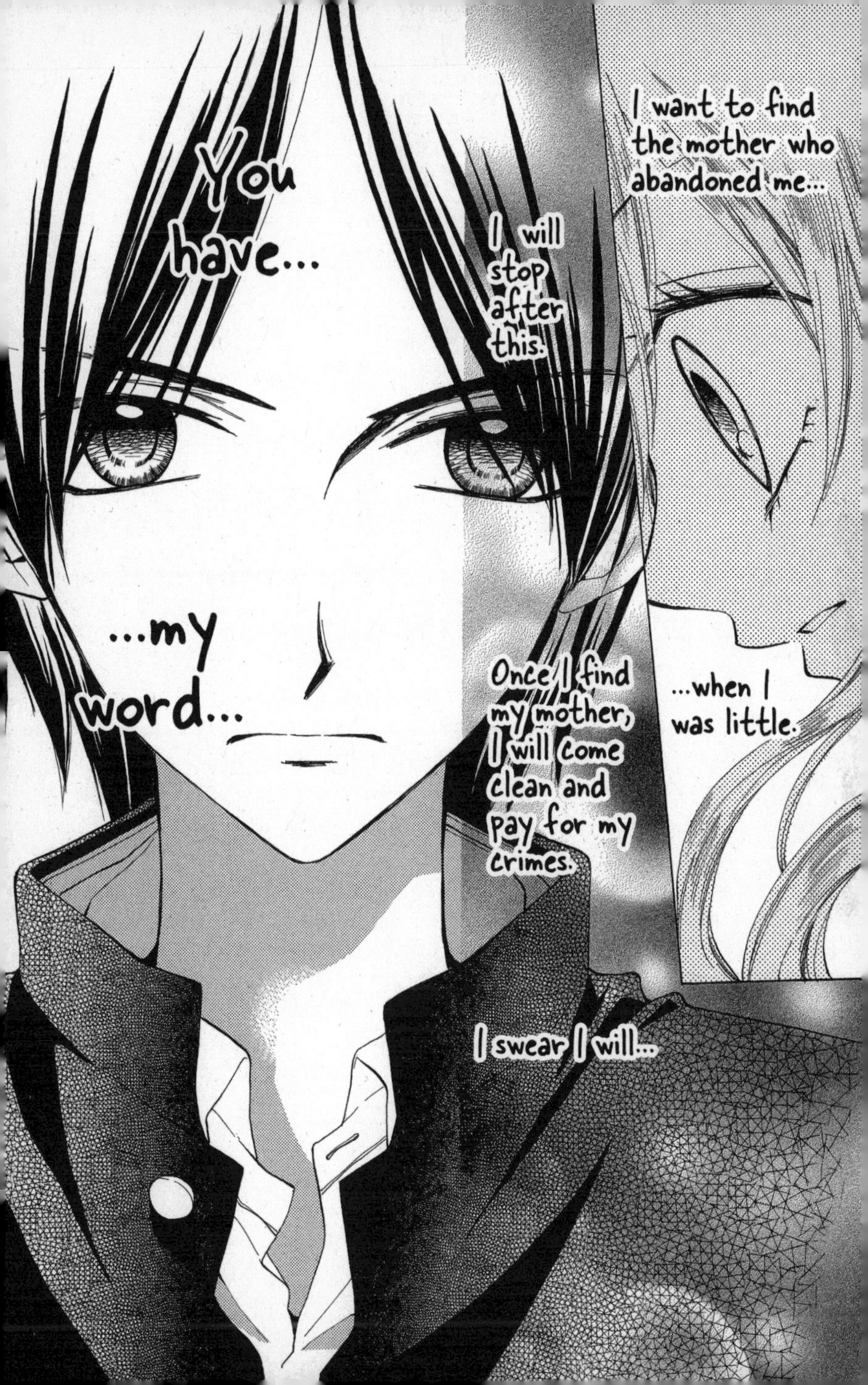
I want to find the mother who abandoned me...
...when I was little.
I will stop after this.
You have...
Once I find my mother, I will come clean and pay for my crimes.
...my word...
I swear I will...

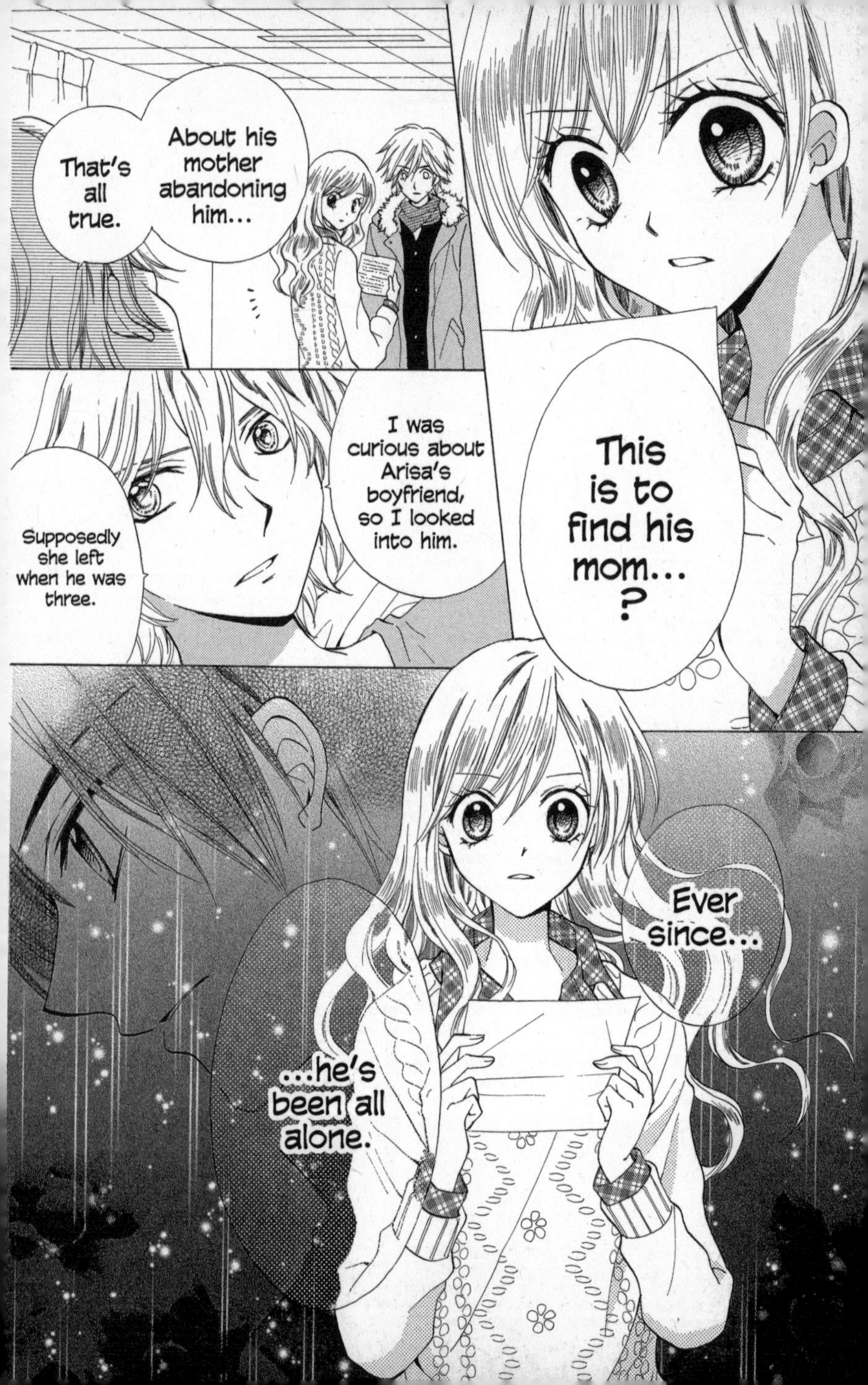
This is to find his mom...?
About his mother abandoning him...
That's all true.
I was curious about Arisa's boyfriend, so I looked into him.
Supposedly she left when he was three.
Ever since...
...he's been all alone.

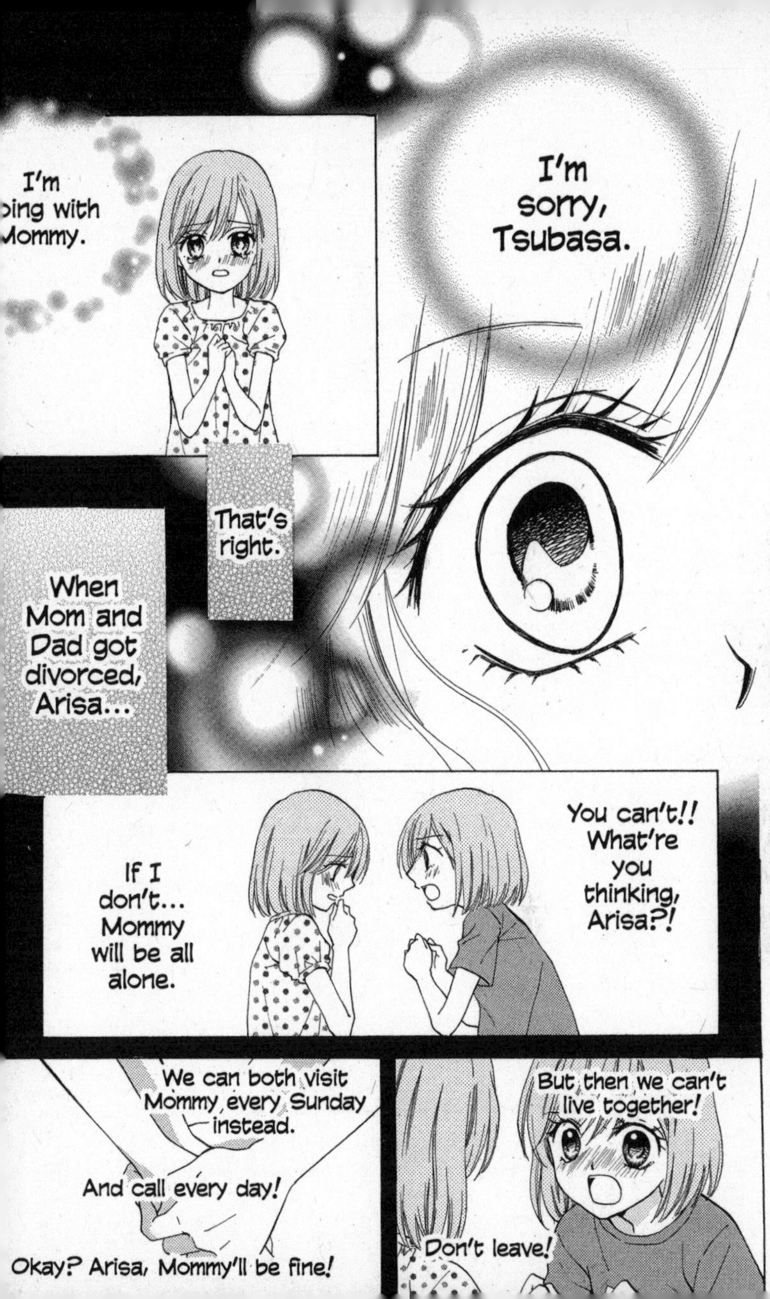
I'm sorry, Tsubasa.
I'm
oing with
Mommy.
That's right.
When Mom and Dad got divorced, Arisa...
You can't!! What're you thinking, Arisa?!
If I don't... Mommy will be all alone.
But then we can't live together!
Don't leave!
We can both visit Mommy every Sunday instead.
And call every day!
Okay? Arisa, Mommy'll be fine!

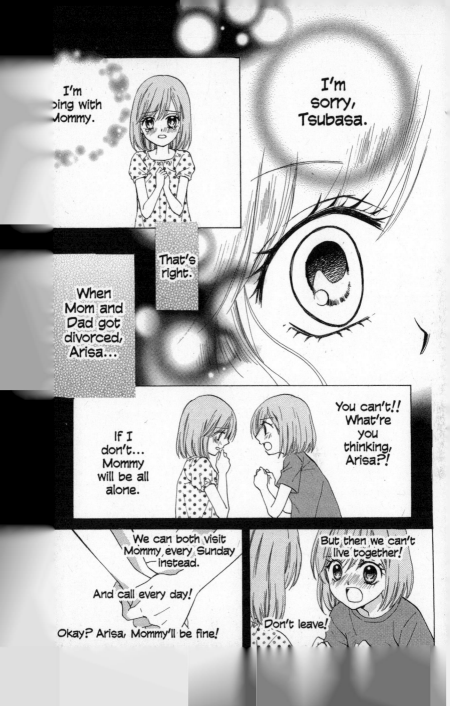

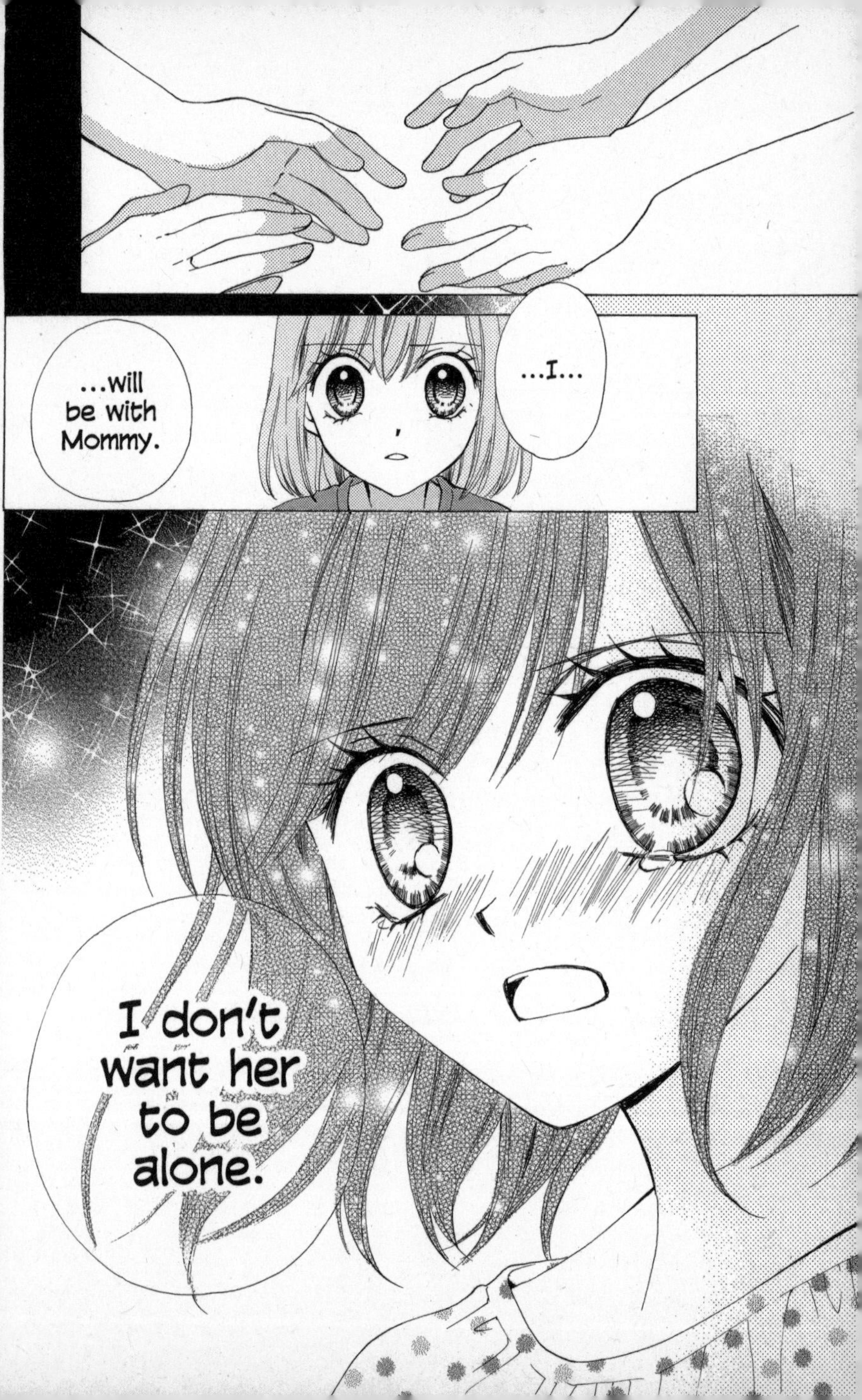
...I...
...will be with Mommy.
I don't want her to be alone.

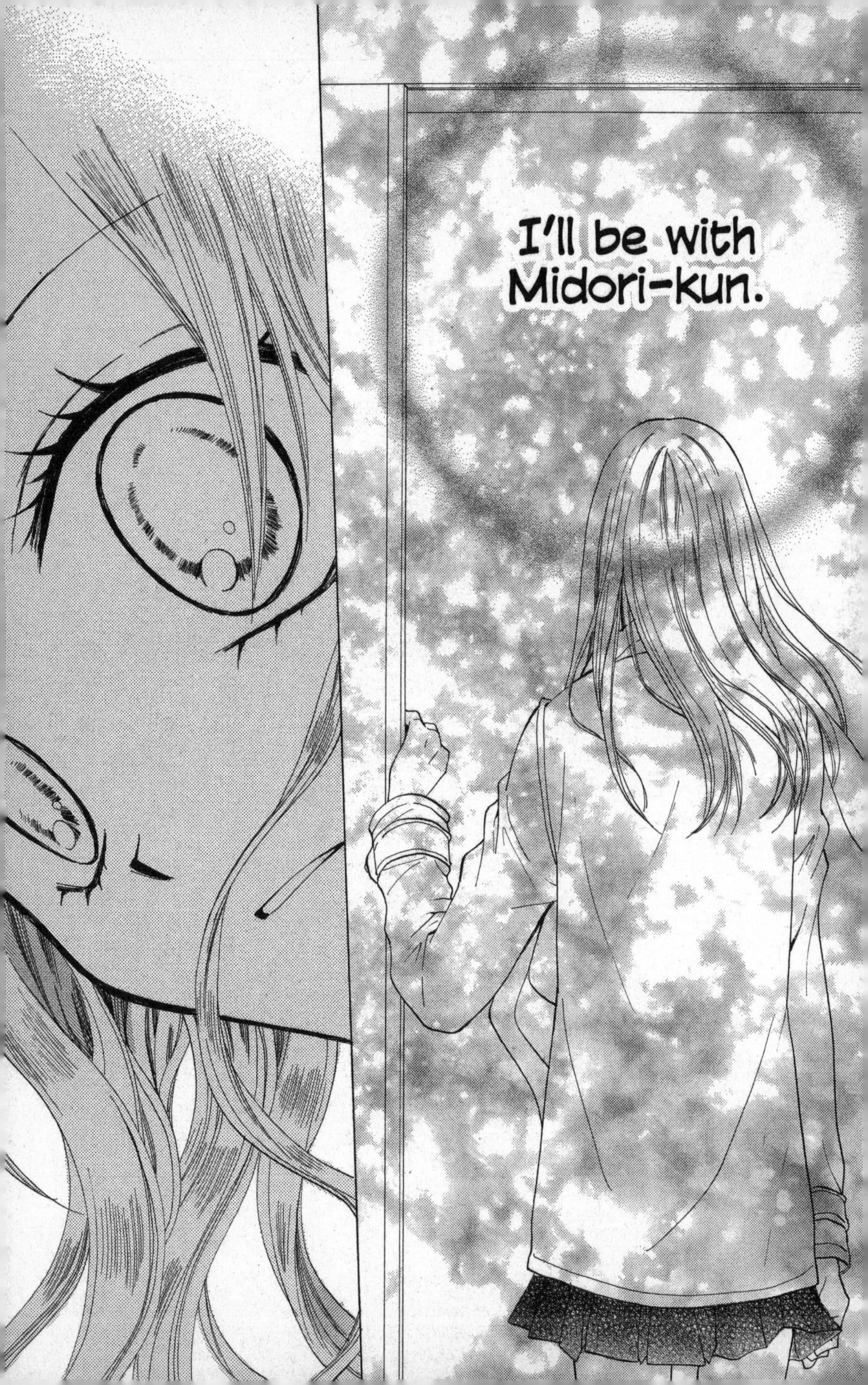
I'll be with Midori-kun.

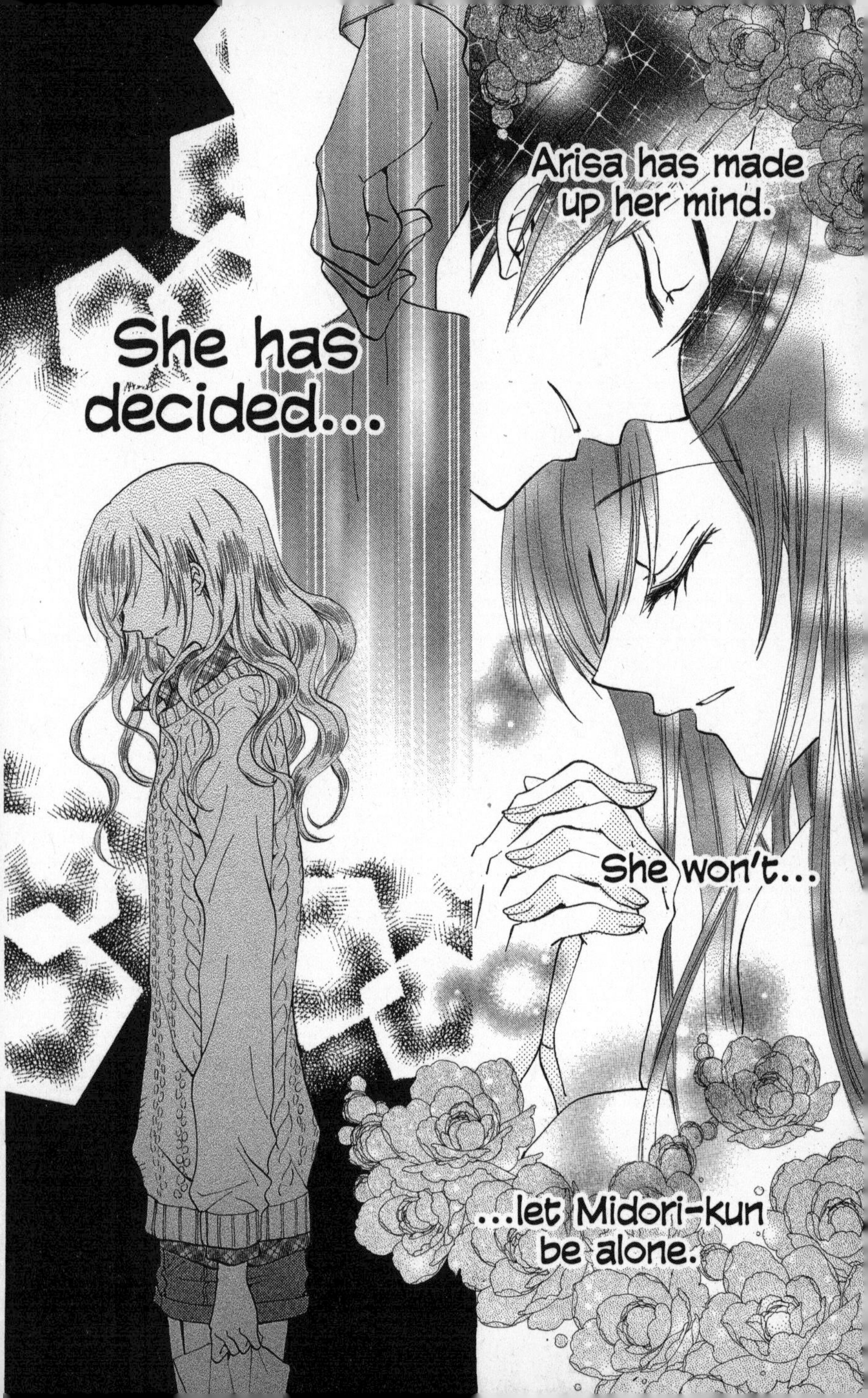
Arisa has made up her mind.
She has decided...
She won't...
...let Midori-kun be alone.

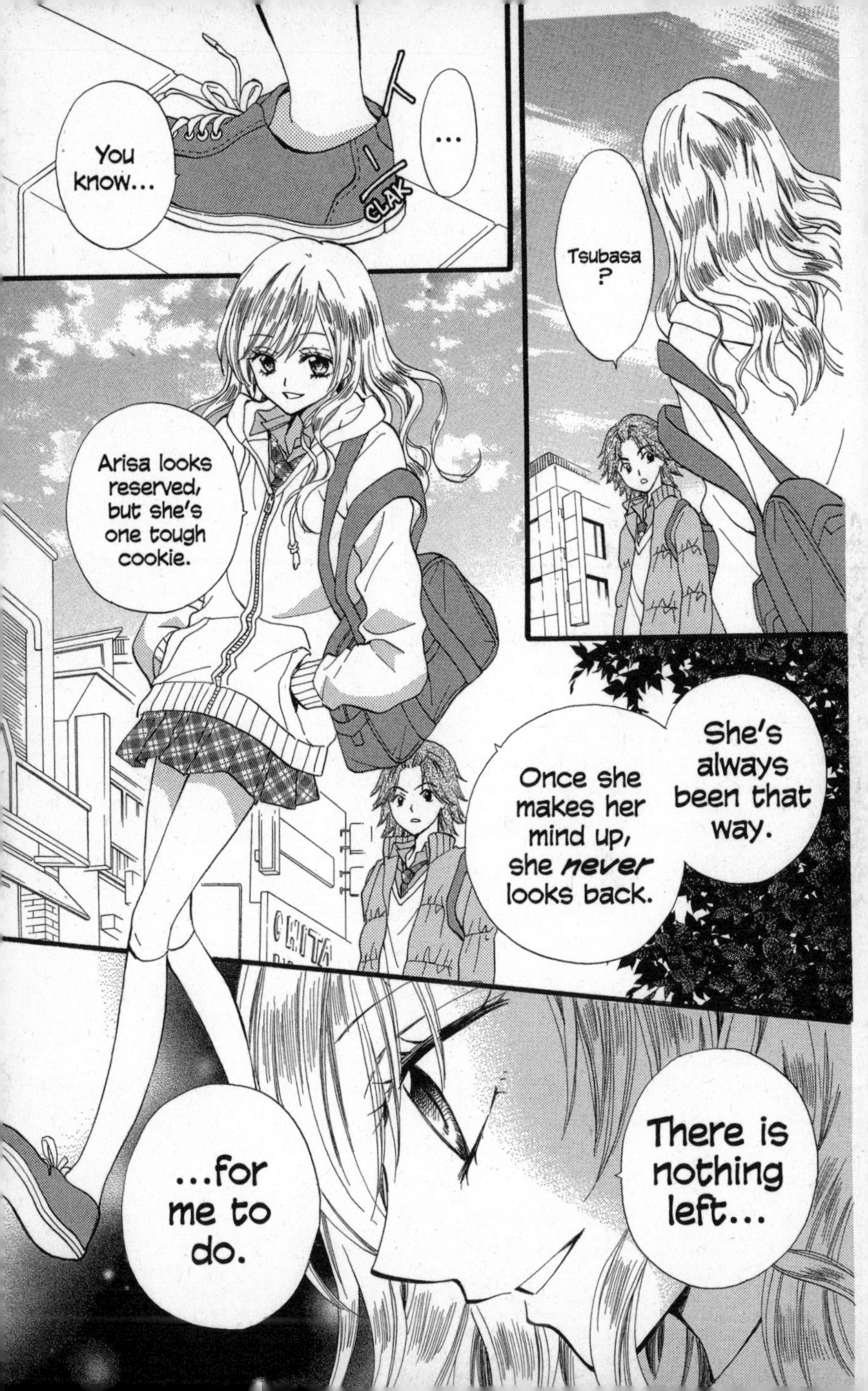
Tsubasa?
...
CLAK
You know...
Arisa looks reserved, but she's one tough cookie.
She's always been that way.
Once she makes her mind up, she *never* looks back.
There is nothing left...
...for me to do.

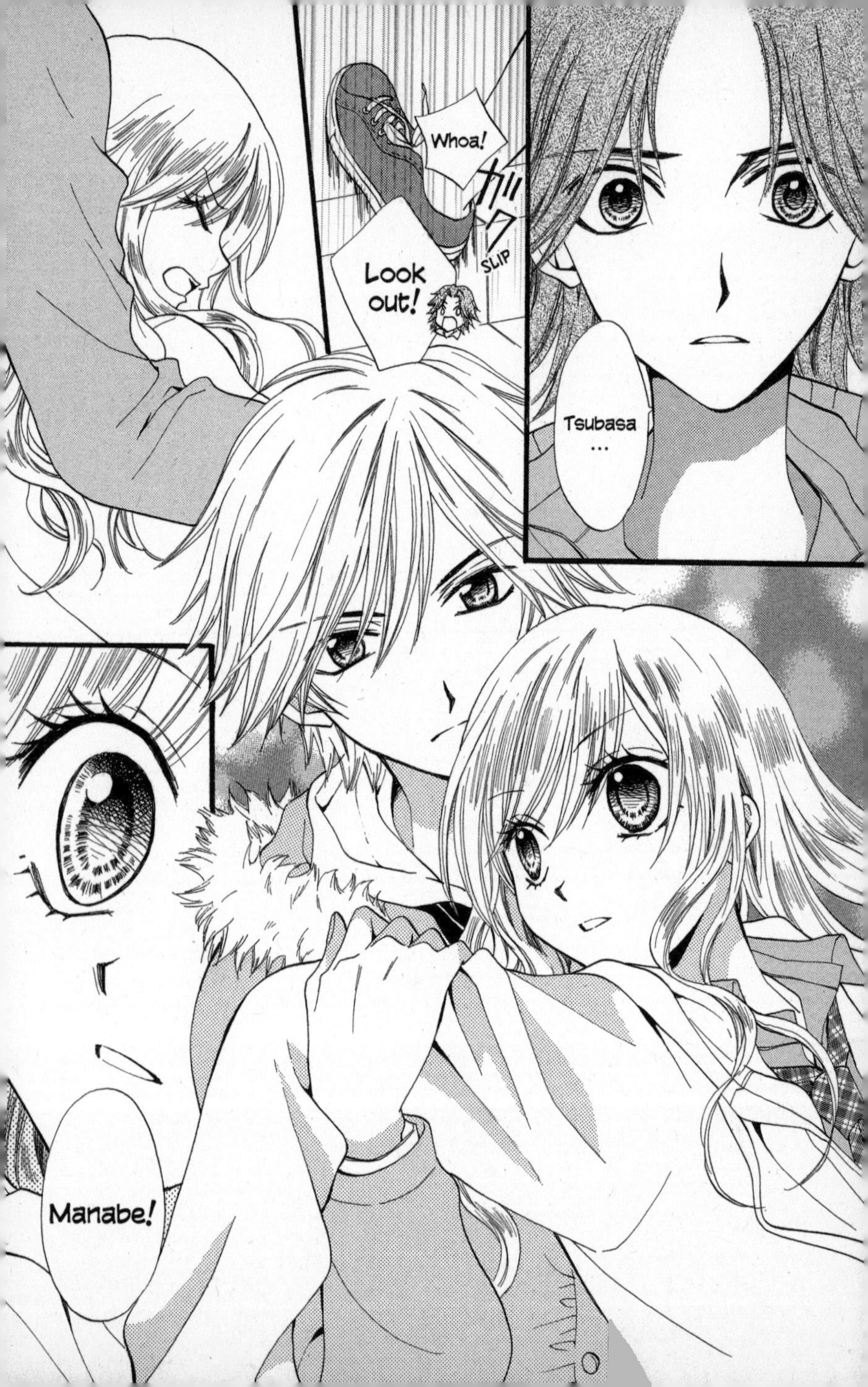
Tsubasa
...
Whoa!
ガク
SLIP
Look out!
Manabe!

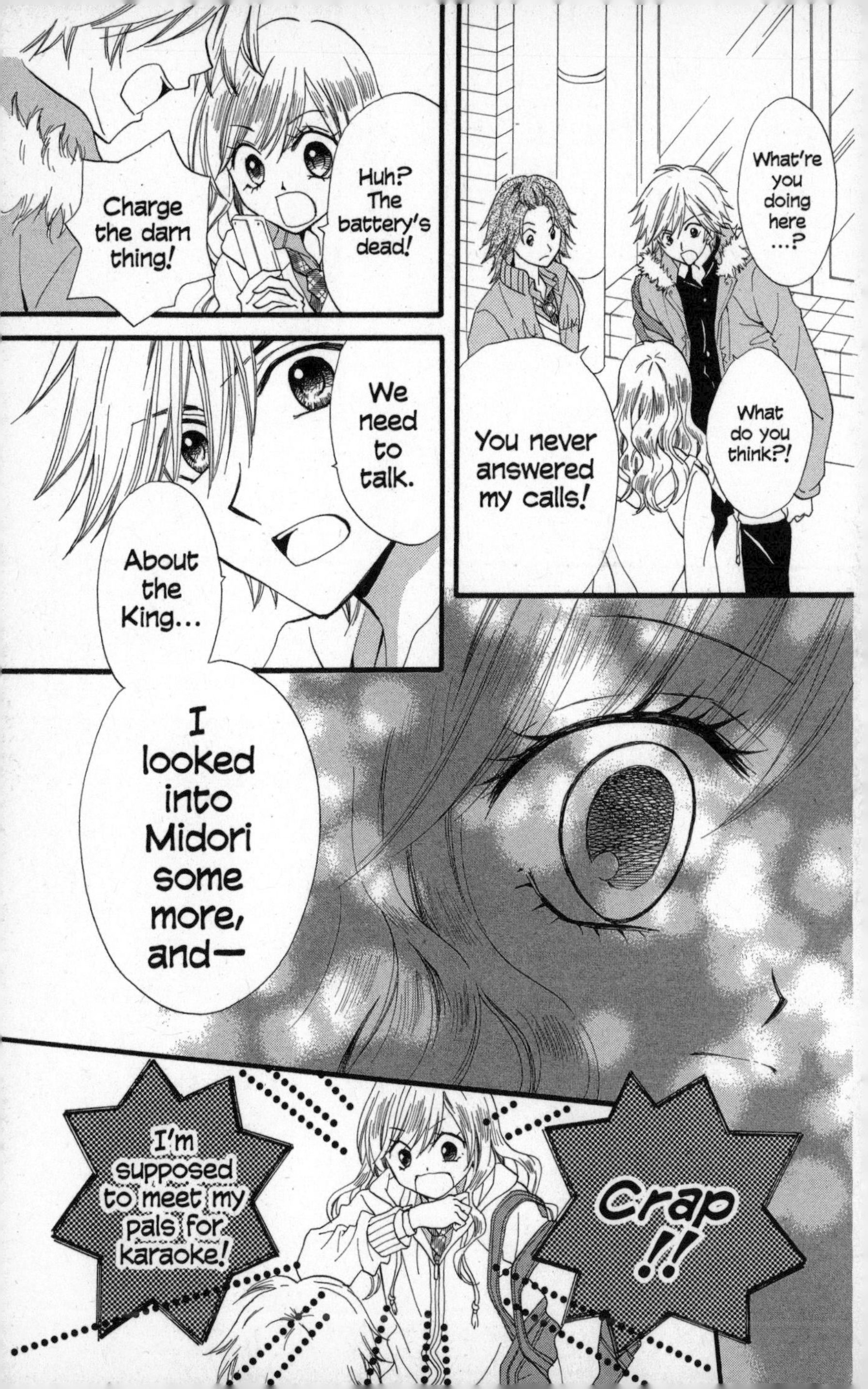
What're you doing here ...?
What do you think?!
You never answered my calls!
Huh? The battery's dead!
Charge the darn thing!
We need to talk.
About the King...
I looked into Midori some more, and—
Crap!!
I'm supposed to meet my pals for karaoke!

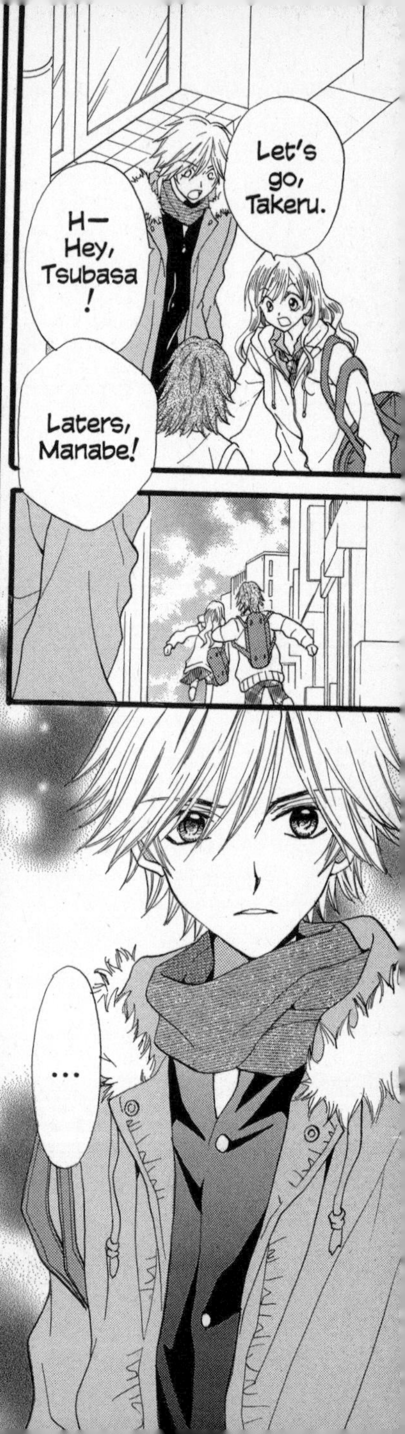
Let's go, Takeru.
H— Hey, Tsubasa!
Laters, Manabe!
...

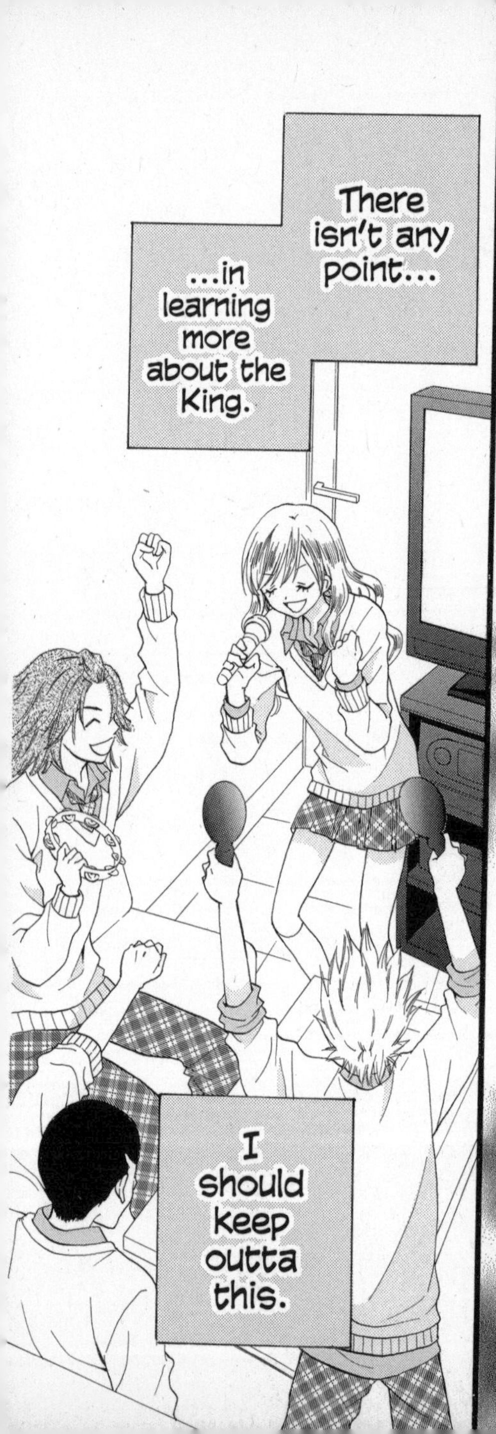
There isn't any point...
...in learning more about the King.
I should keep outta this.

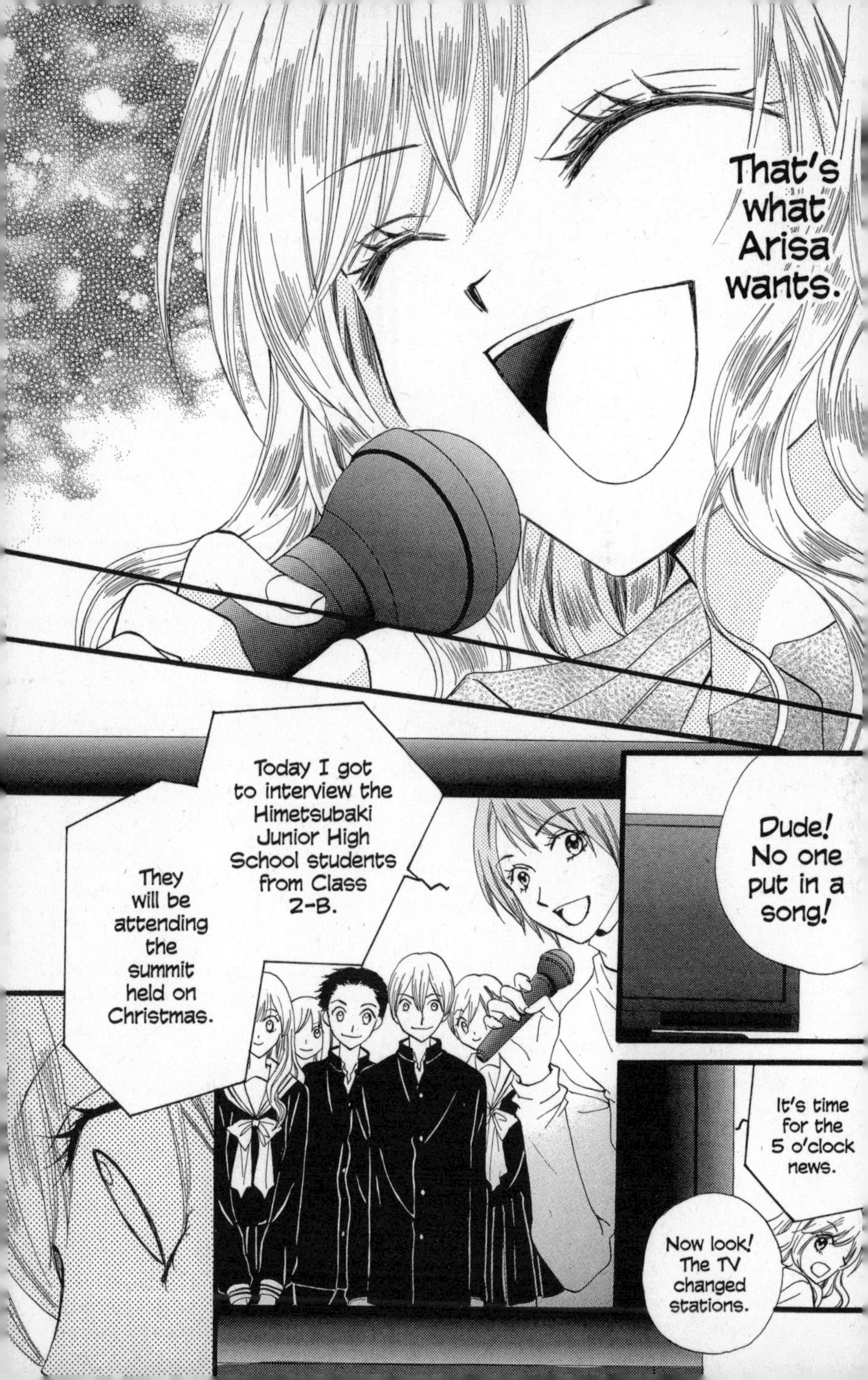
That's what Arisa wants.
Dude! No one put in a song!
It's time for the 5 o'clock news.
Now look! The TV changed stations.
Today I got to interview the Himetsubaki Junior High School students from Class 2-B.
They will be attending the summit held on Christmas.

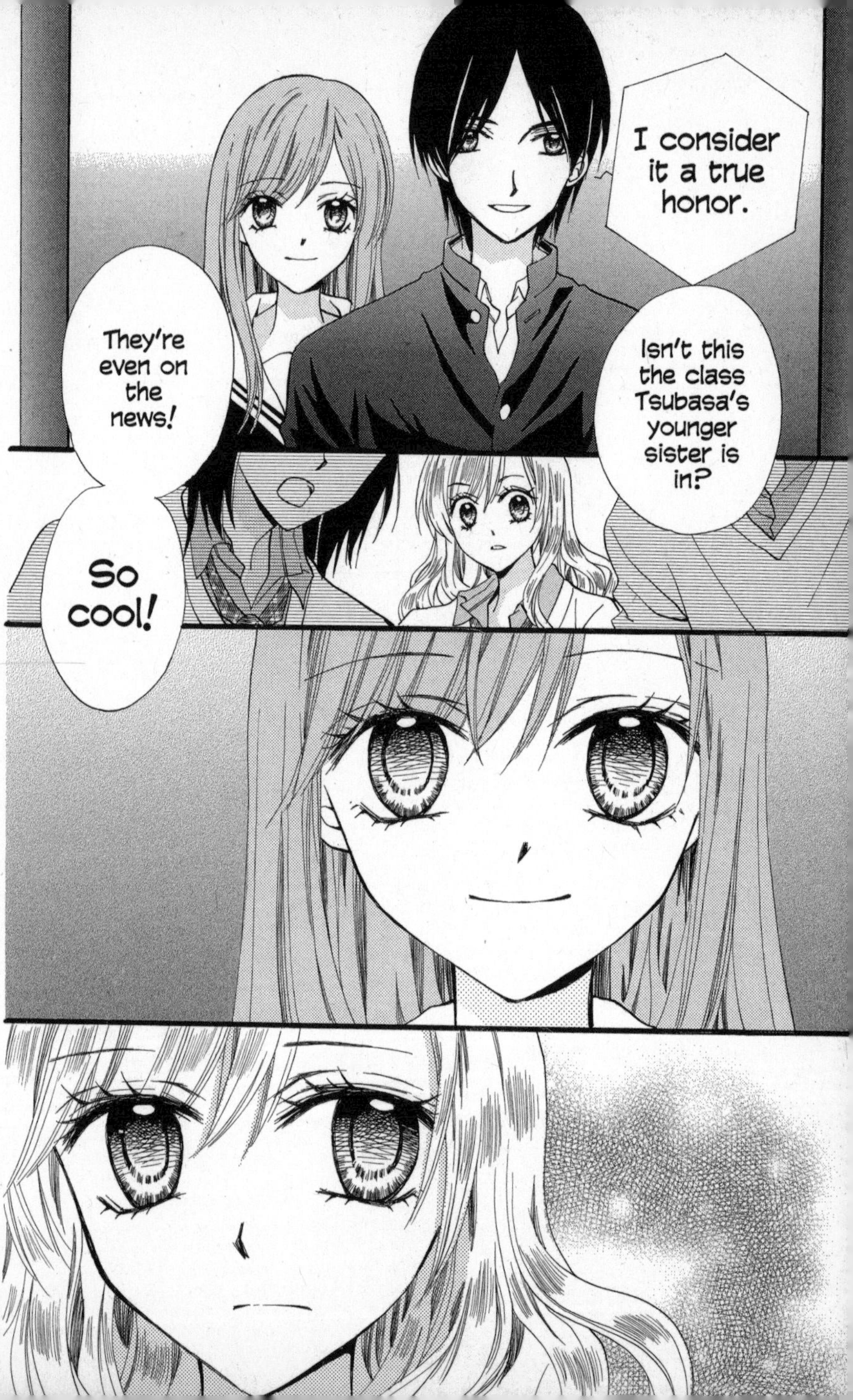
I consider it a true honor.
They're even on the news!
Isn't this the class Tsubasa's younger sister is in?
So cool!

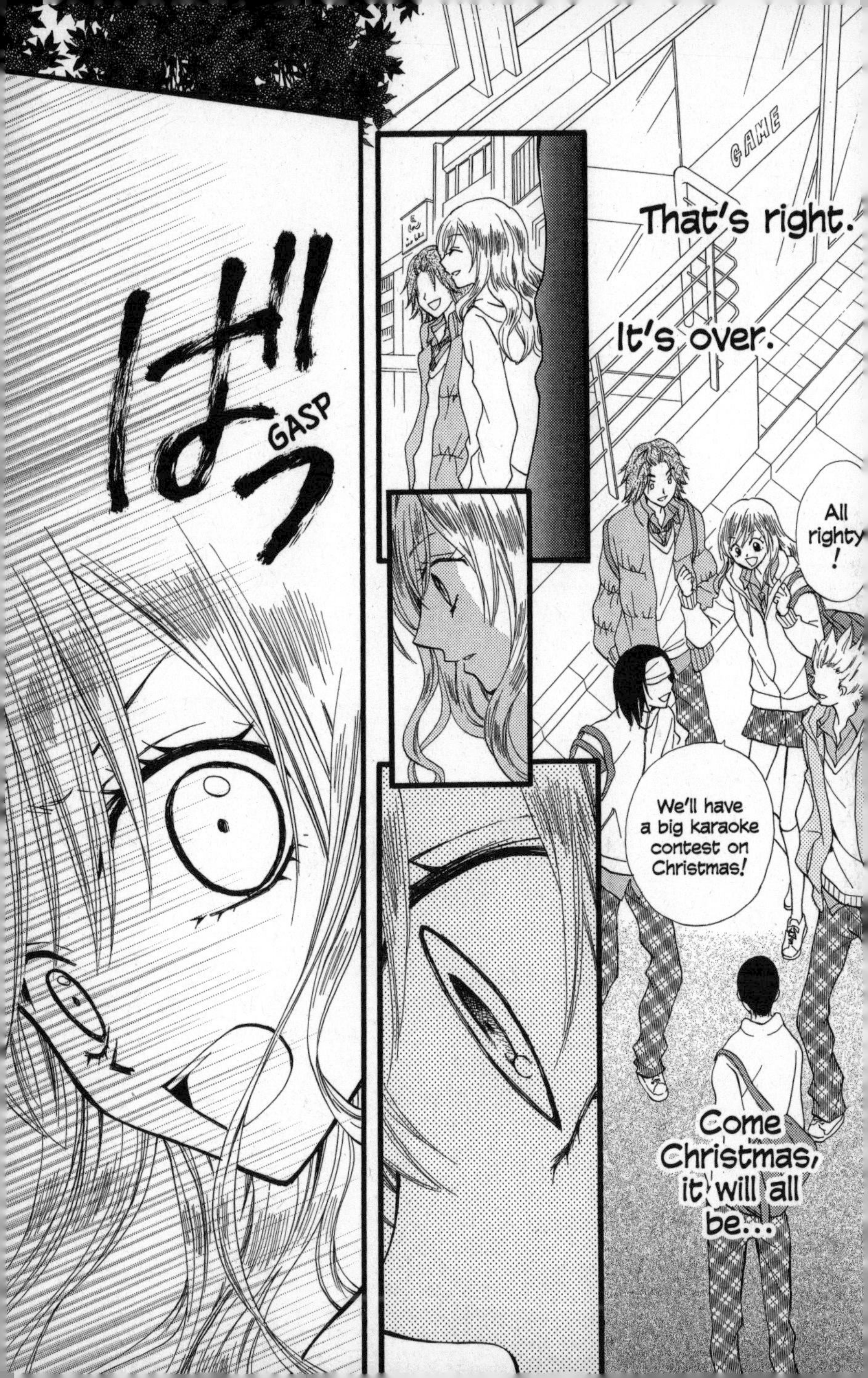
That's right.
It's over.
All righty!
We'll have a big karaoke contest on Christmas!
Come Christmas, it will all be...
GAME
はっ
GASP

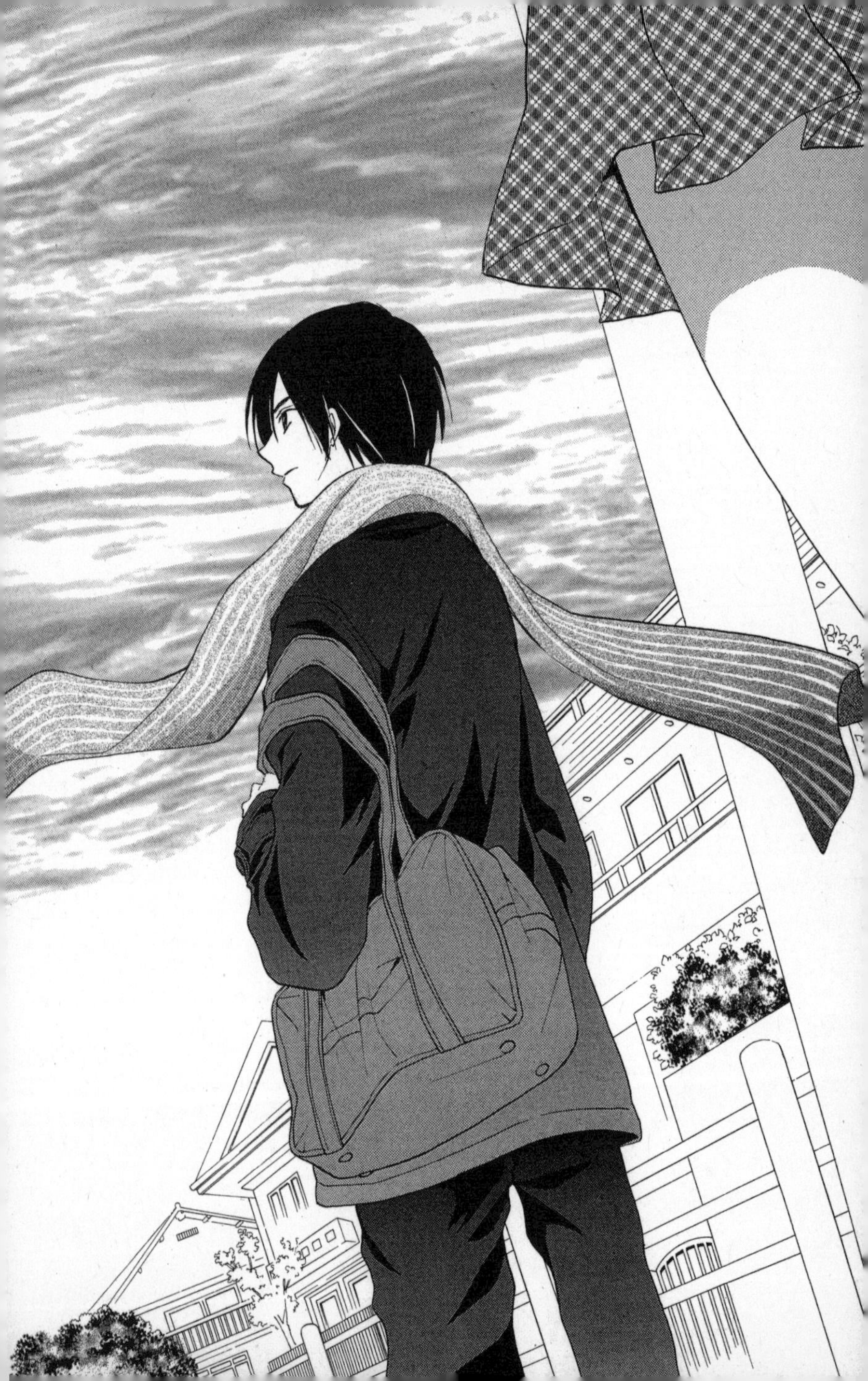

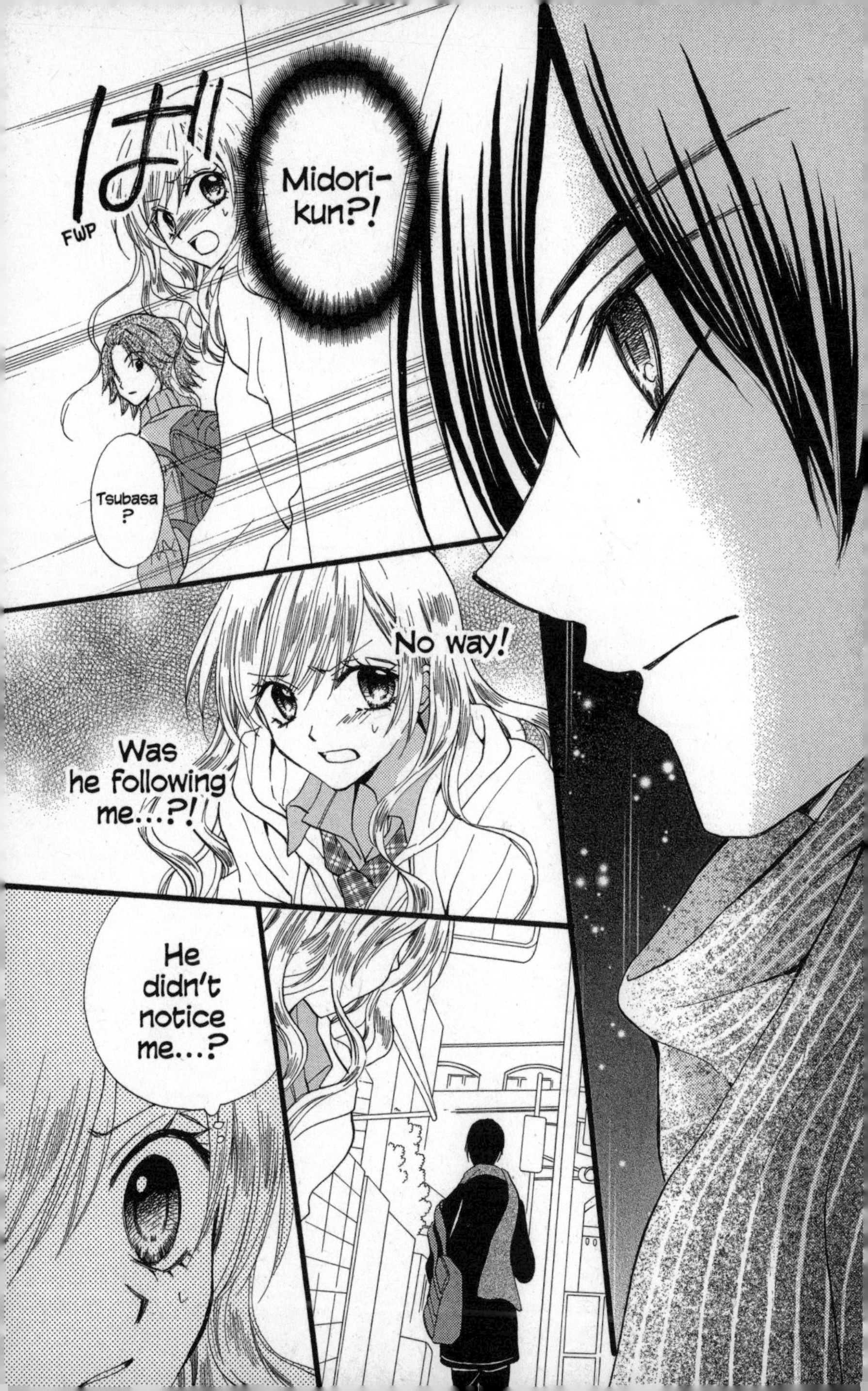

Midori-kun?!
は!
FWP
Tsubasa?
No way!
Was he following me...?!
He didn't notice me...?

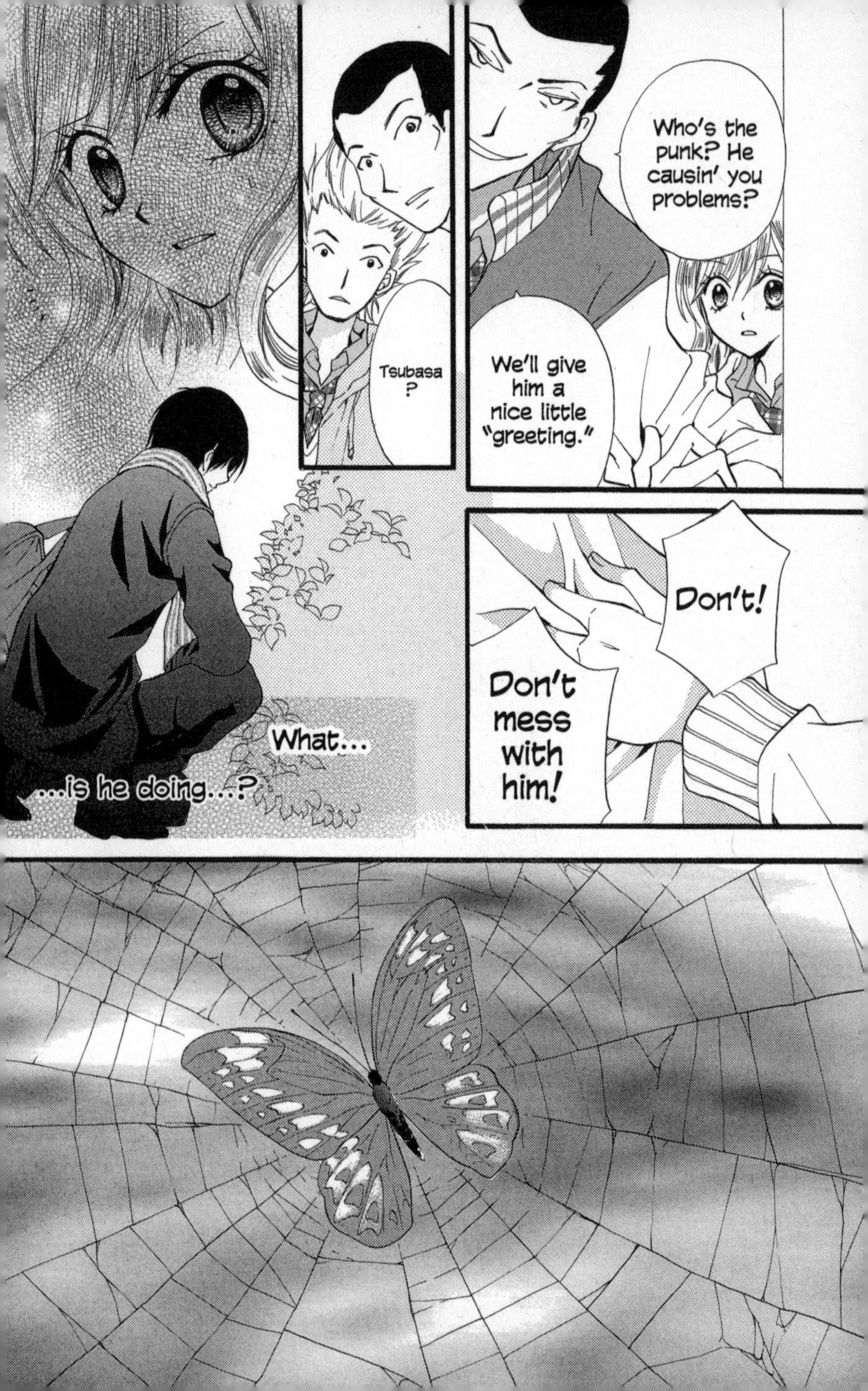
Who's the punk? He causin' you problems?
We'll give him a nice little "greeting."
Tsubasa?
Don't!
Don't mess with him!
What...
...is he doing...?

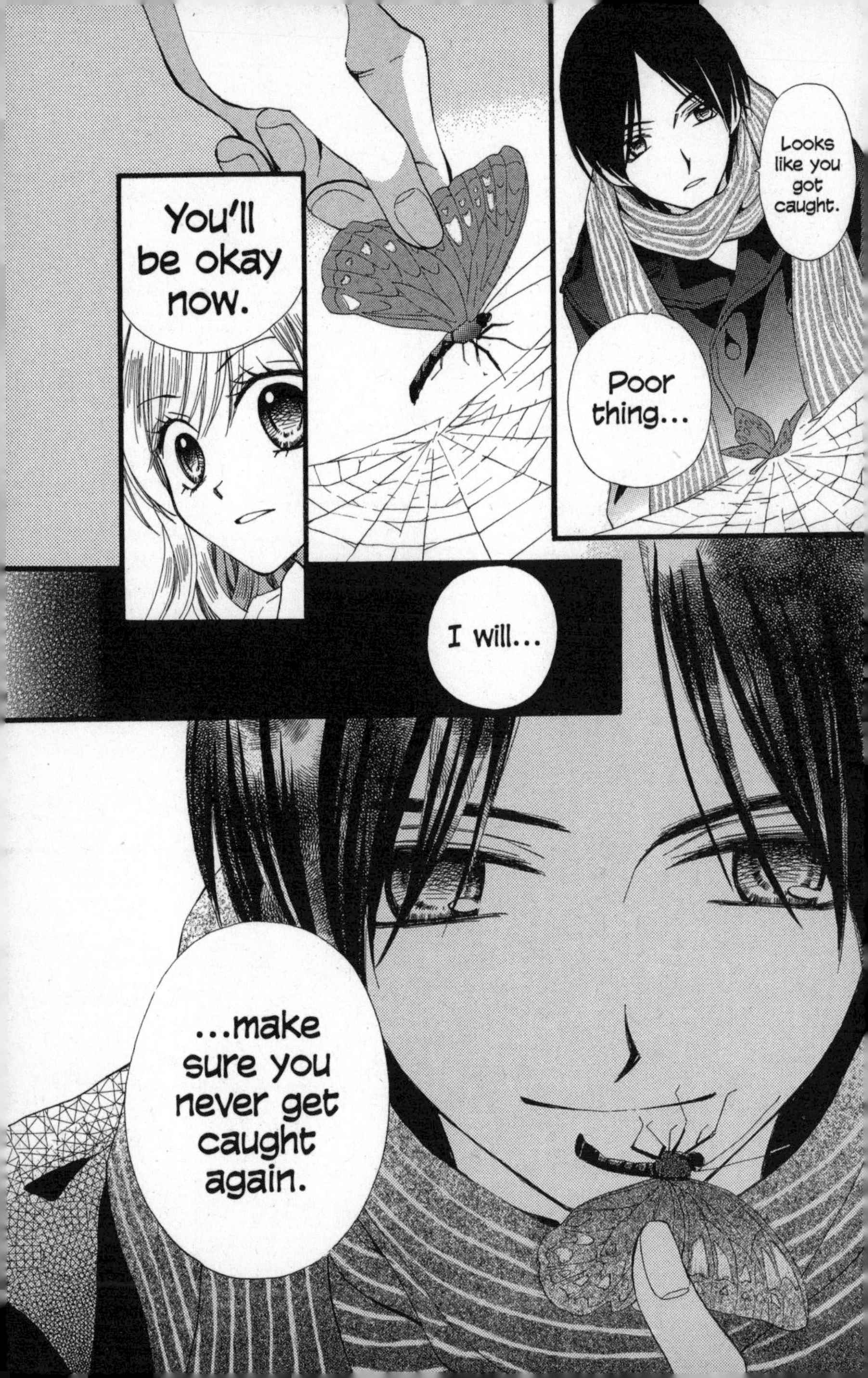
Looks like you got caught.
Poor thing...
You'll be okay now.
I will...
...make sure you never get caught again.

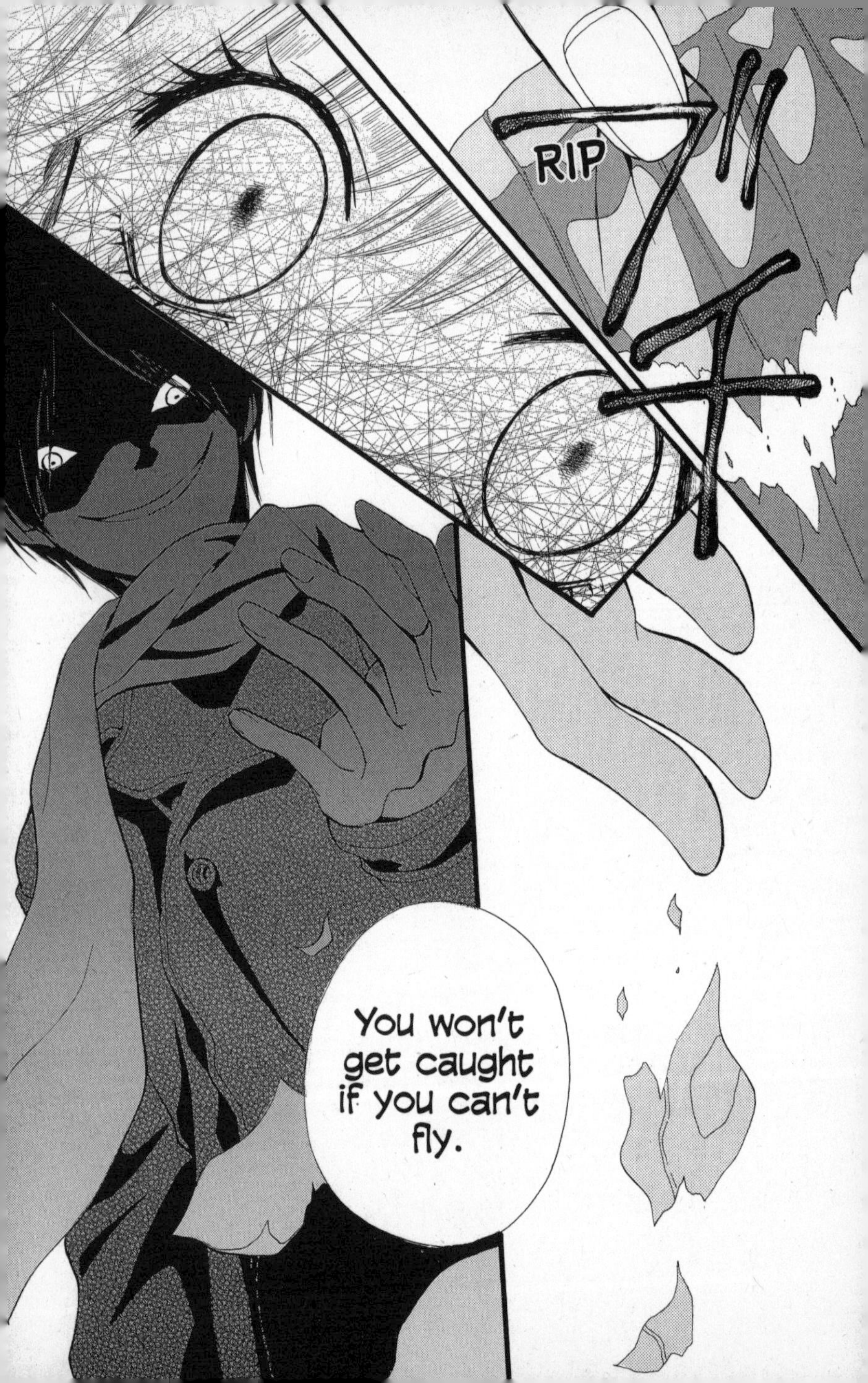
RIP
You won't get caught if you can't fly.

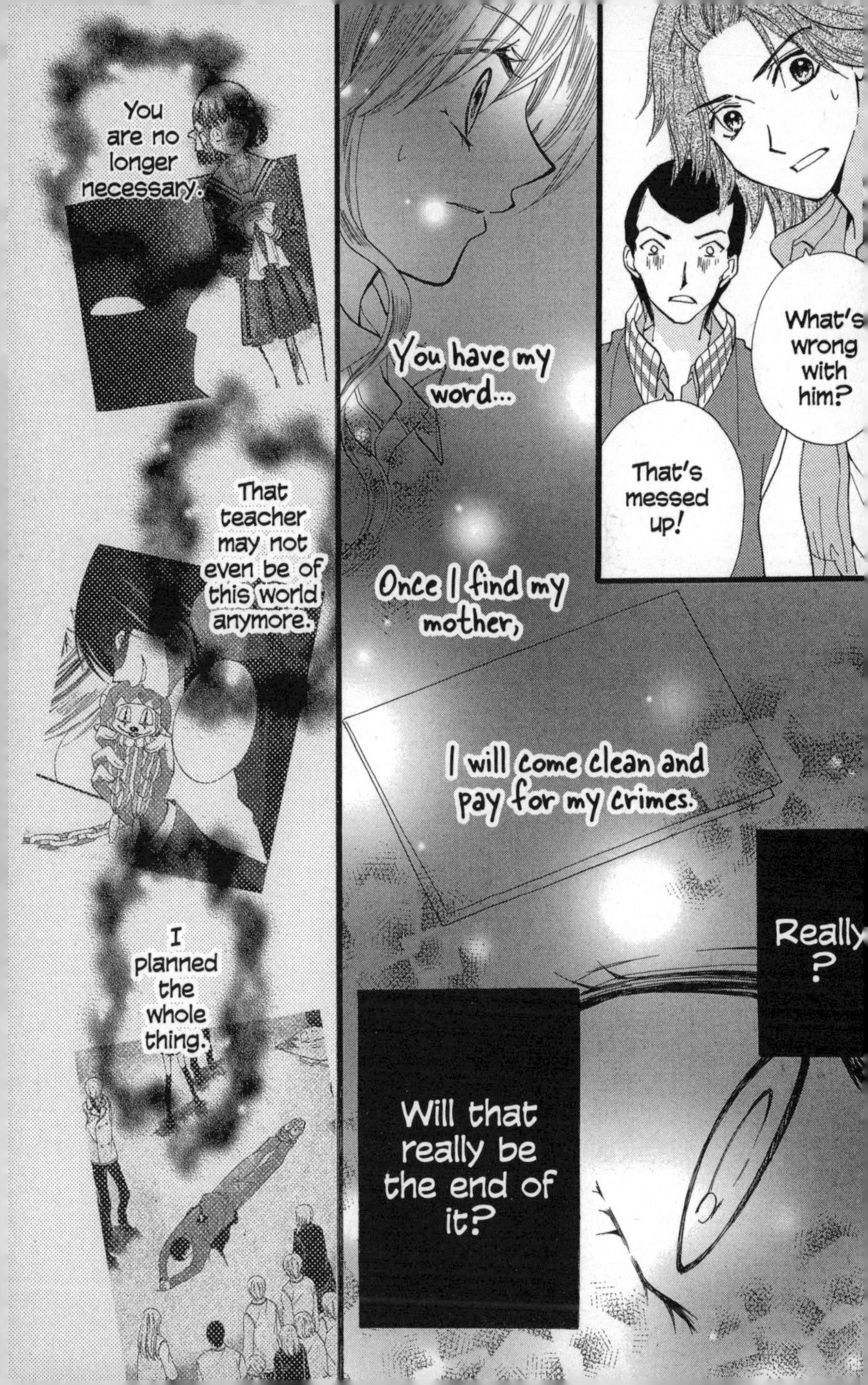
What's wrong with him?
That's messed up!
You have my word...
Once I find my mother,
I will come clean and pay for my crimes.
Really?
Will that really be the end of it?
You are no longer necessary.
That teacher may not even be of this world anymore.
I planned the whole thing.

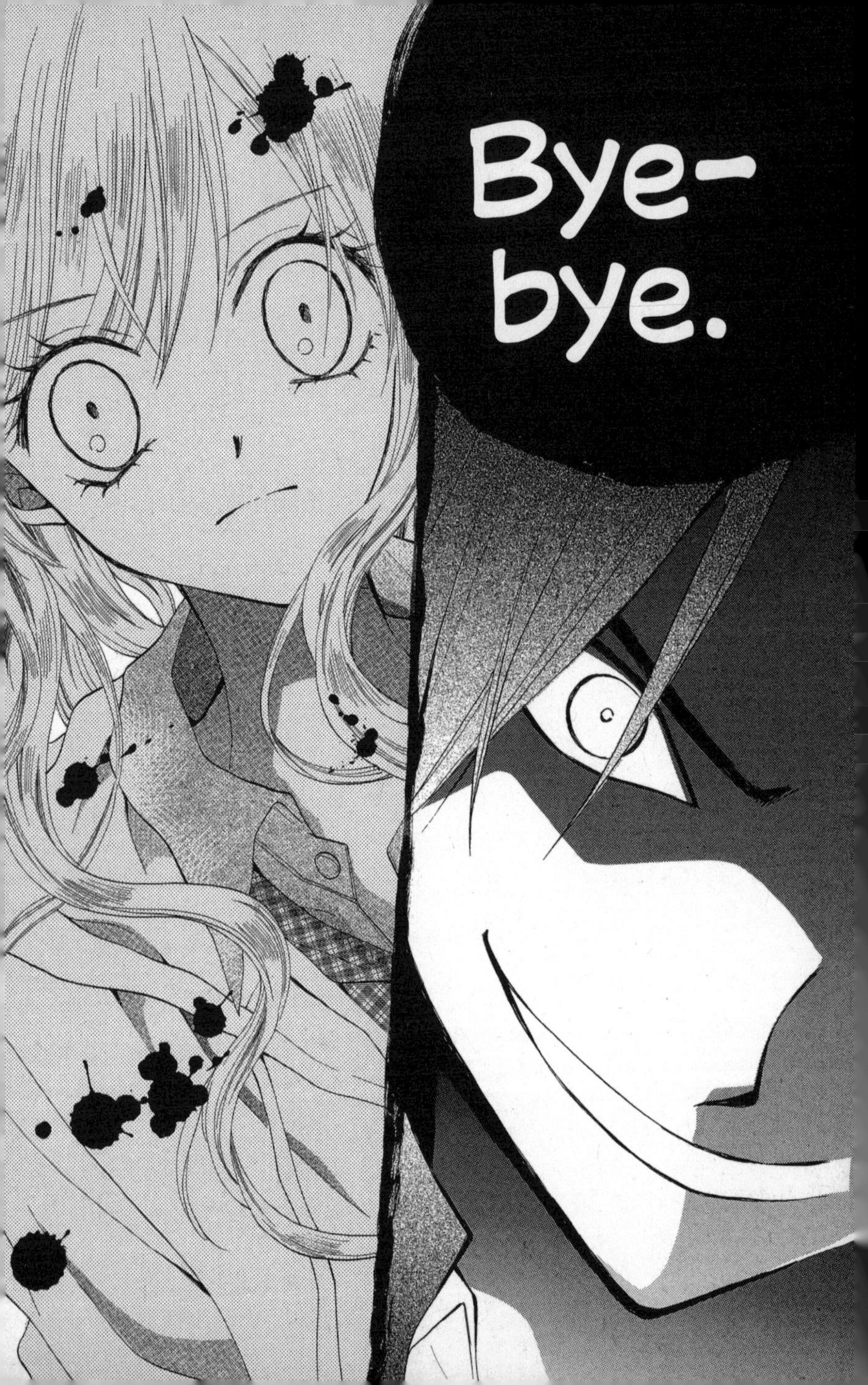
Bye-bye.

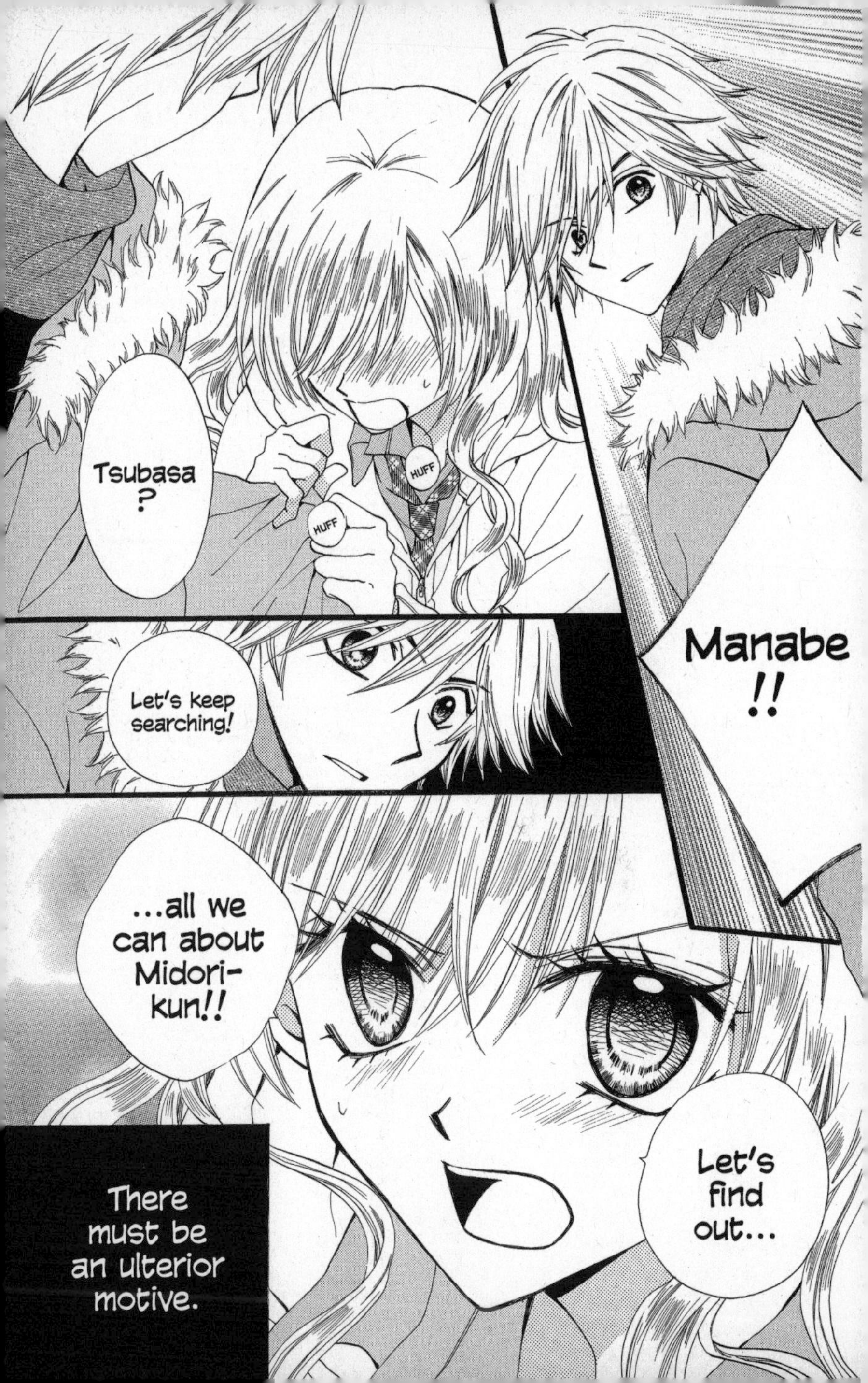
Manabe !!
Tsubasa ?
HUFF
HUFF
Let's keep searching!
Let's find out...
...all we can about Midori-kun!!
There must be an ulterior motive.

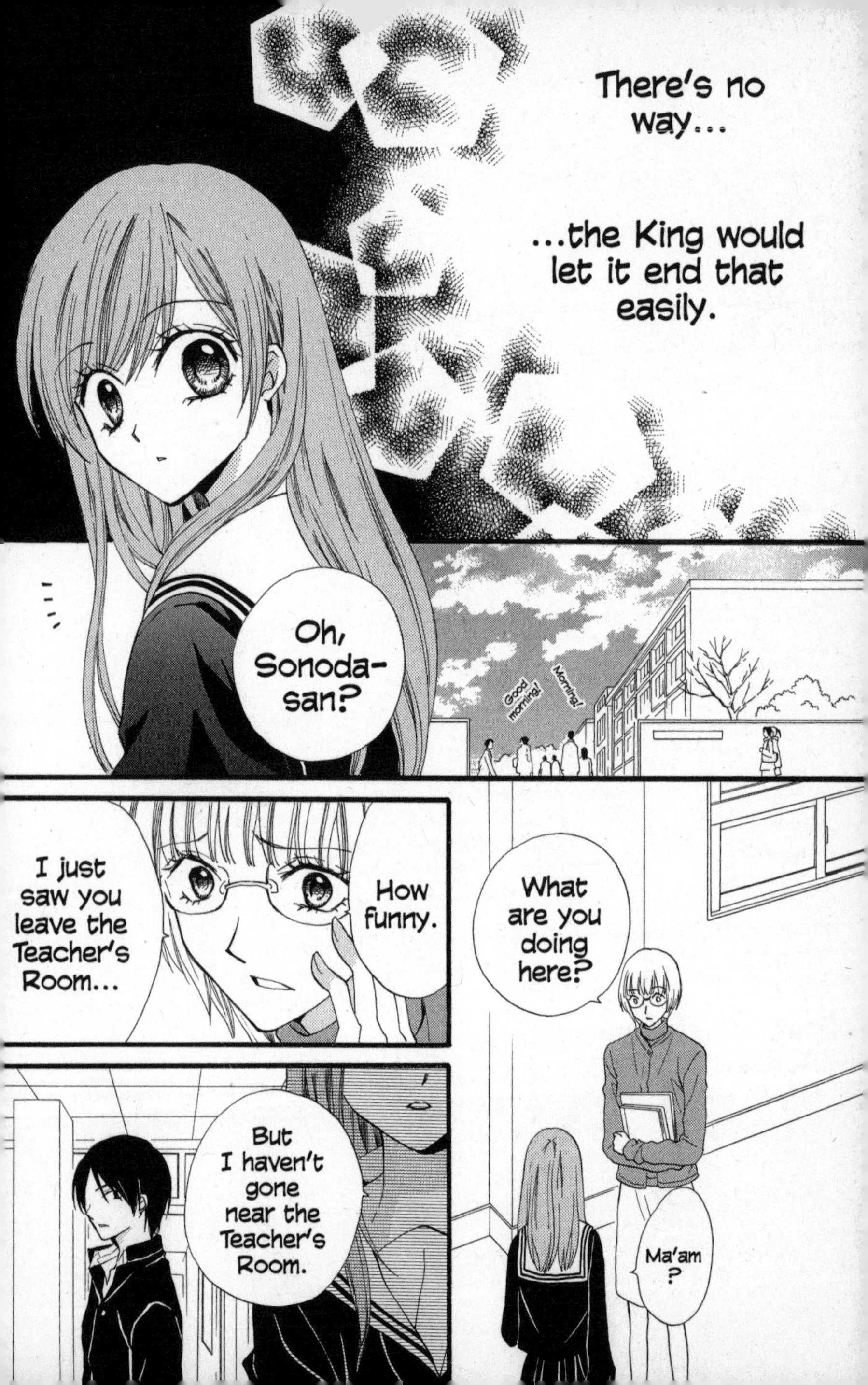
There's no way...
...the King would let it end that easily.
Morning!
Good morning!
Oh, Sonoda-san?
What are you doing here?
Ma'am?
How funny.
I just saw you leave the Teacher's Room...
But I haven't gone near the Teacher's Room.

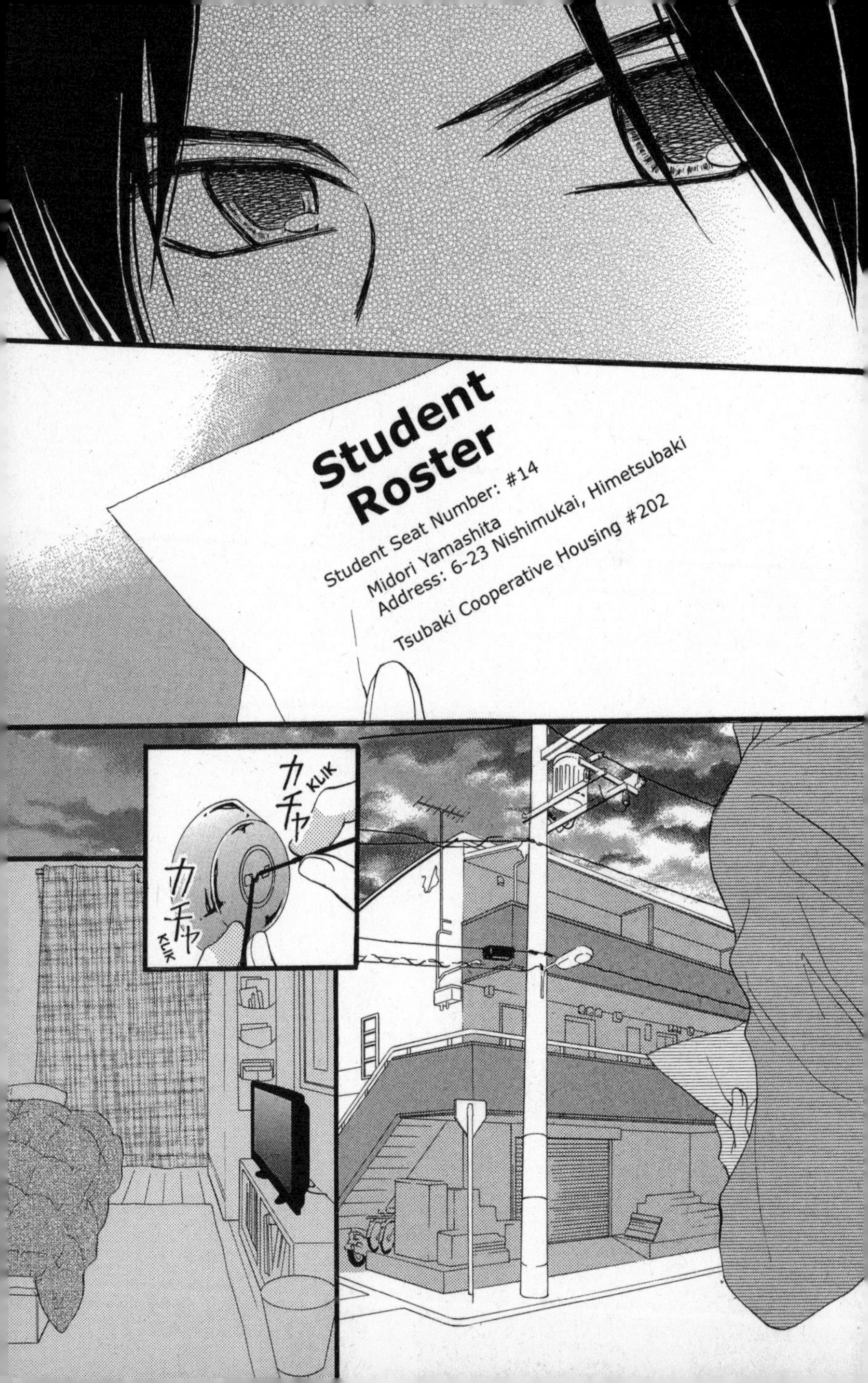
Student Roster
Student Seat Number: #14
Midori Yamashita
Address: 6-23 Nishimukai, Himetsubaki
Tsubaki Cooperative Housing #202
カチャ KLIK
カチャ KLIK

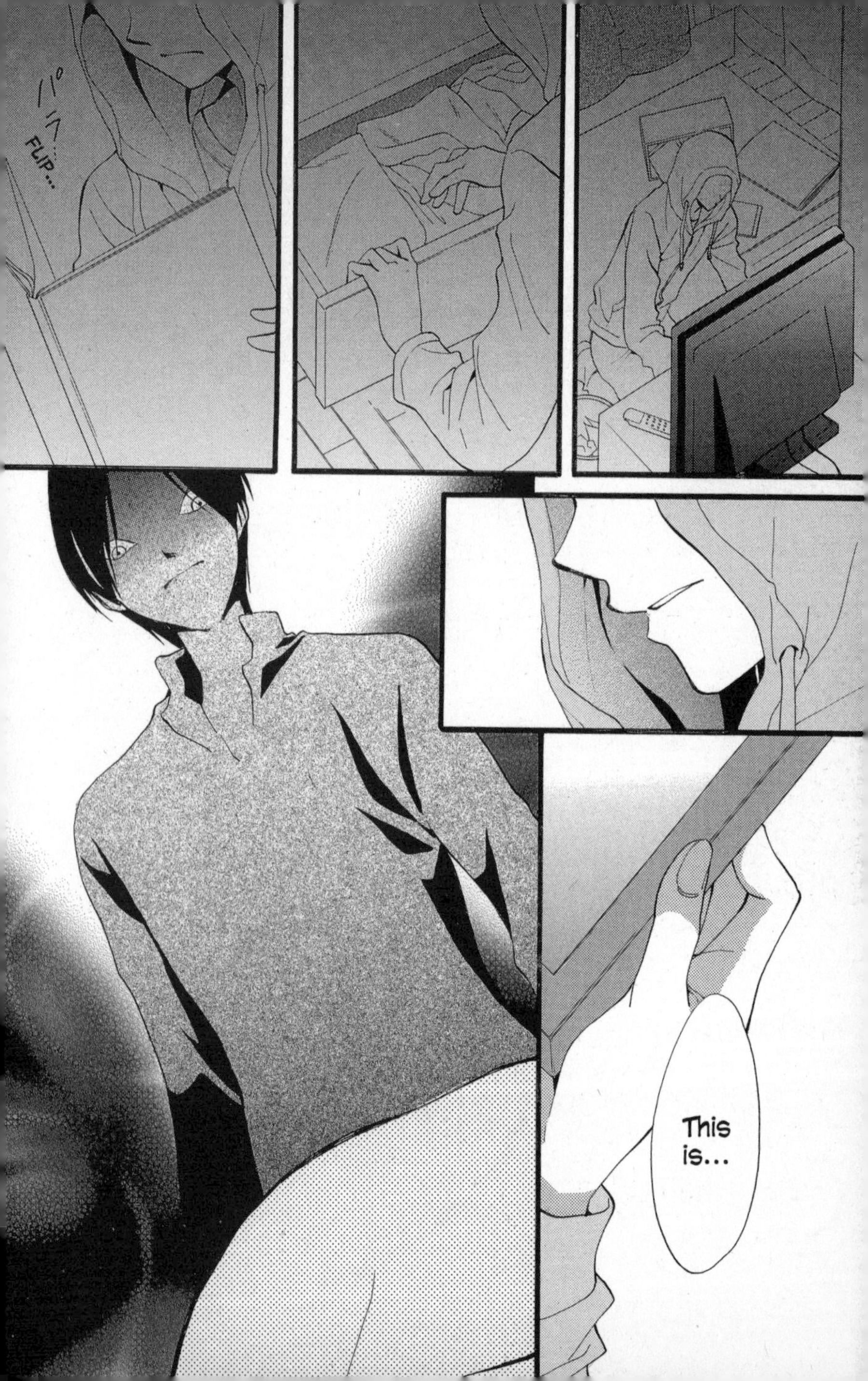
パラ
FLIP...
This is...

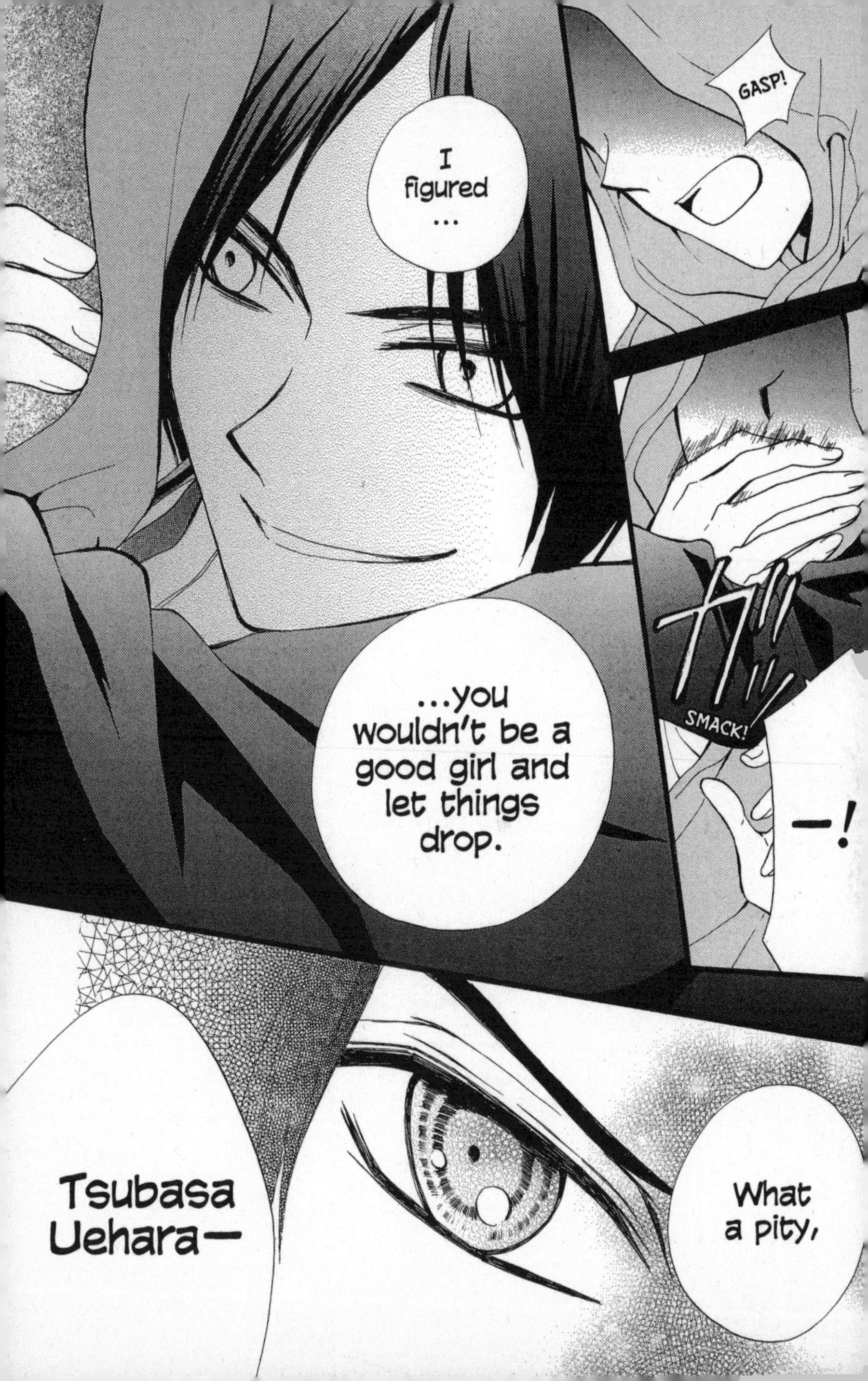
GASP!
SMACK!
—!
I figured ...
...you wouldn't be a good girl and let things drop.
What a pity,
Tsubasa Uehara—

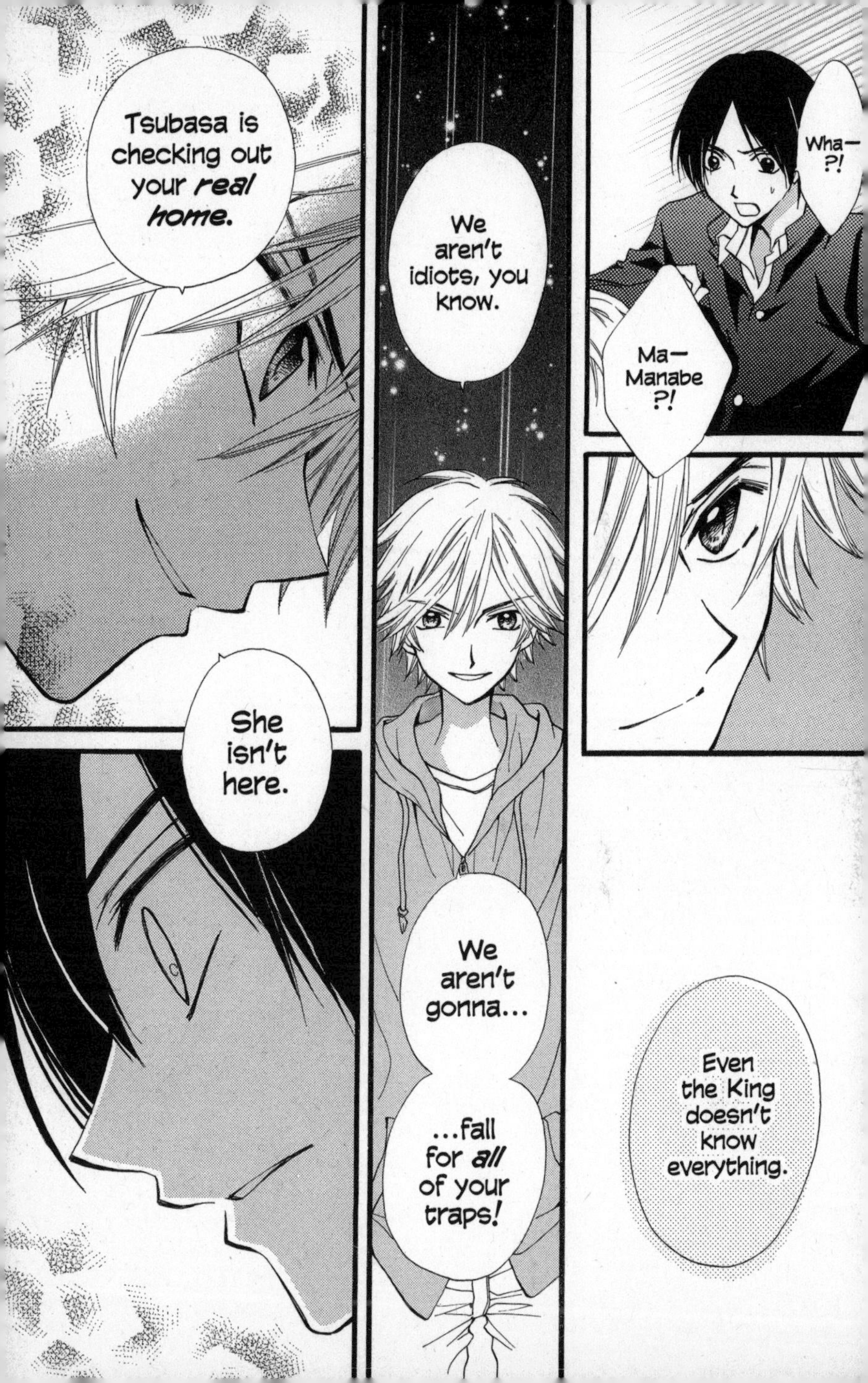
Wha—?!
Ma—Manabe?!
Even the King doesn't know everything.
We aren't idiots, you know.
We aren't gonna...
...fall for *all* of your traps!
Tsubasa is checking out your *real home*.
She isn't here.

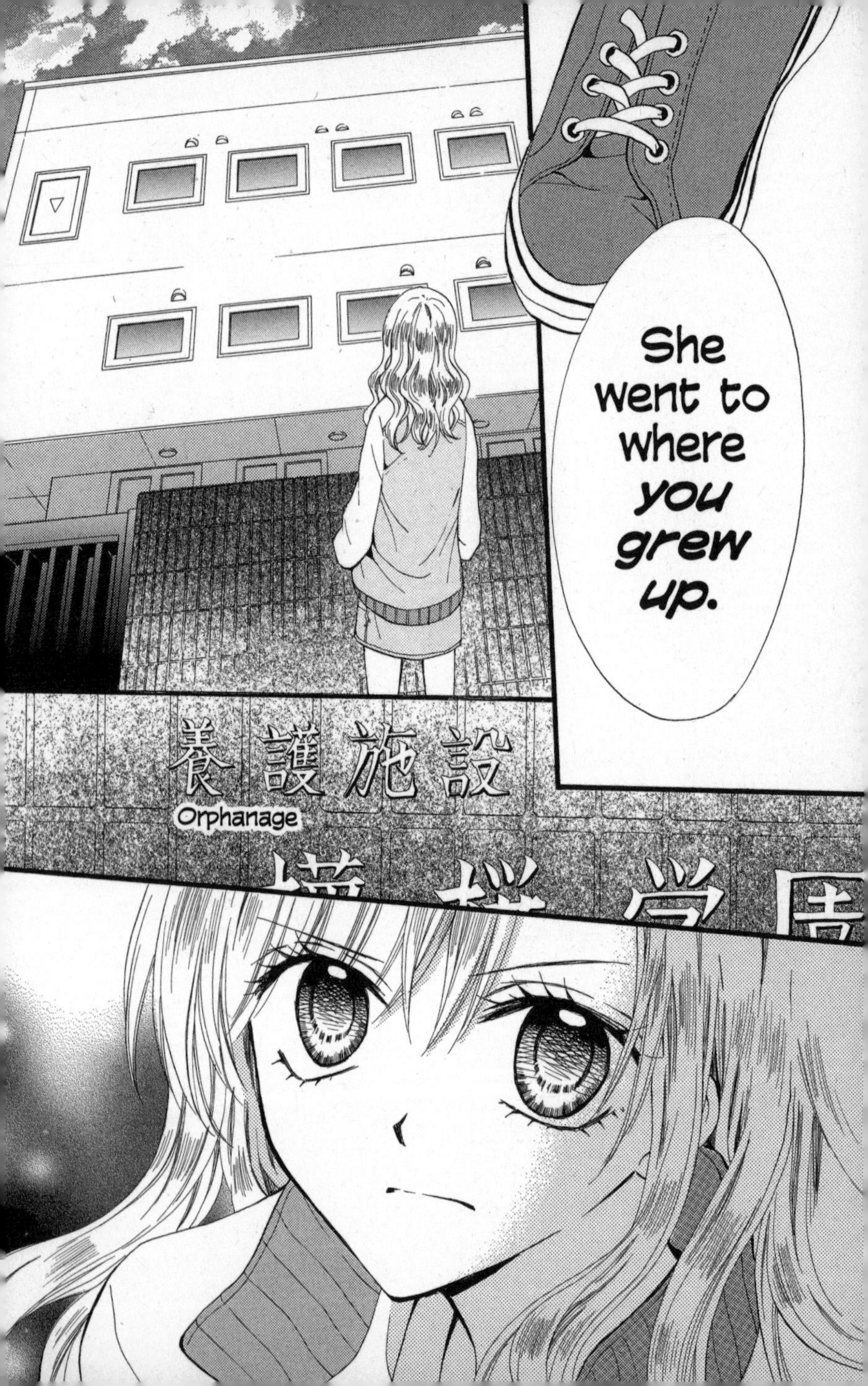
She went to where you grew up.
養護施設
Orphanage

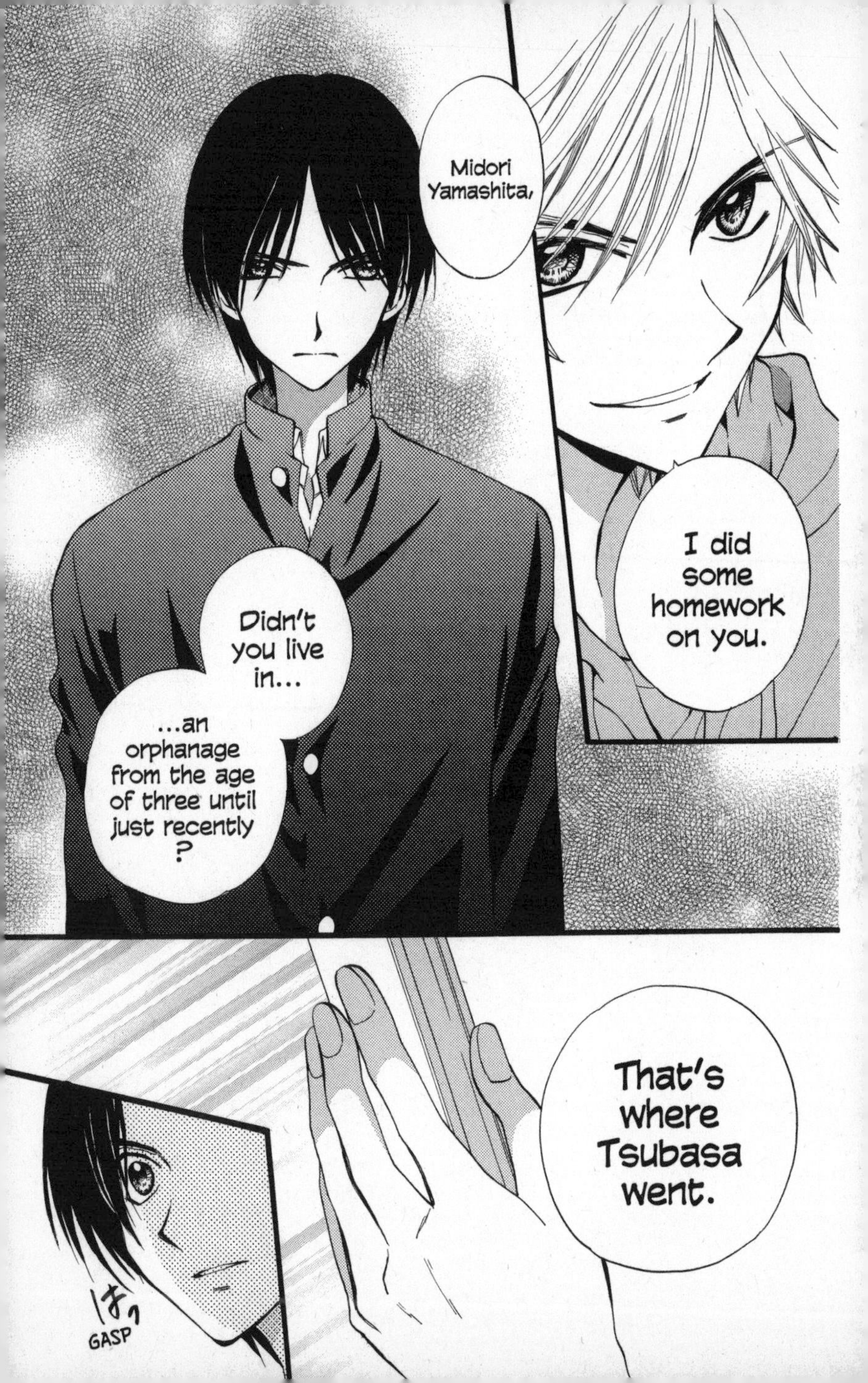
Midori Yamashita,
I did some homework on you.
Didn't you live in...
...an orphanage from the age of three until just recently?
That's where Tsubasa went.
は
GASP

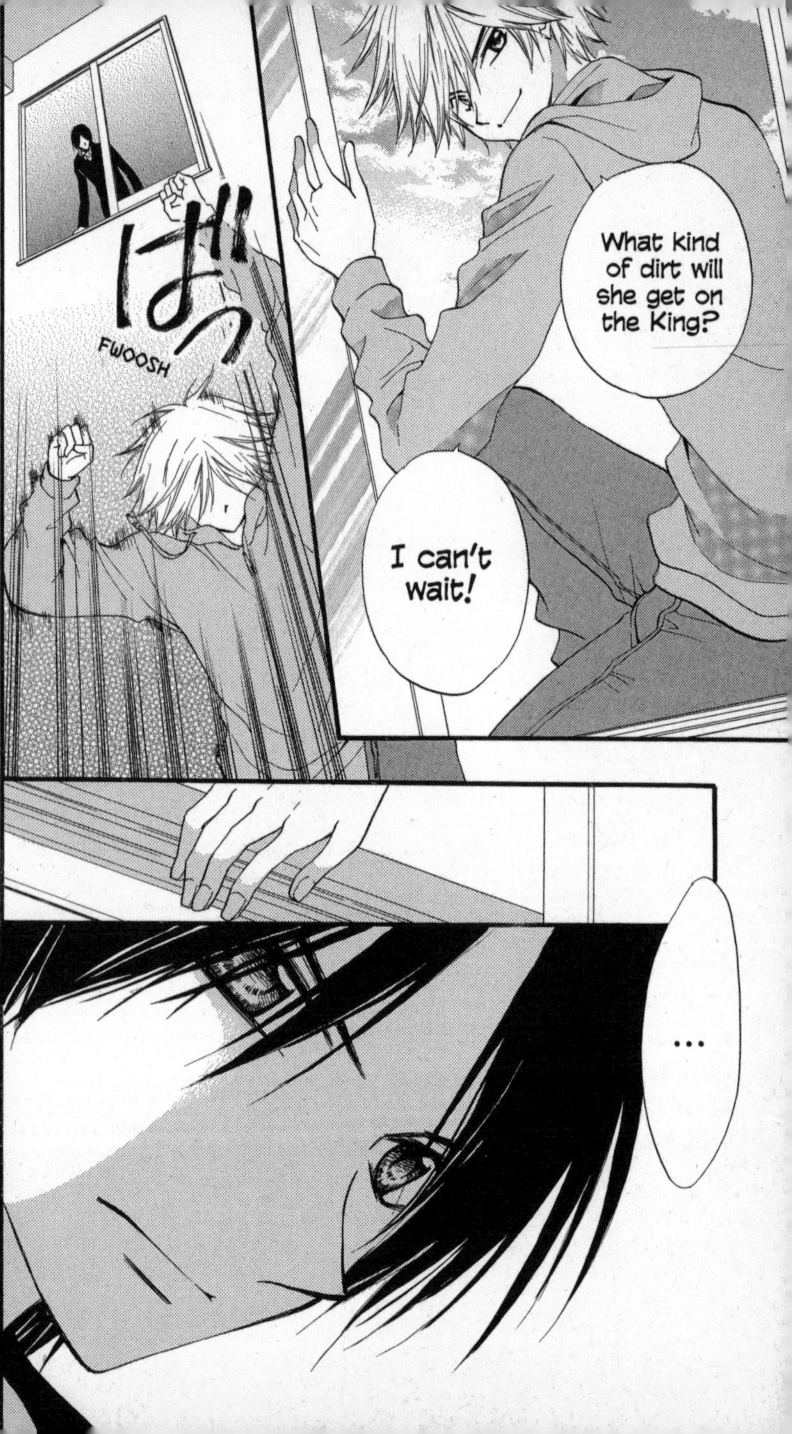
What kind of dirt will she get on the King?
I can't wait!
ばっ
FWOOSH
...

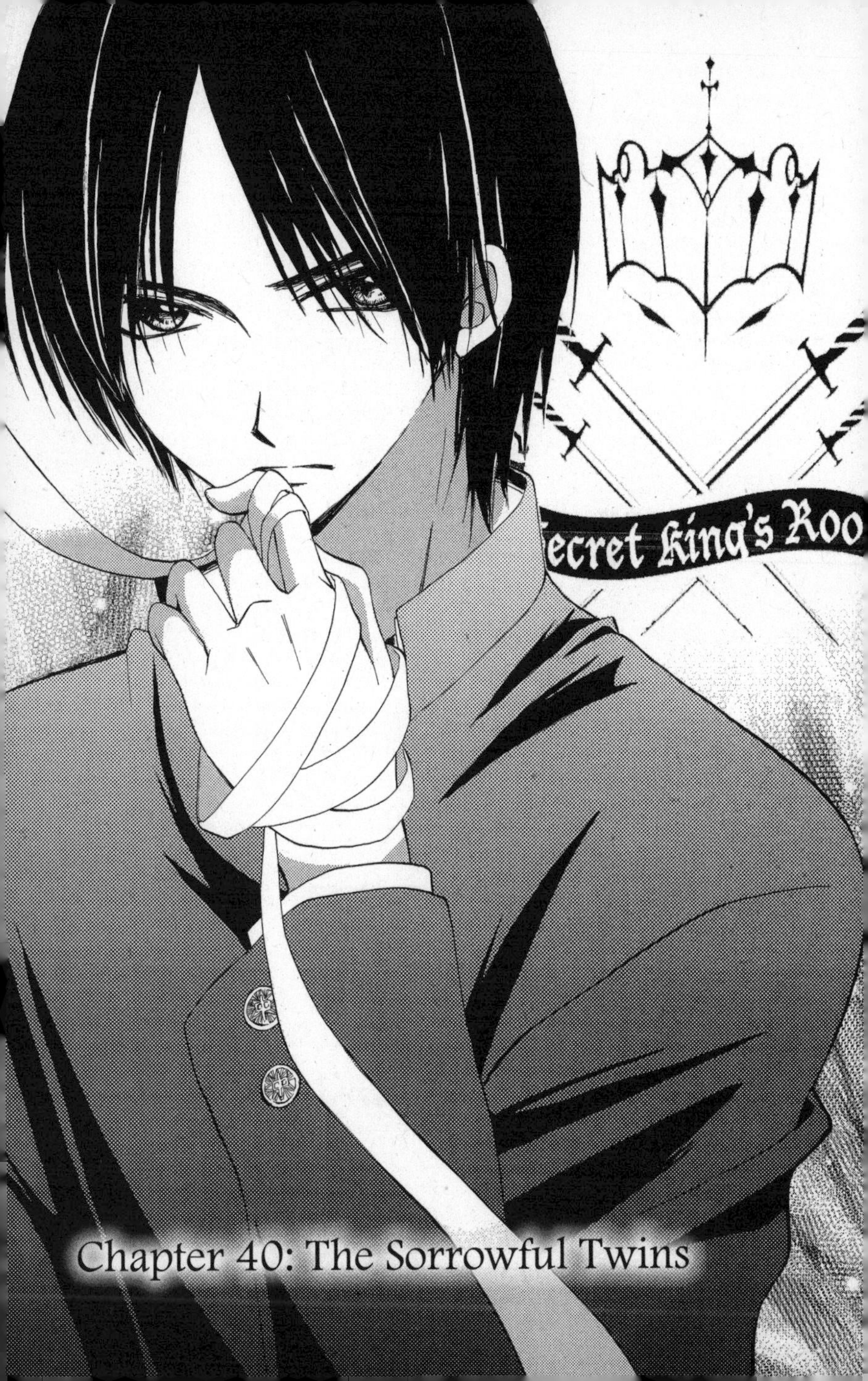
ecret King's Roo

Chapter 40: The Sorrowful Twins

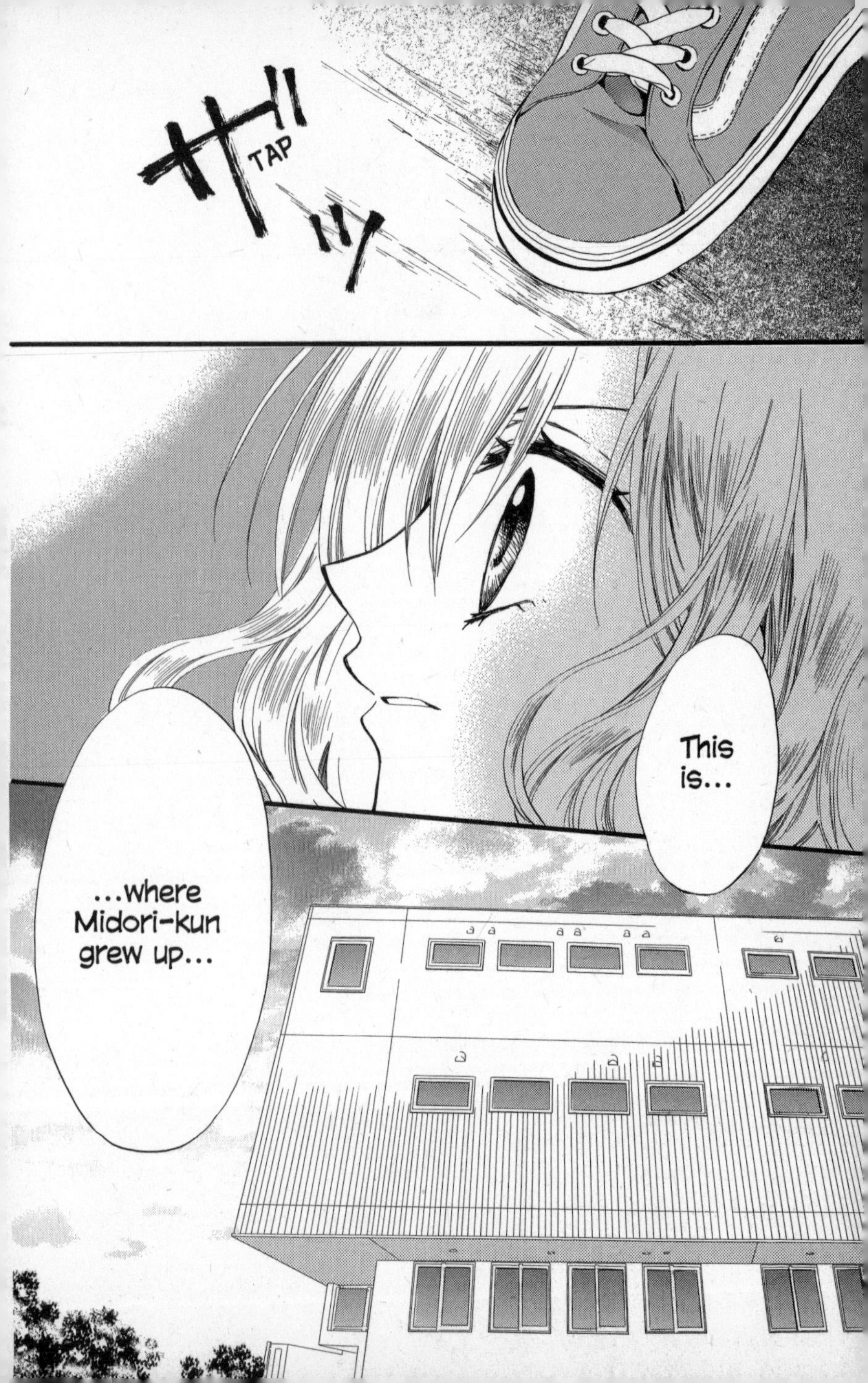
ザッ
TAP
This is...
...where Midori-kun grew up...

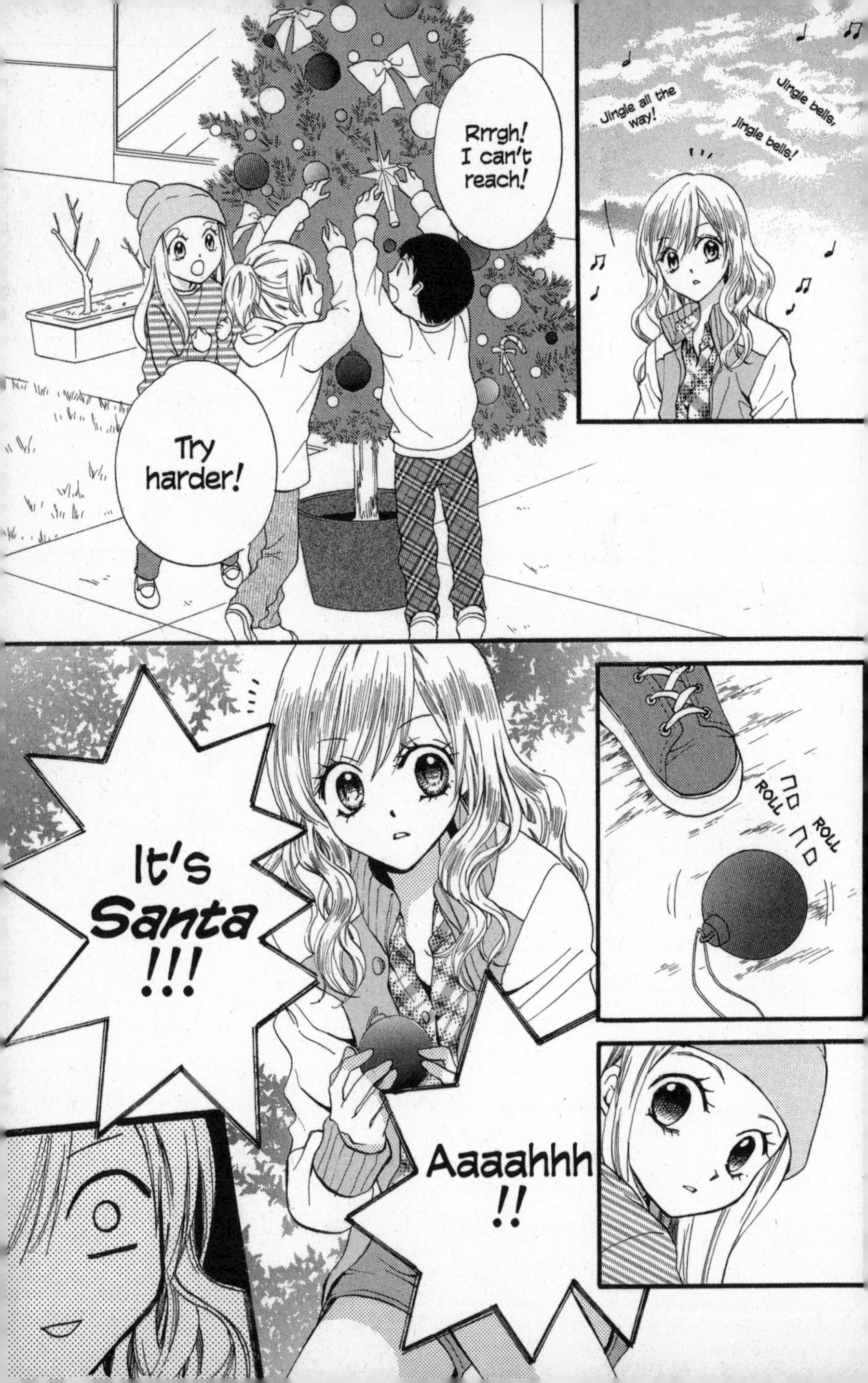

Jingle bells,
jingle bells!
Jingle all the way!
Rrrgh! I can't reach!
Try harder!
ROLL
ROLL
It's Santa!!!
Aaaahhh!!

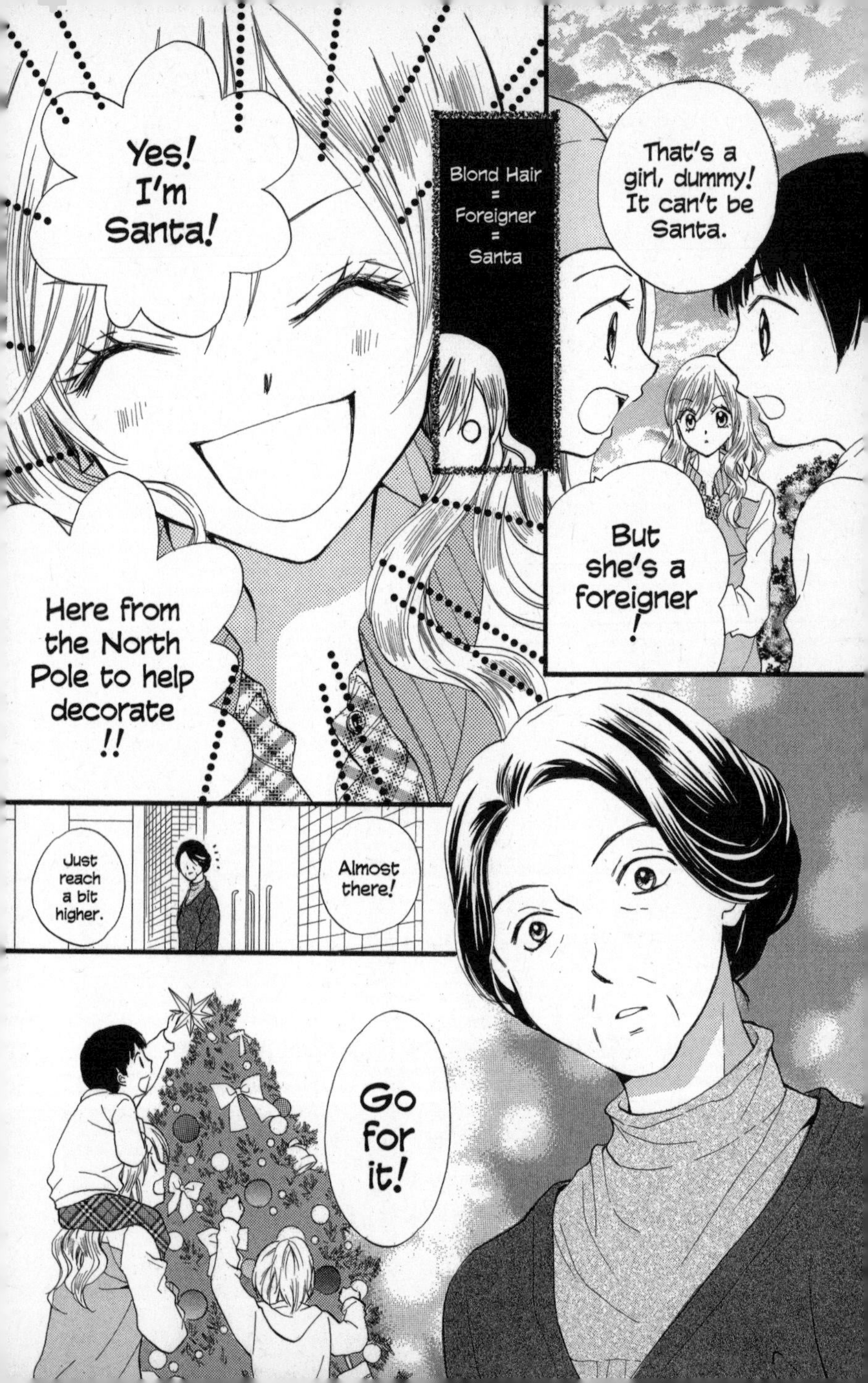
That's a girl, dummy! It can't be Santa.
But she's a foreigner!
Yes! I'm Santa!
Blond Hair = Foreigner = Santa
Here from the North Pole to help decorate!!
Almost there!
Just reach a bit higher.
Go for it!

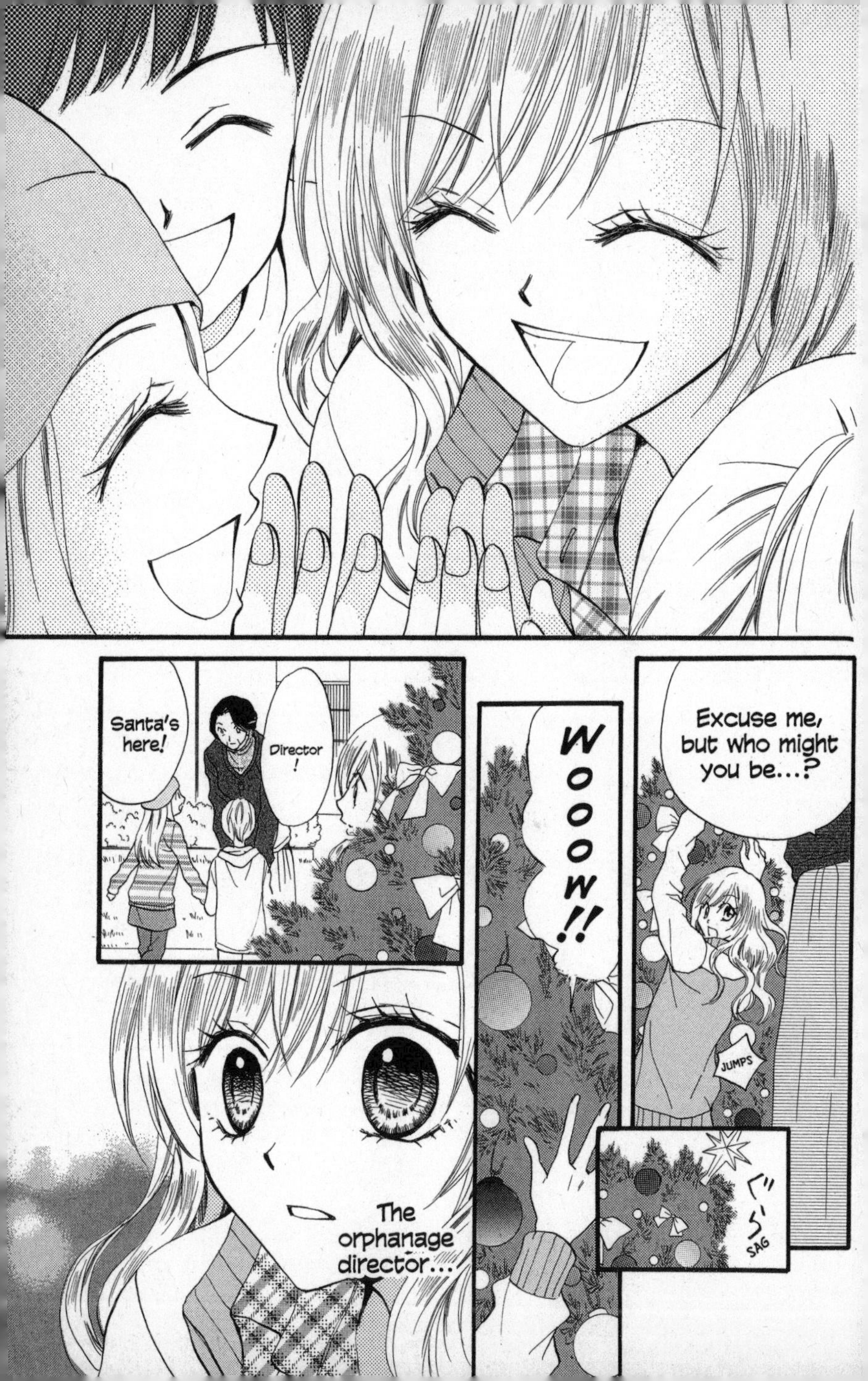

Excuse me, but who might you be...?
JUMPS
SAG
WOOOOW!!
Director!
Santa's here!
The orphanage director...

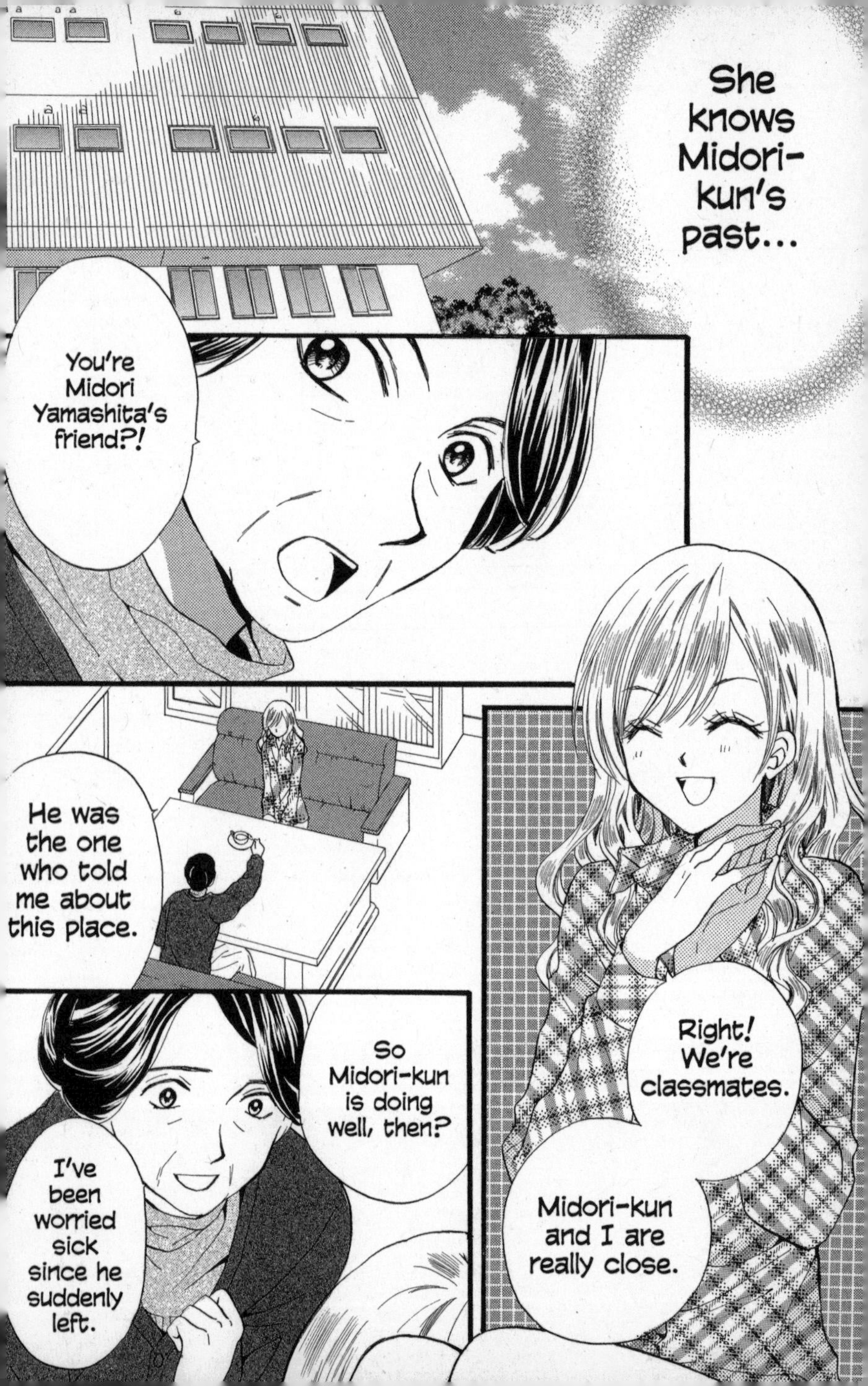
She knows Midori-kun's past...
You're Midori Yamashita's friend?!
Right! We're classmates.
Midori-kun and I are really close.
He was the one who told me about this place.
So Midori-kun is doing well, then?
I've been worried sick since he suddenly left.

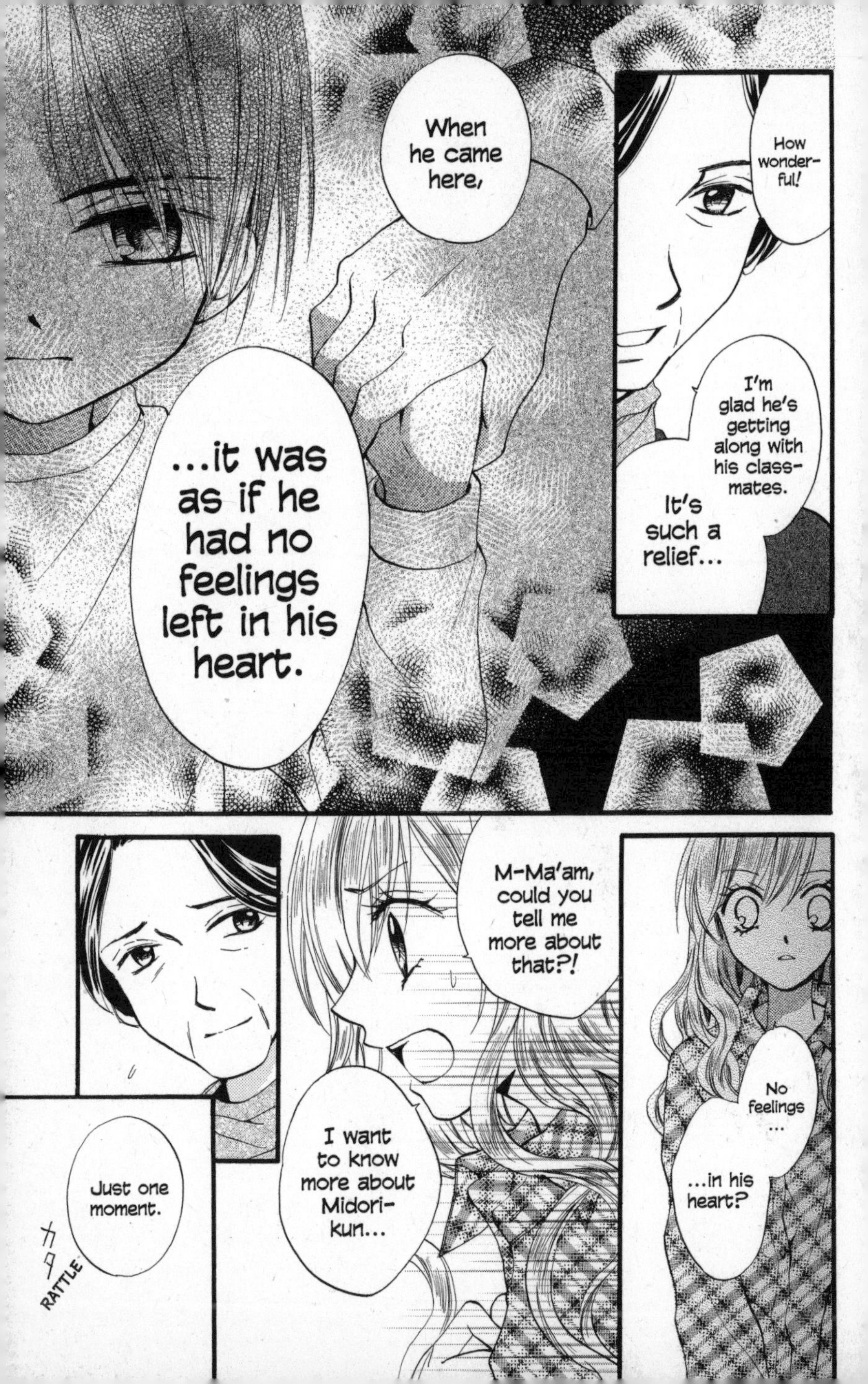
How wonderful!
I'm glad he's getting along with his classmates.
It's such a relief...
When he came here,
...it was as if he had no feelings left in his heart.
No feelings ...
...in his heart?
M-Ma'am, could you tell me more about that?!
I want to know more about Midori-kun...
Just one moment.
カタ
RATTLE

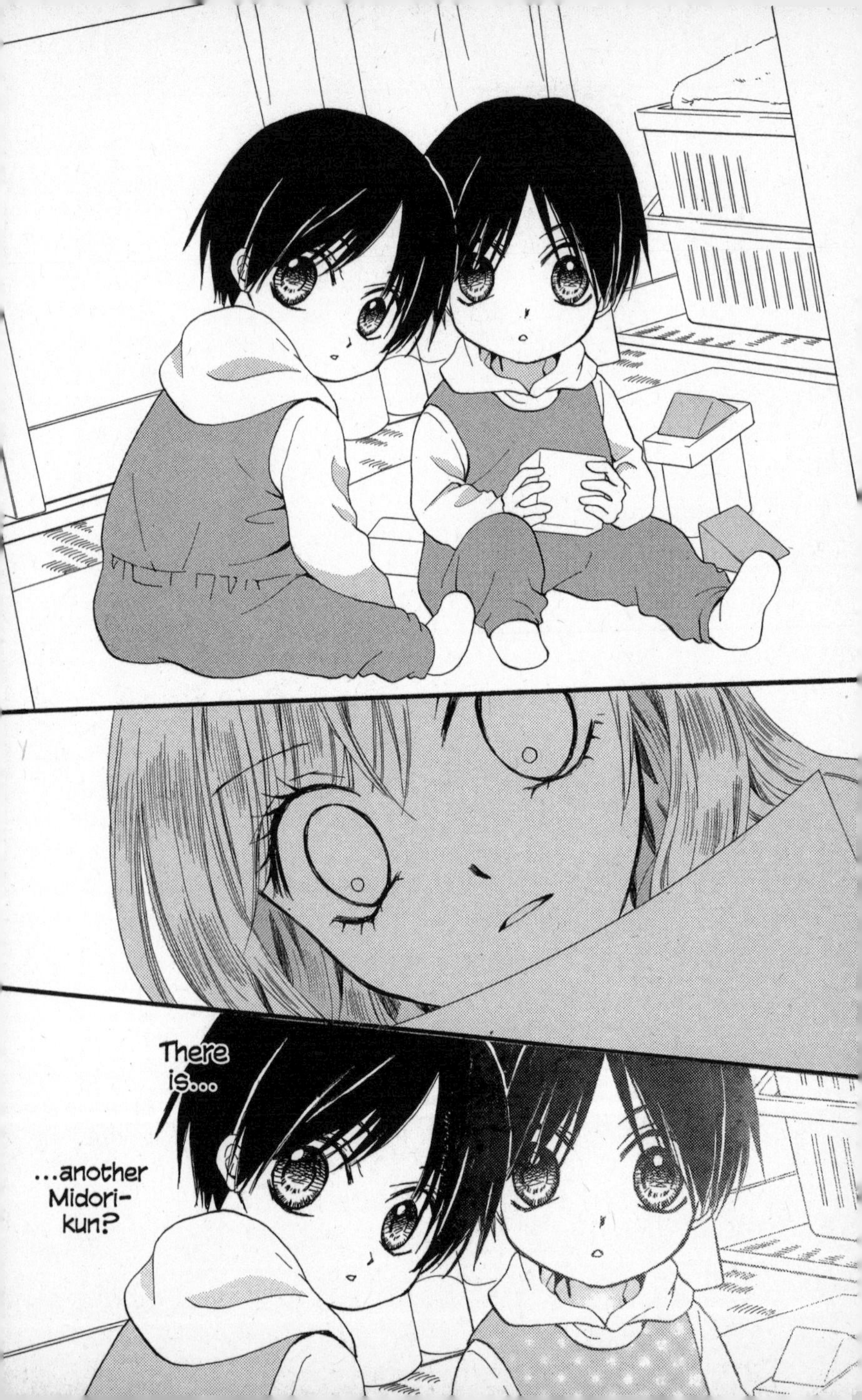
There is...
...another Midori-kun?

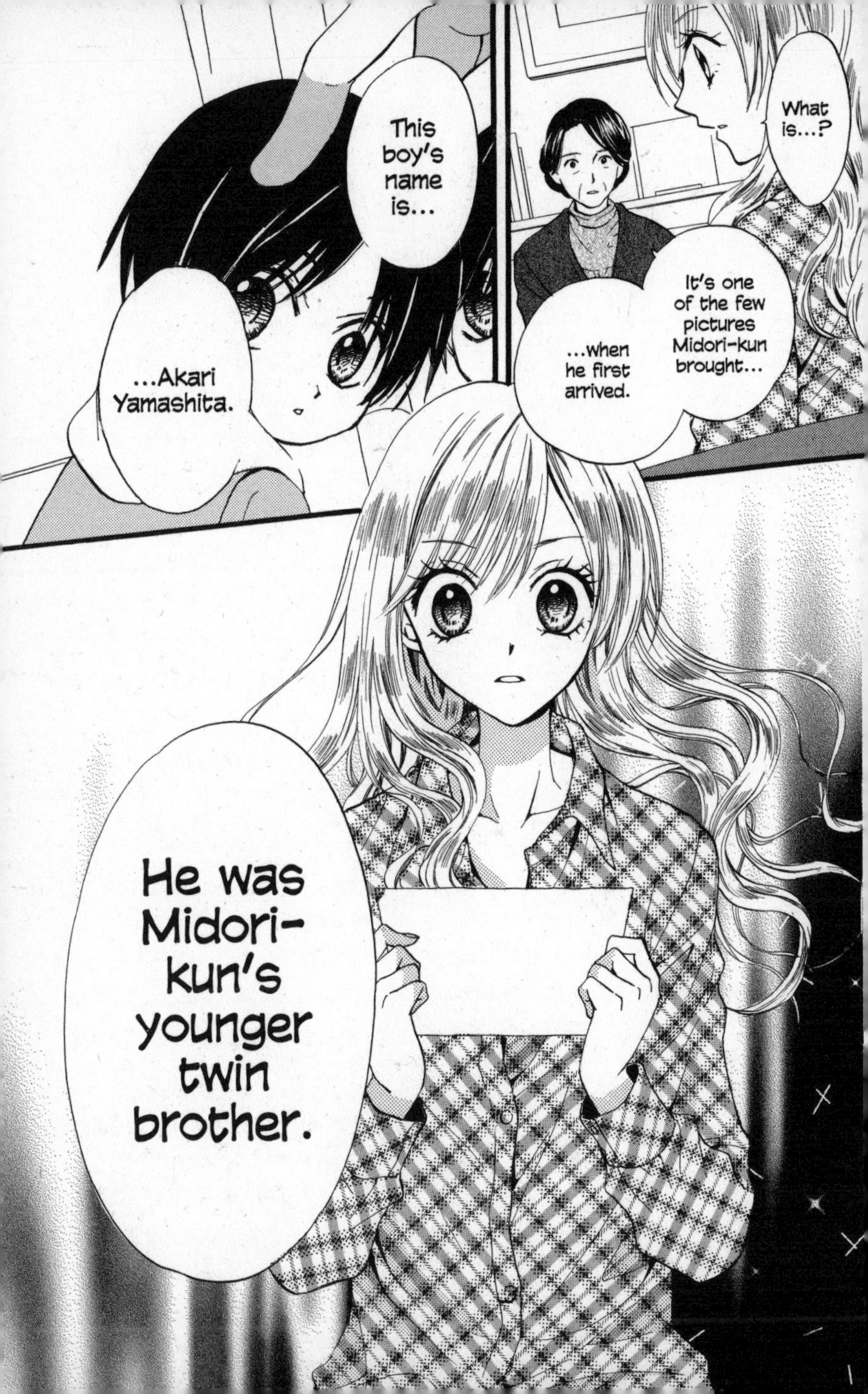
What is...?
It's one of the few pictures Midori-kun brought...
...when he first arrived.
This boy's name is...
...Akari Yamashita.
He was Midori-kun's younger twin brother.

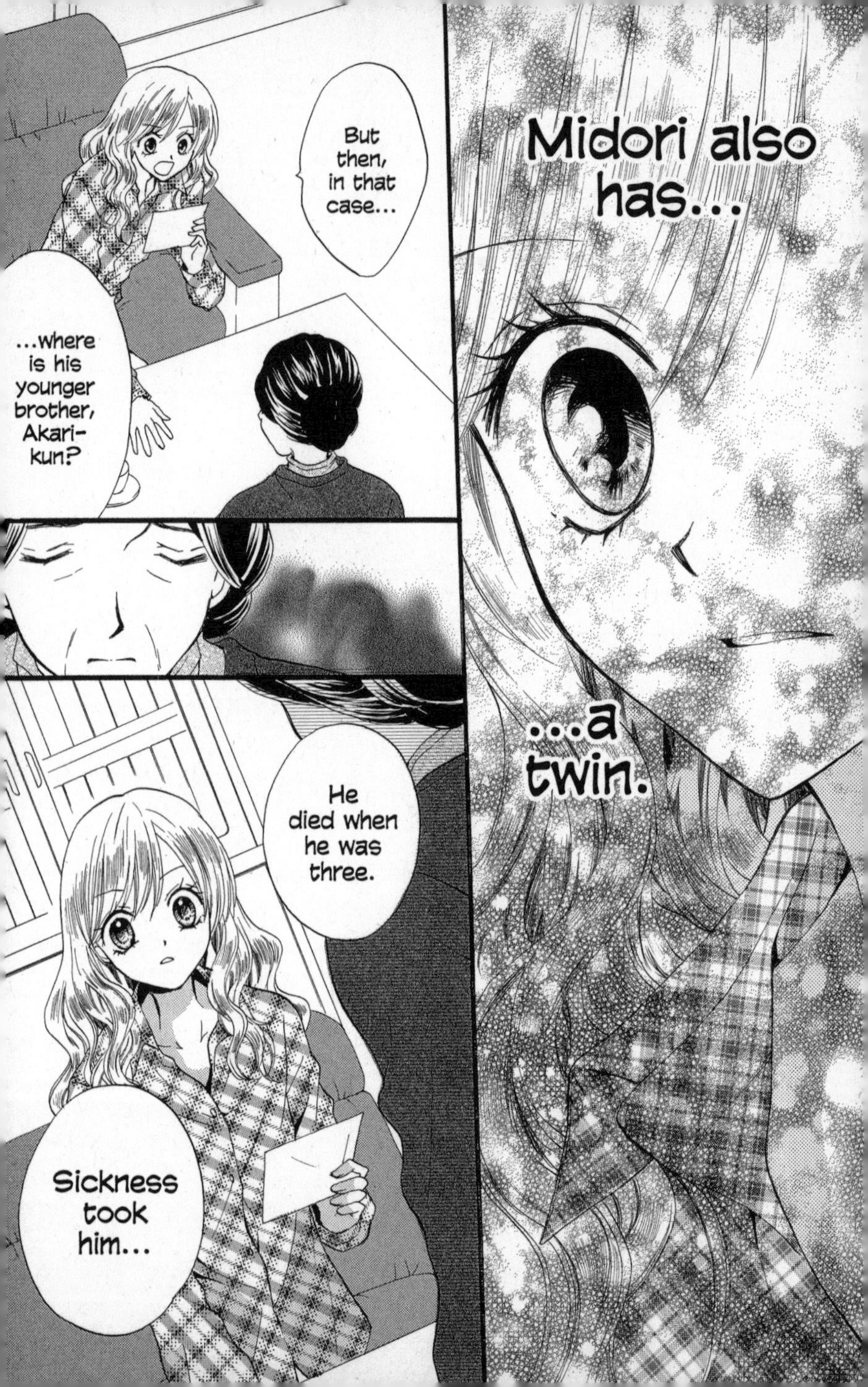
Midori also has...
...a twin.
But then, in that case...
...where is his younger brother, Akari-kun?
He died when he was three.
Sickness took him...

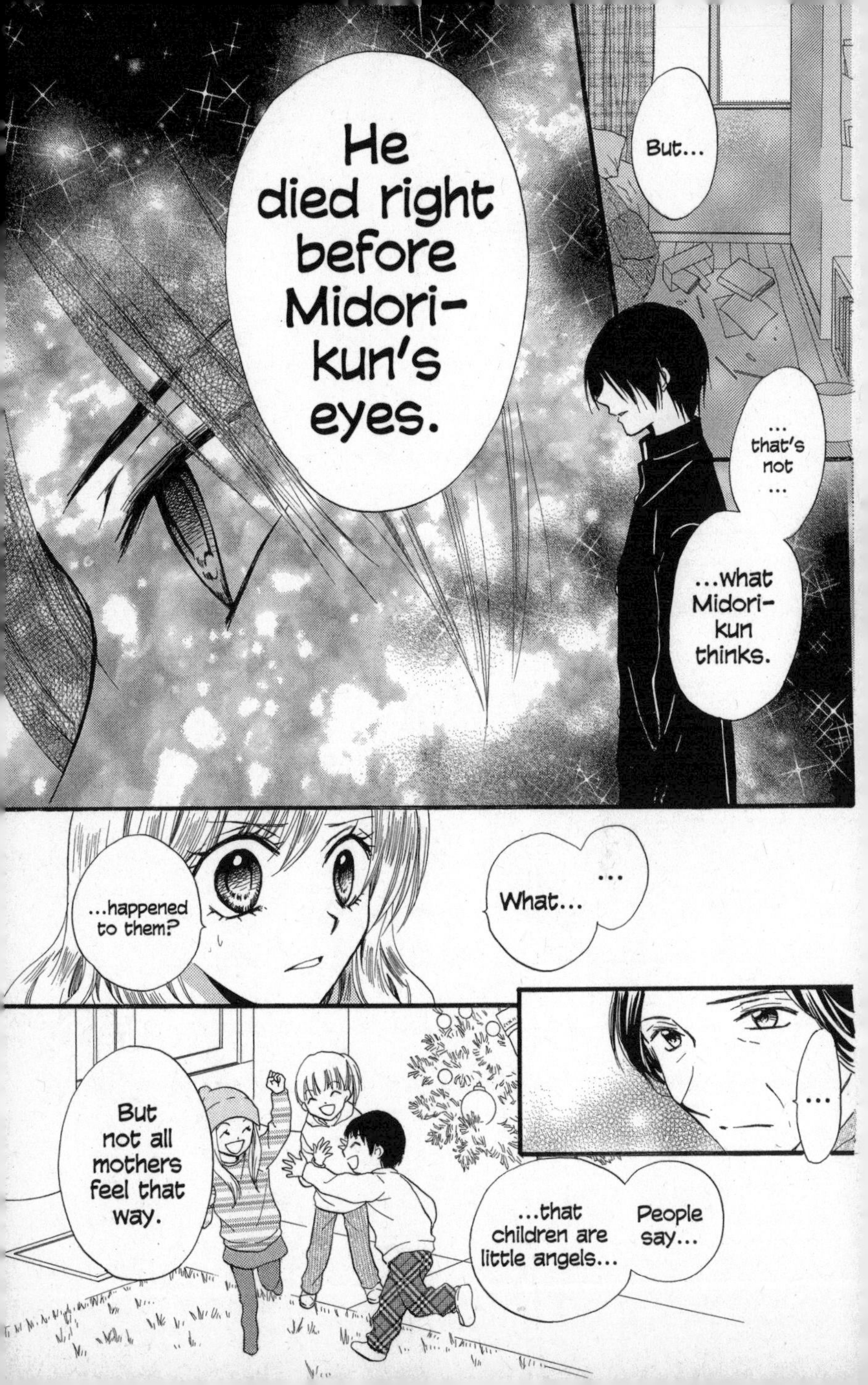
But...
...that's not...
...what Midori-kun thinks.
He died right before Midori-kun's eyes.
...
What...
...happened to them?
...
People say...
...that children are little angels...
But not all mothers feel that way.

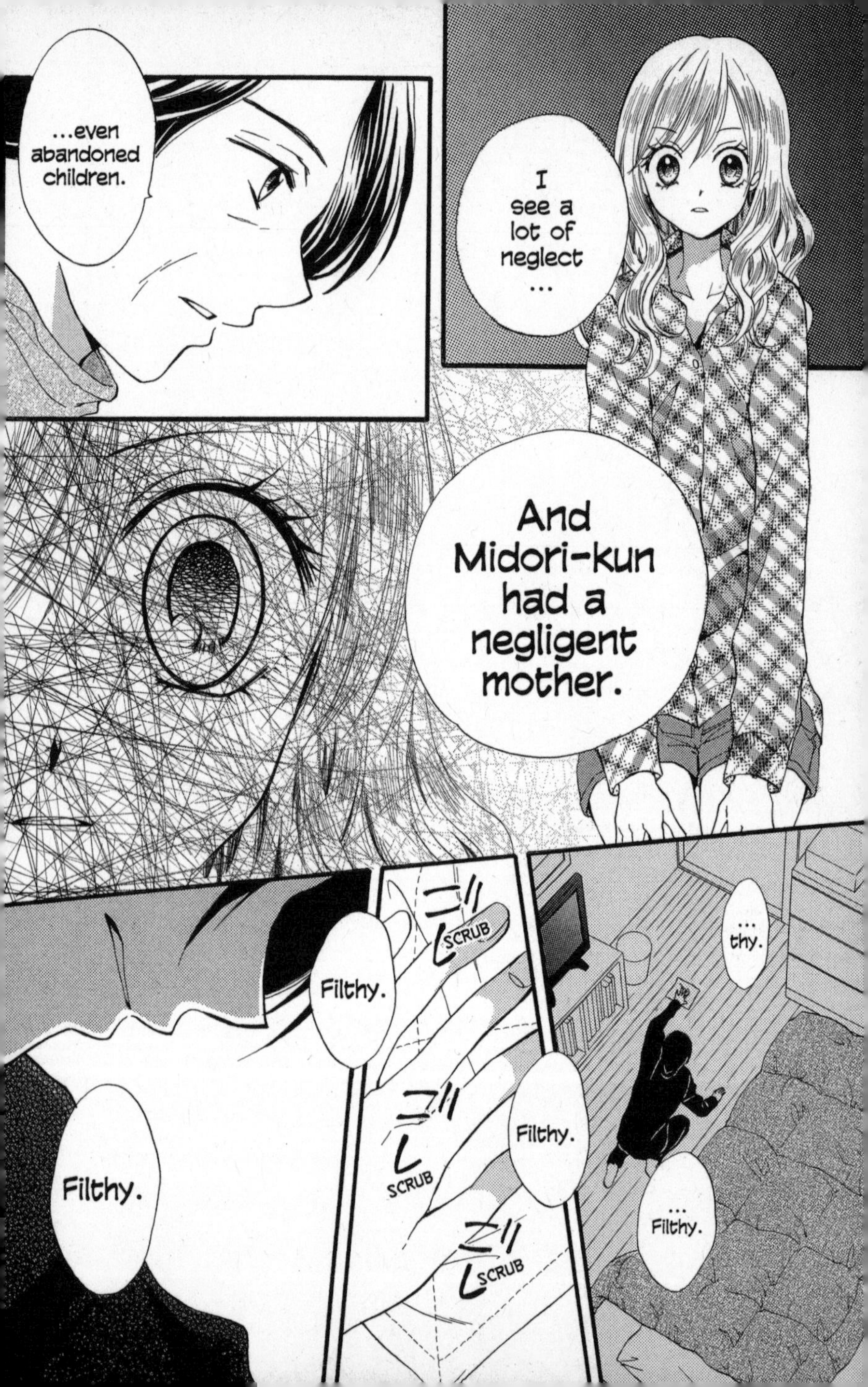
I see a lot of neglect ...
...even abandoned children.
And Midori-kun had a negligent mother.
...thy.
Filthy.
...Filthy.
SCRUB
Filthy.
SCRUB
SCRUB
Filthy.

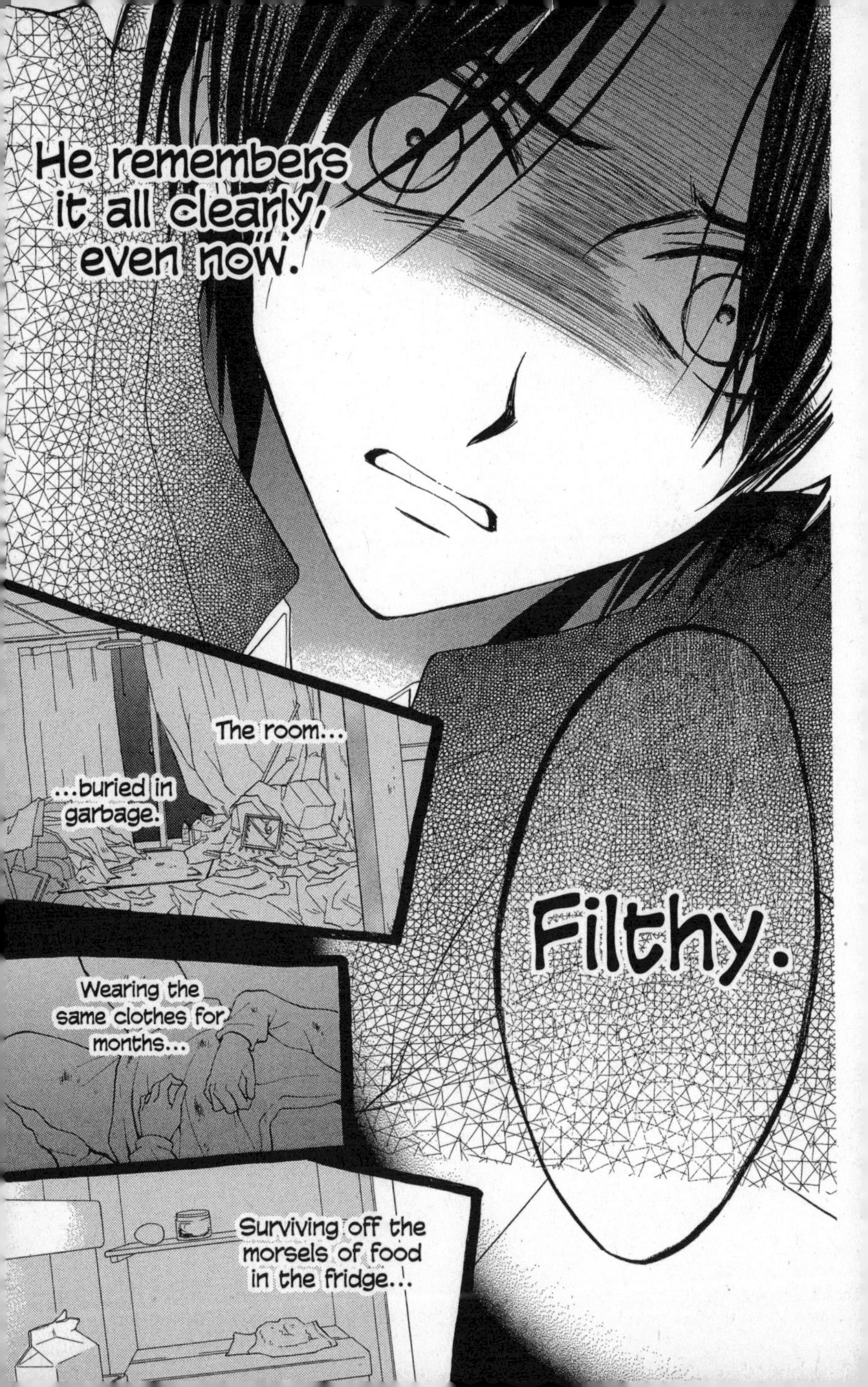

He remembers it all clearly, even now.
Filthy.
The room...
...buried in garbage.
Wearing the same clothes for months...
Surviving off the morsels of food in the fridge...

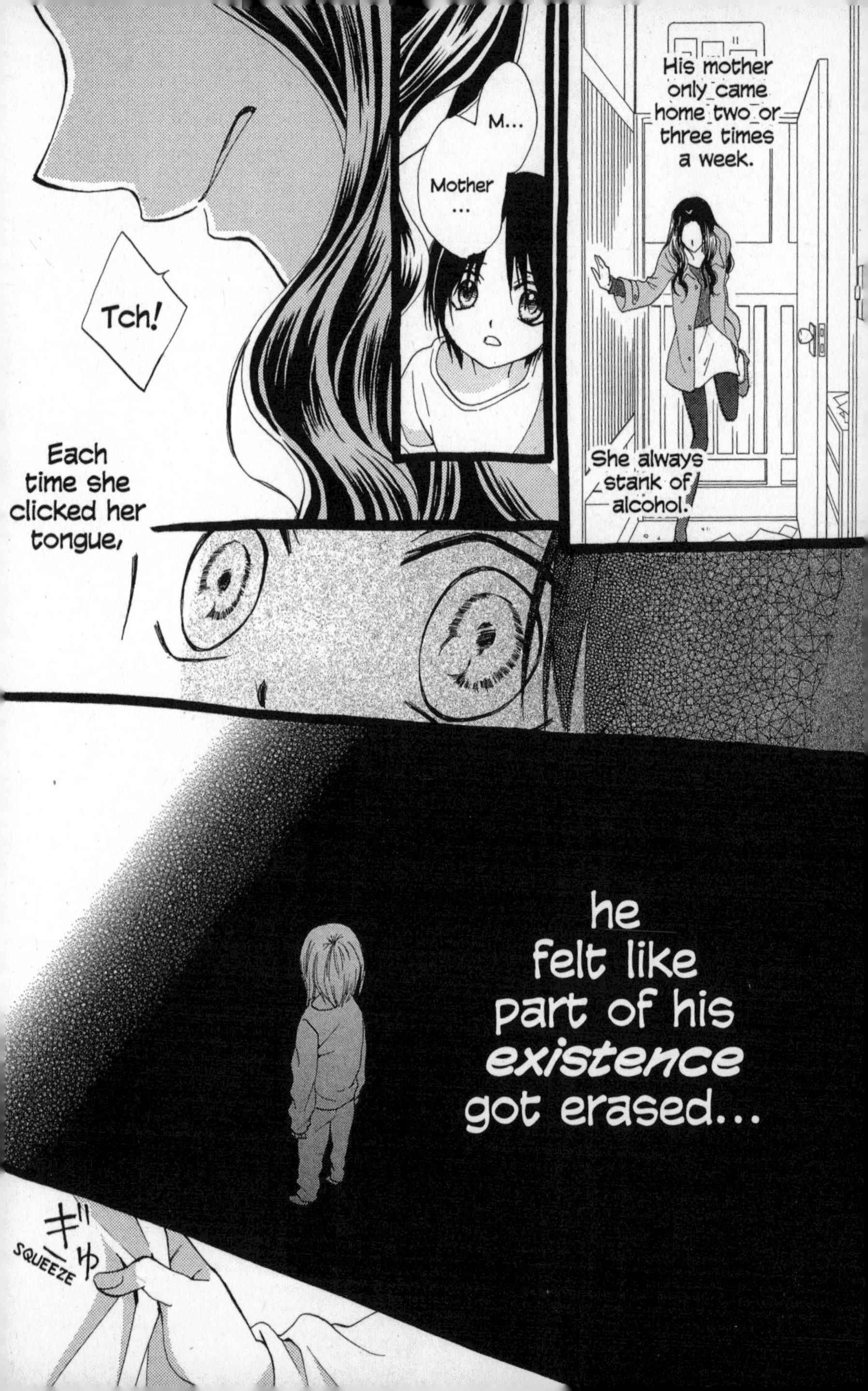
His mother only came home two or three times a week.
She always stank of alcohol.
M...
Mother...
Tch!
Each time she clicked her tongue,
he felt like part of his *existence* got erased...
ぎゅ
SQUEEZE

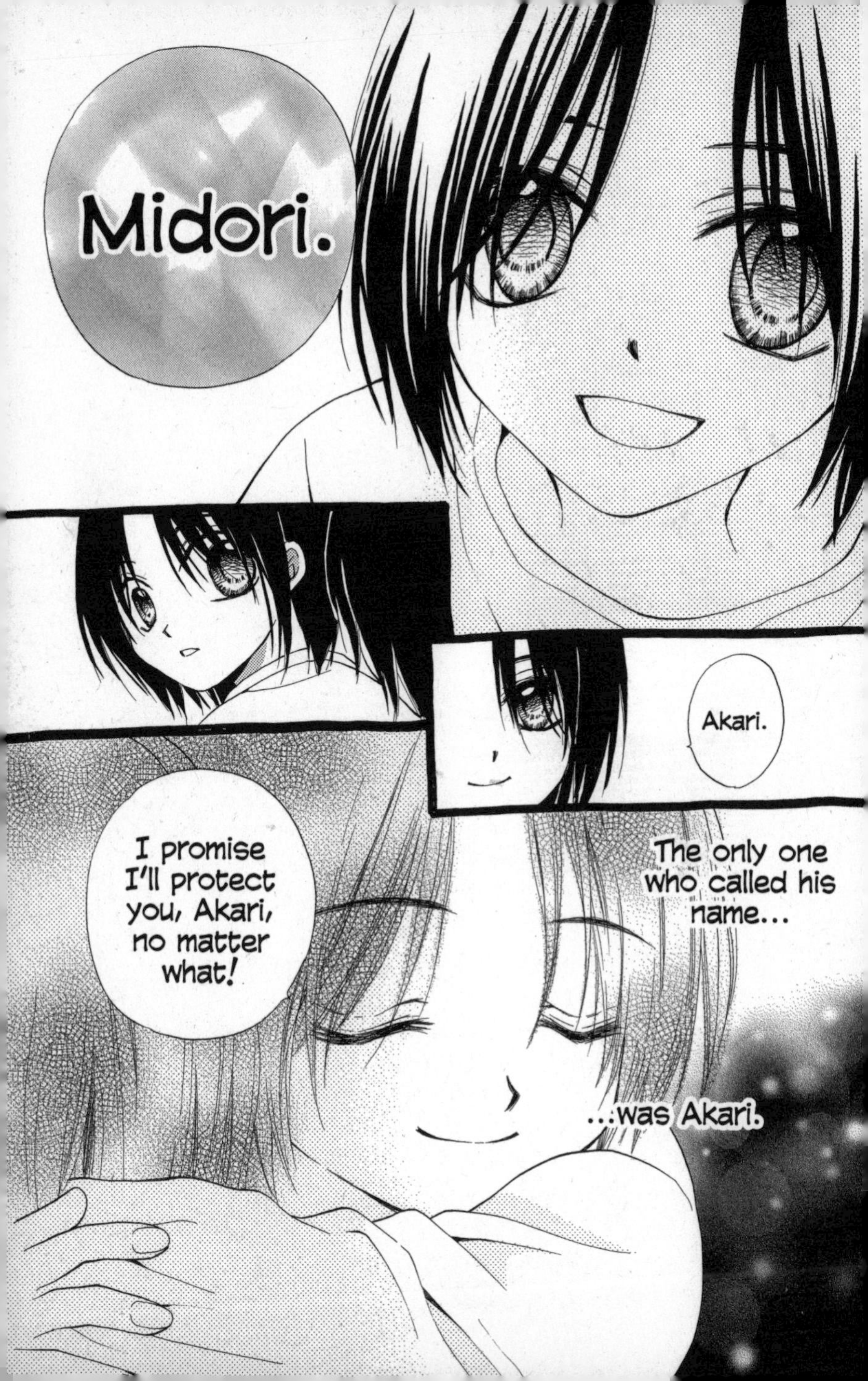
Midori.
Akari.
The only one who called his name...
I promise I'll protect you, Akari, no matter what!
...was Akari.

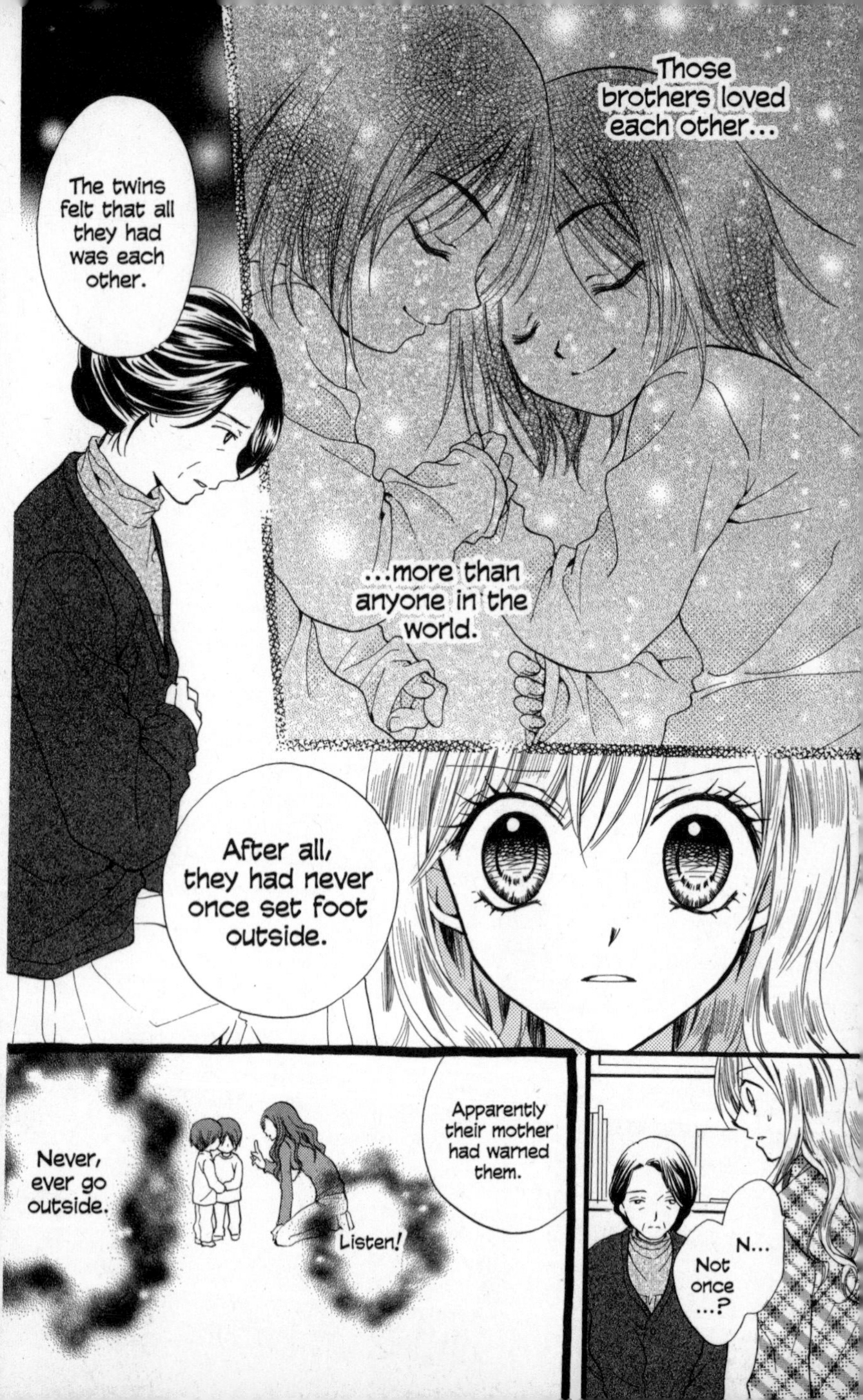
The twins felt that all they had was each other.
Those brothers loved each other...
...more than anyone in the world.
After all, they had never once set foot outside.
N... Not once ...?
Apparently their mother had warned them.
Listen!
Never, ever go outside.

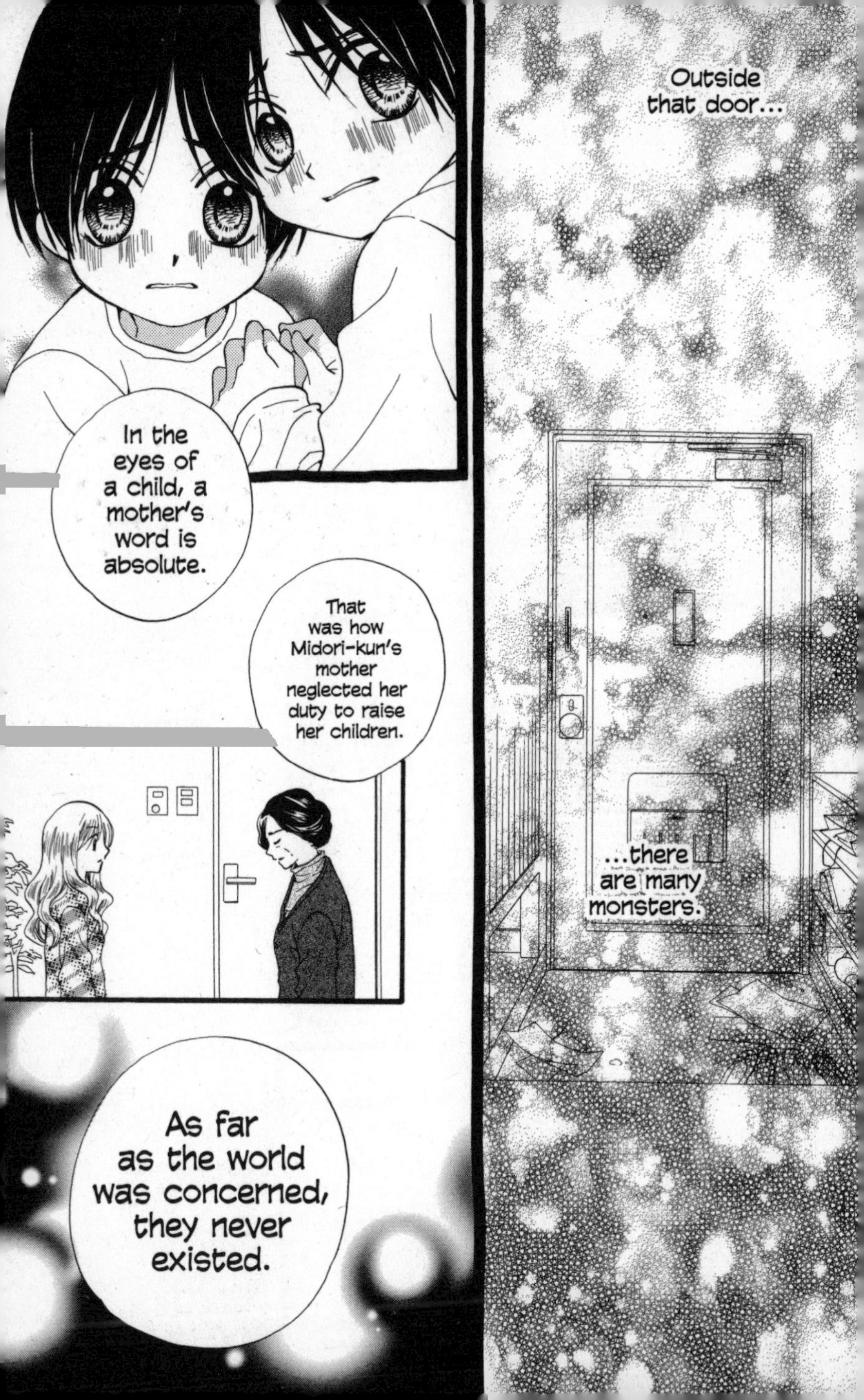
Outside that door...
...there are many monsters.
In the eyes of a child, a mother's word is absolute.
That was how Midori-kun's mother neglected her duty to raise her children.
As far as the world was concerned, they never existed.

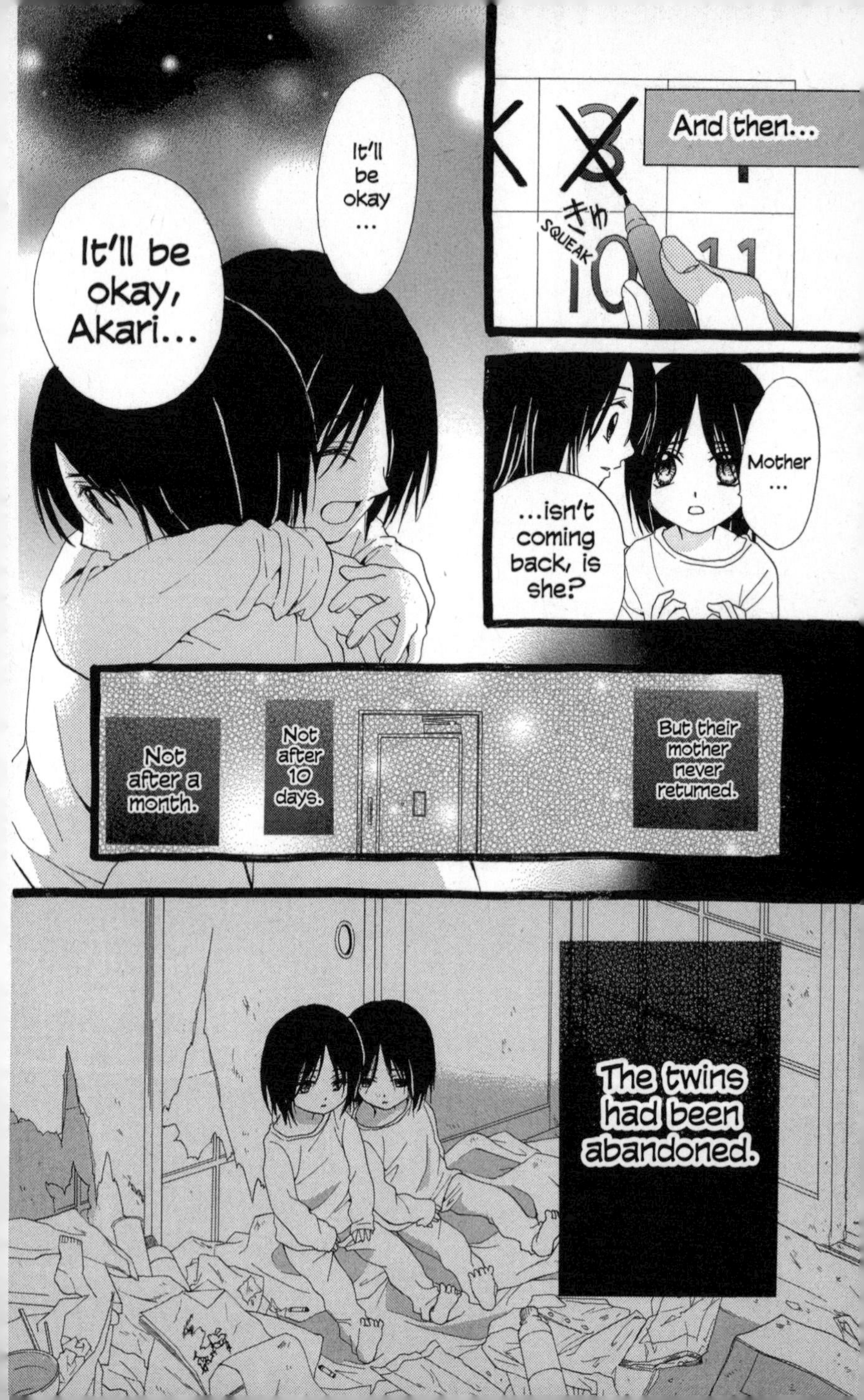
And then...
きゅ
SQUEAK
Mother...
...isn't coming back, is she?
It'll be okay...
It'll be okay, Akari...
But their mother never returned.
Not after 10 days.
Not after a month.
The twins had been abandoned.

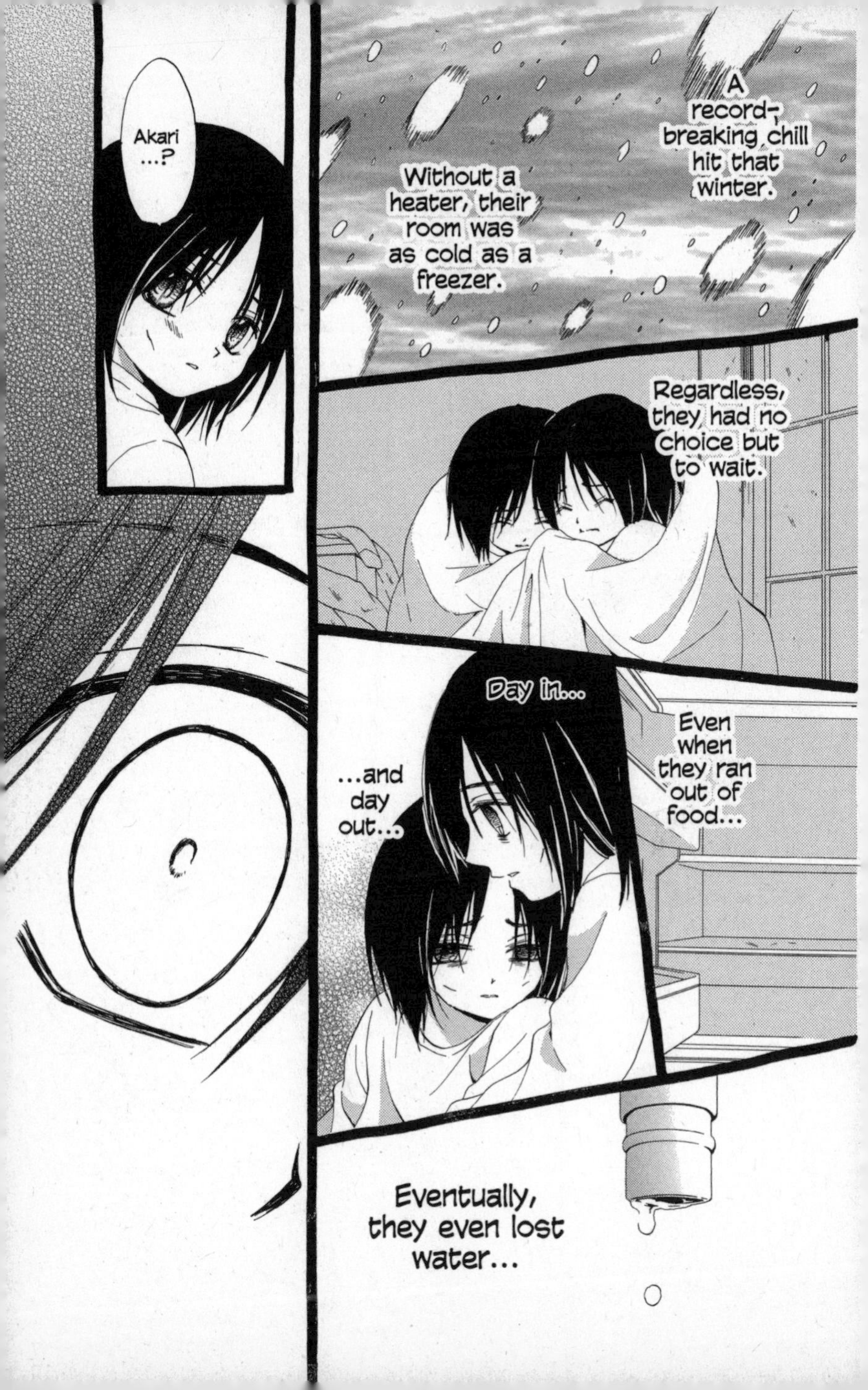
A record-breaking chill hit that winter.
Without a heater, their room was as cold as a freezer.
Regardless, they had no choice but to wait.
Even when they ran out of food...
Day in...
...and day out...
Eventually, they even lost water...
Akari ...?

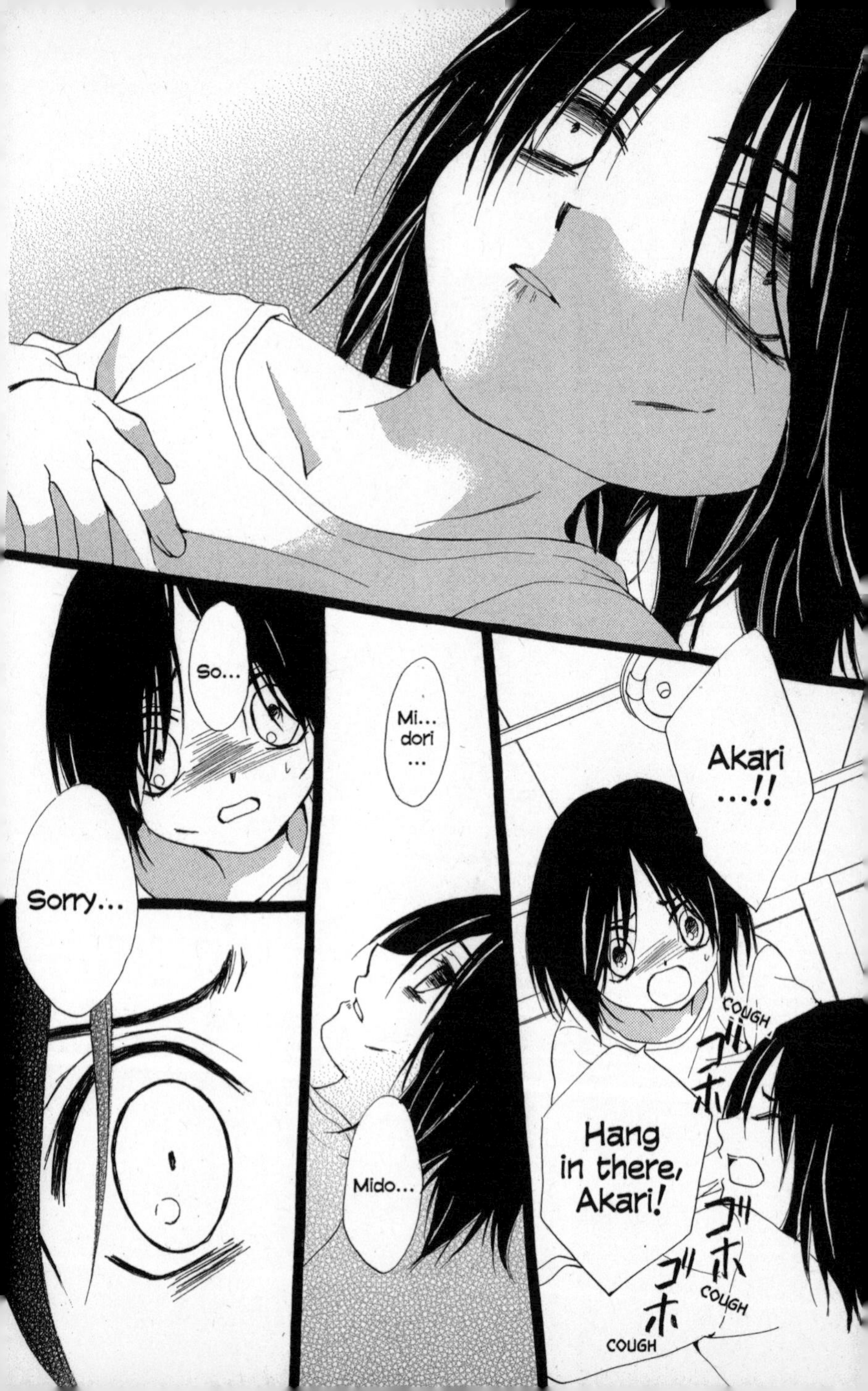
Akari ...!!
COUGH
ゴホ
Hang in there, Akari!
ゴホ
COUGH
ゴホ
COUGH
Mi... dori ...
Mido...
So...
Sorry...

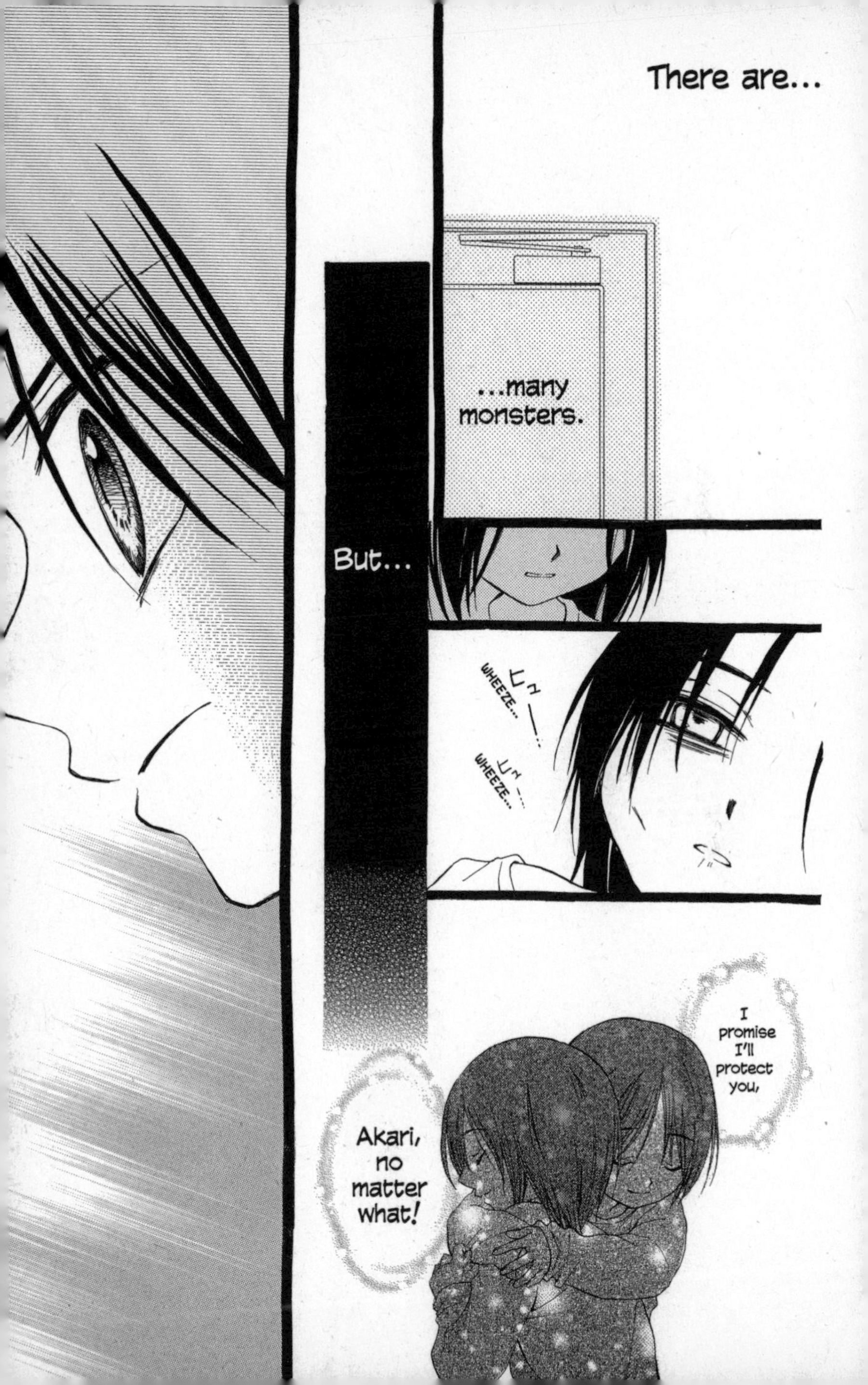
There are...
...many monsters.
But...
WHEEZE...
WHEEZE...
I promise I'll protect you,
Akari, no matter what!

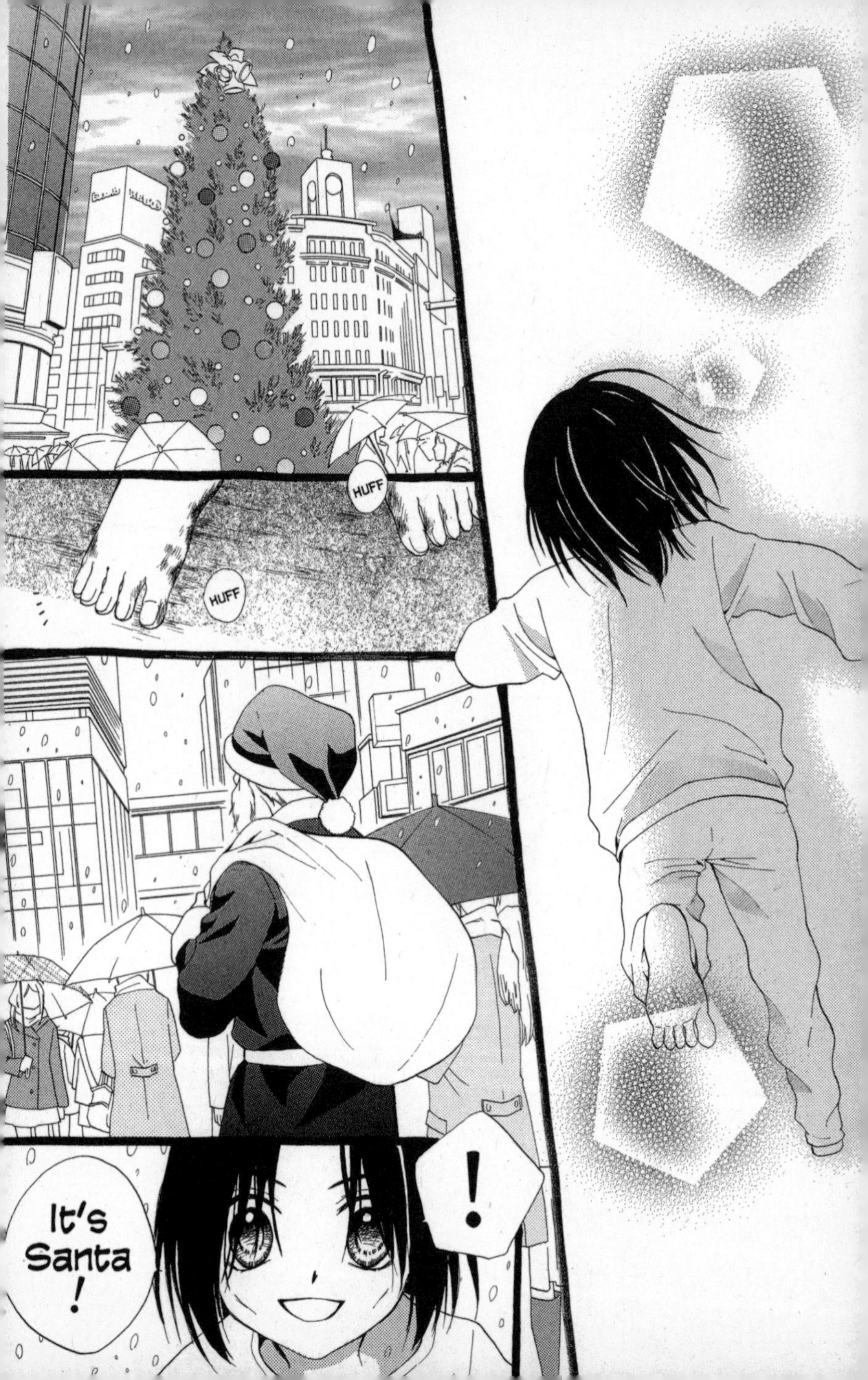
HUFF
HUFF
!
It's Santa!

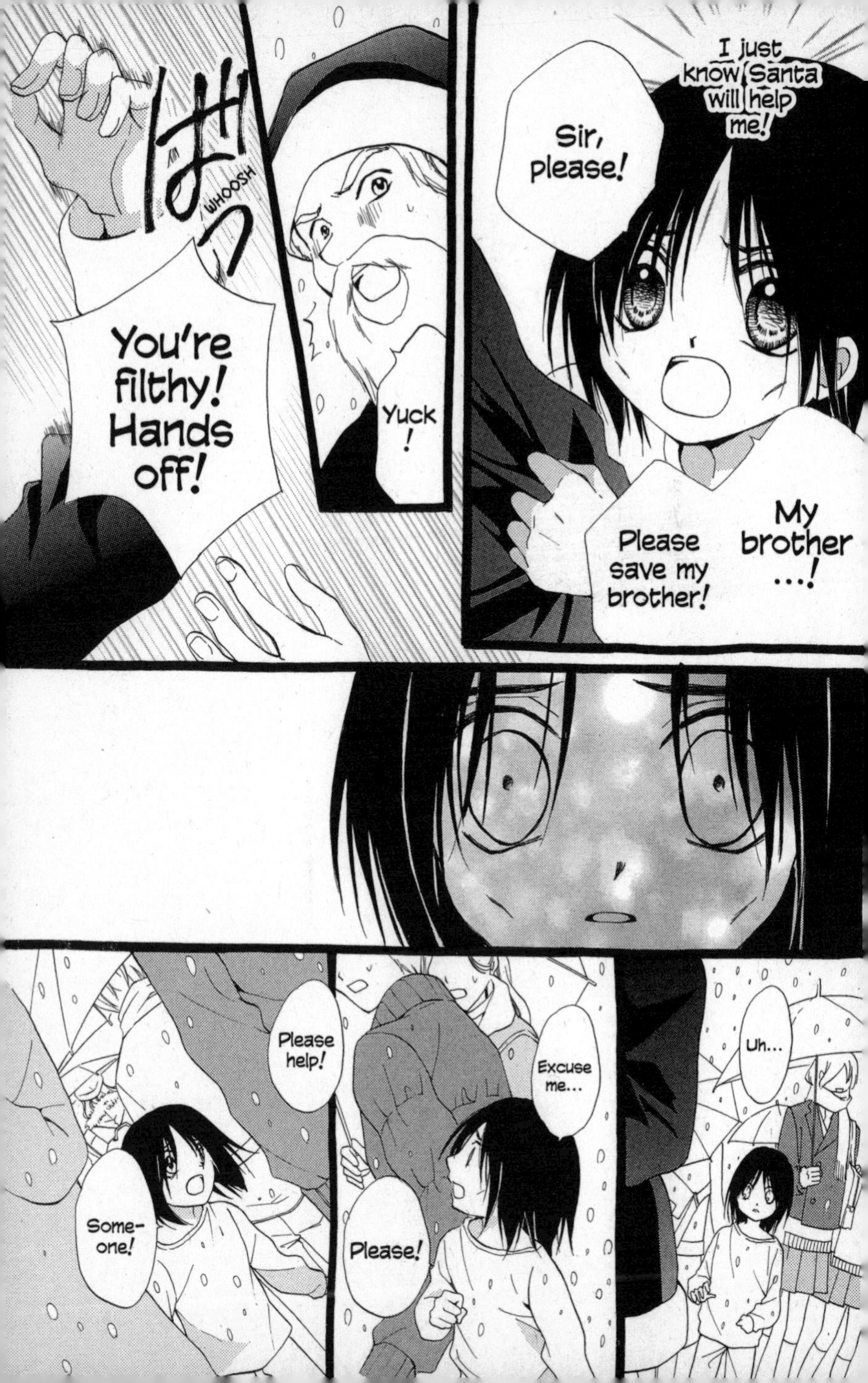
I just know Santa will help me!
Sir, please!
My brother ...!
Please save my brother!
Yuck!
はっ
WHOOSH
You're filthy! Hands off!
Uh...
Excuse me...
Please!
Please help!
Some-one!

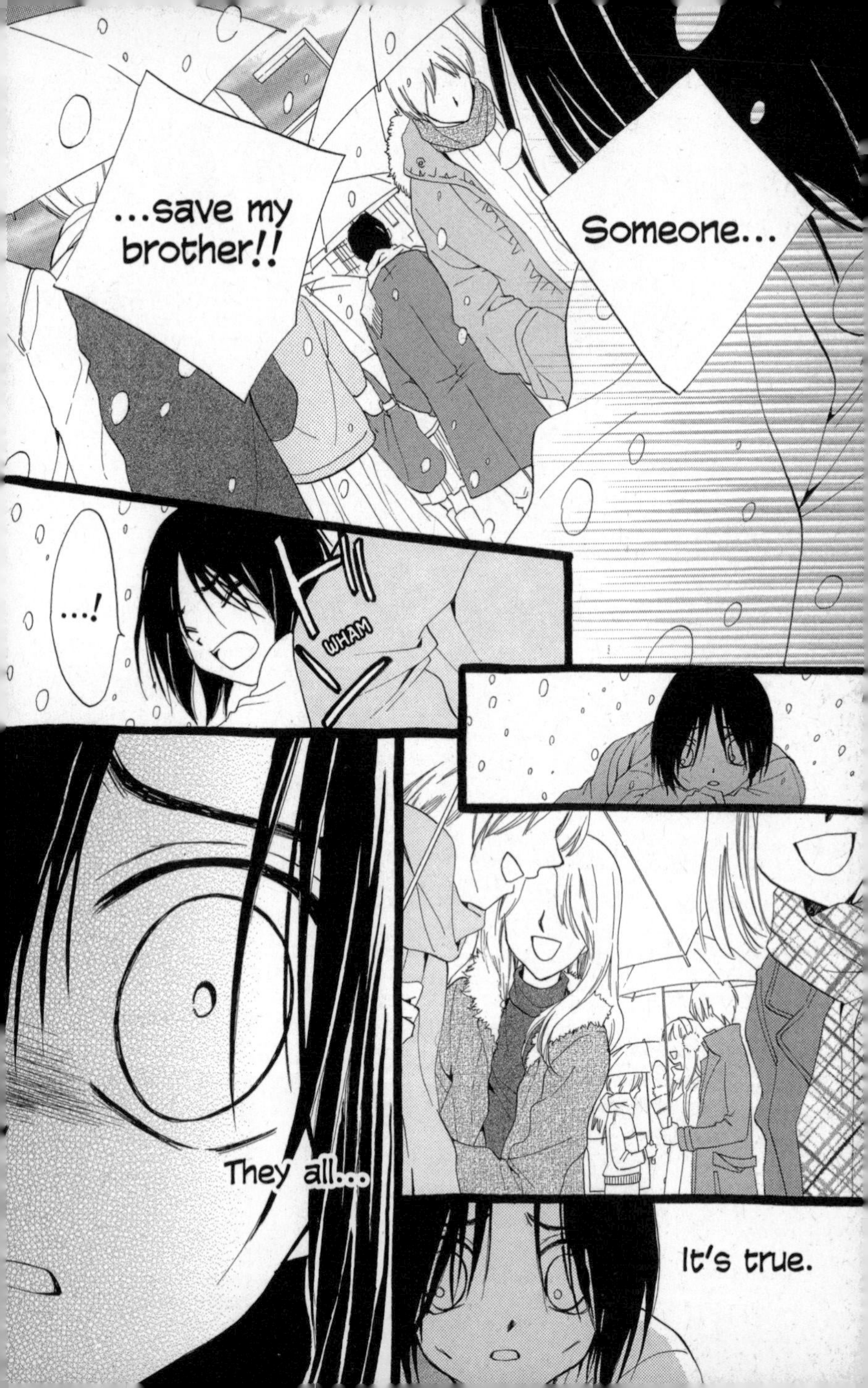
Someone...
...save my brother!!
WHAM
...!
They all...
It's true.

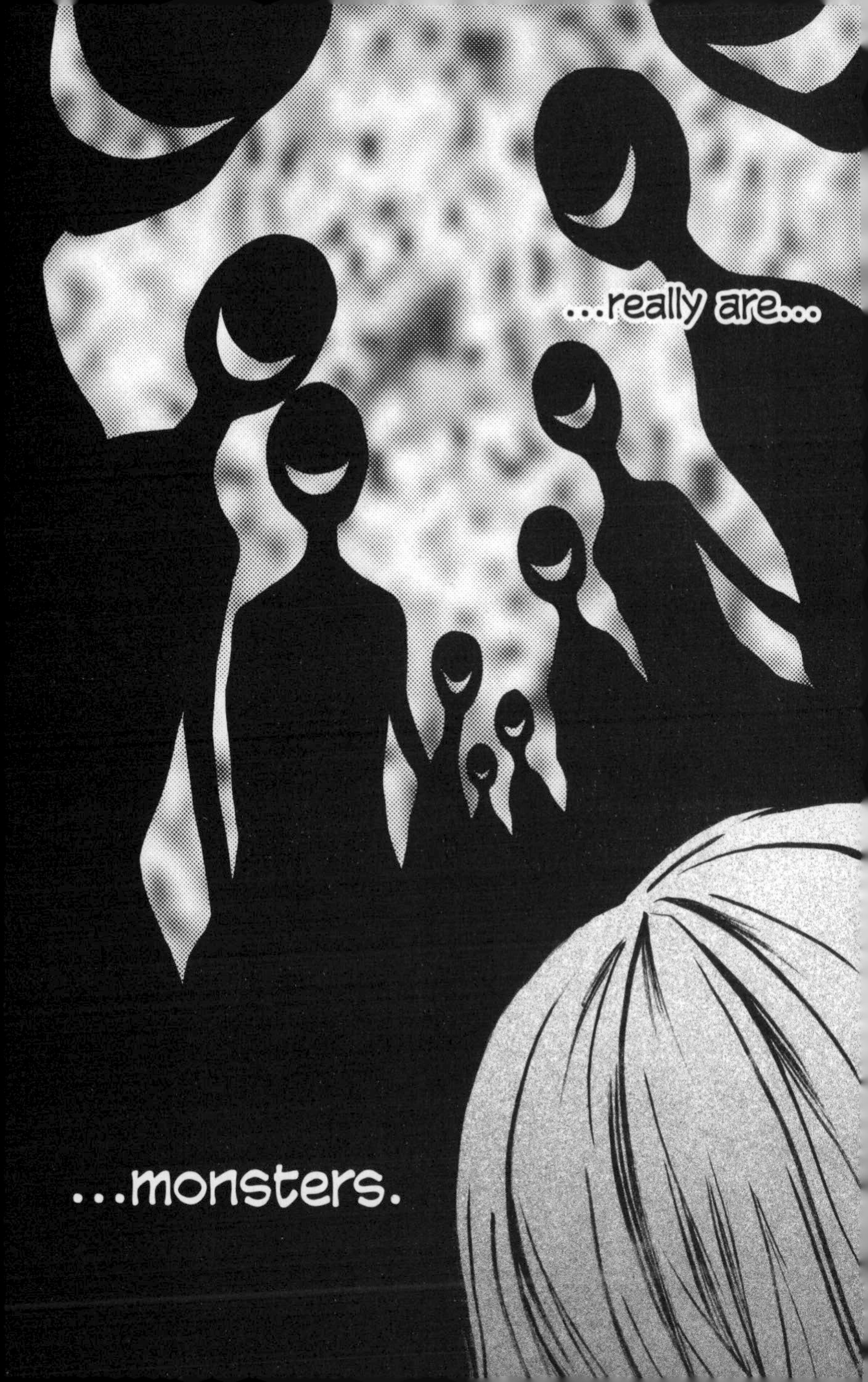
...really are...
...monsters.

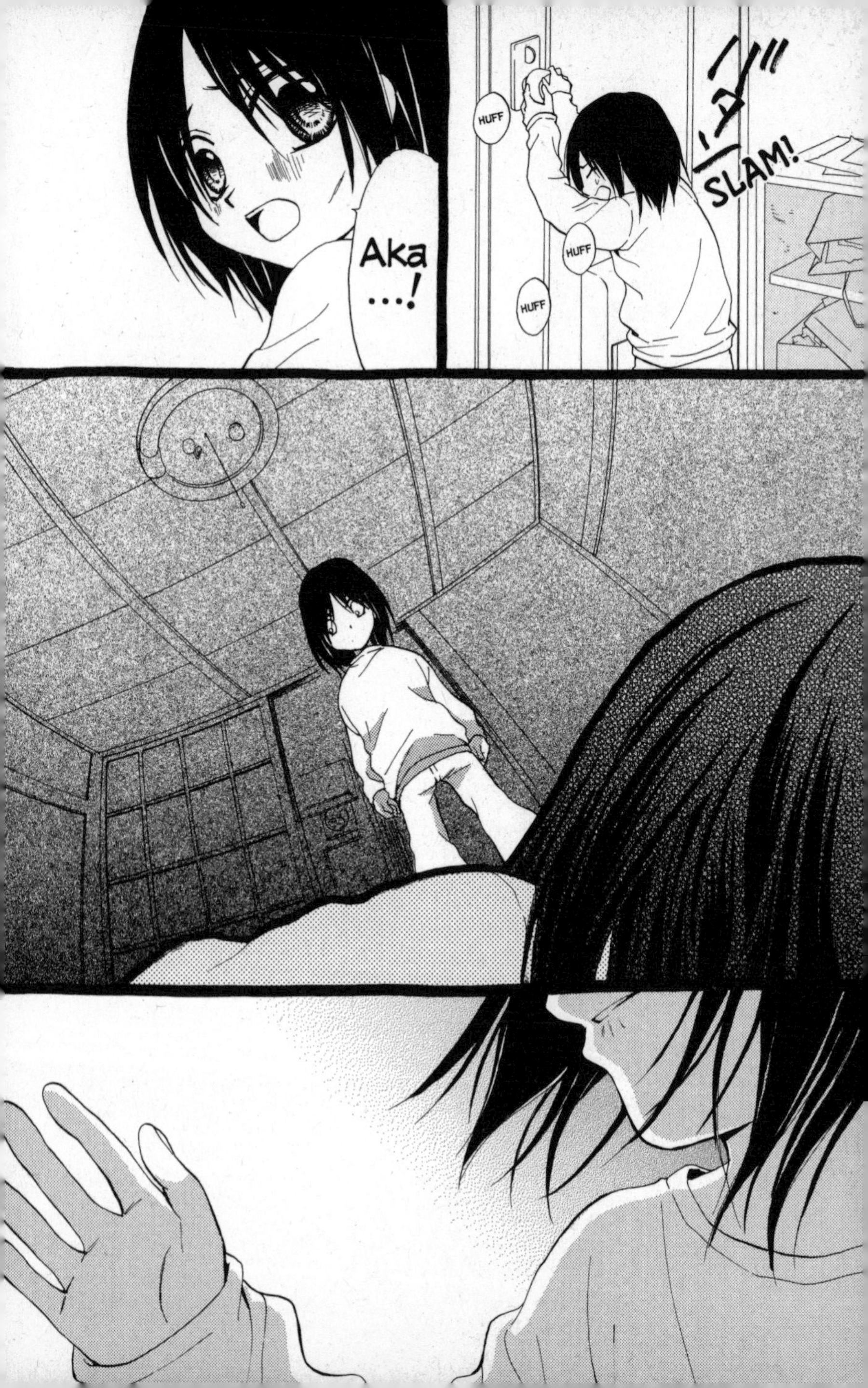
SLAM!
HUFF
HUFF
HUFF
Aka ...!

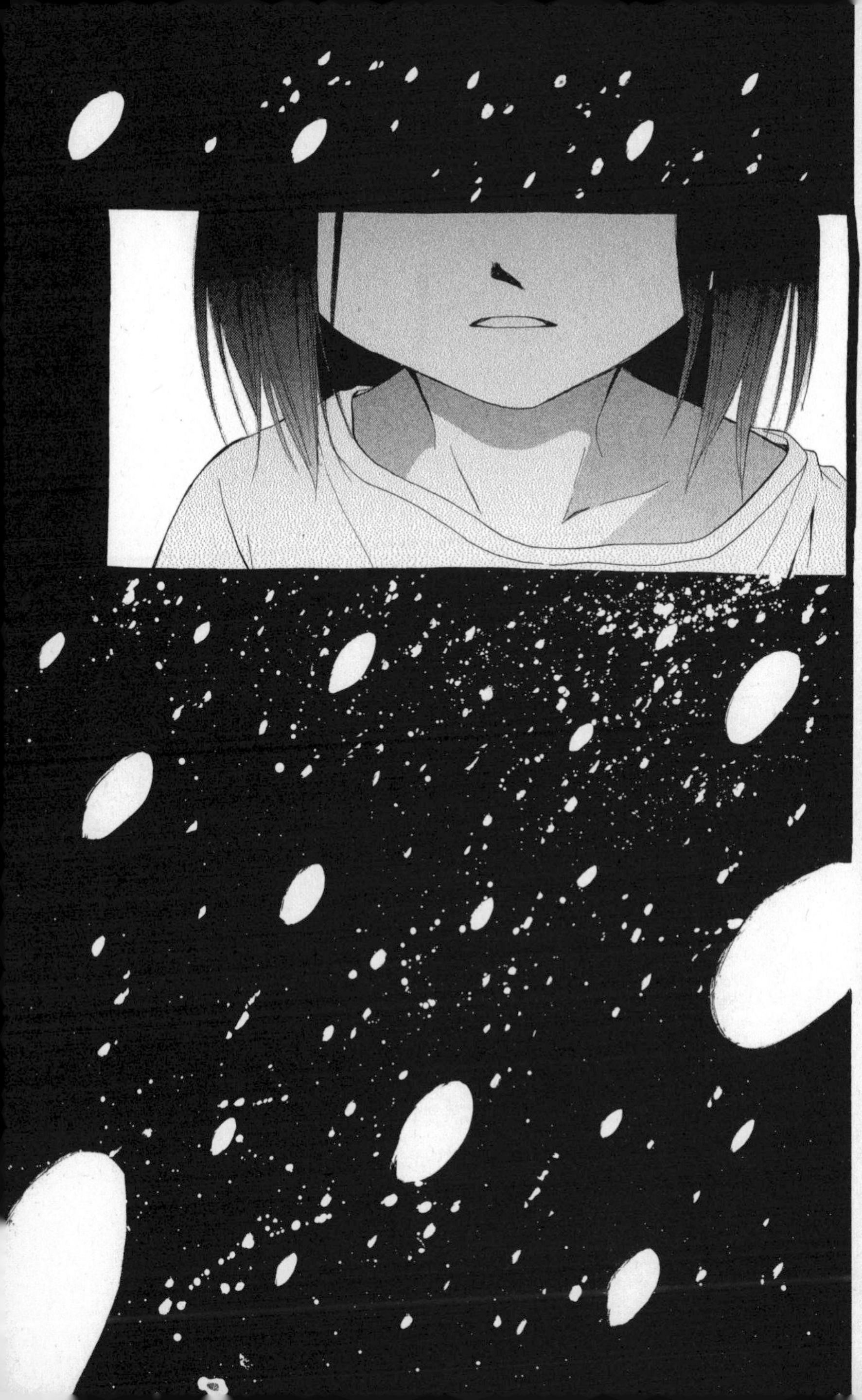

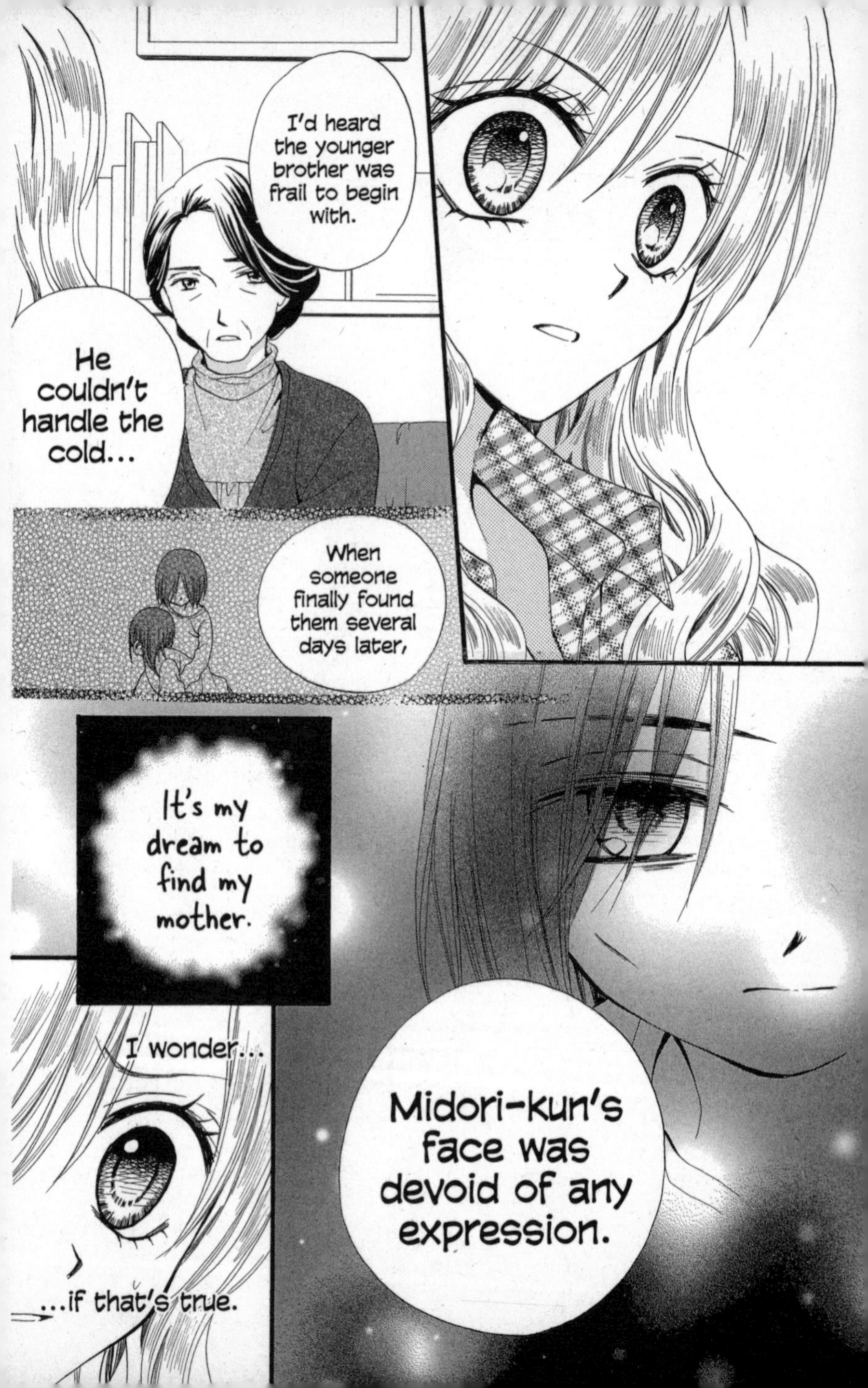
I'd heard the younger brother was frail to begin with.
He couldn't handle the cold...
When someone finally found them several days later,
Midori-kun's face was devoid of any expression.
It's my dream to find my mother.
I wonder...
...if that's true.

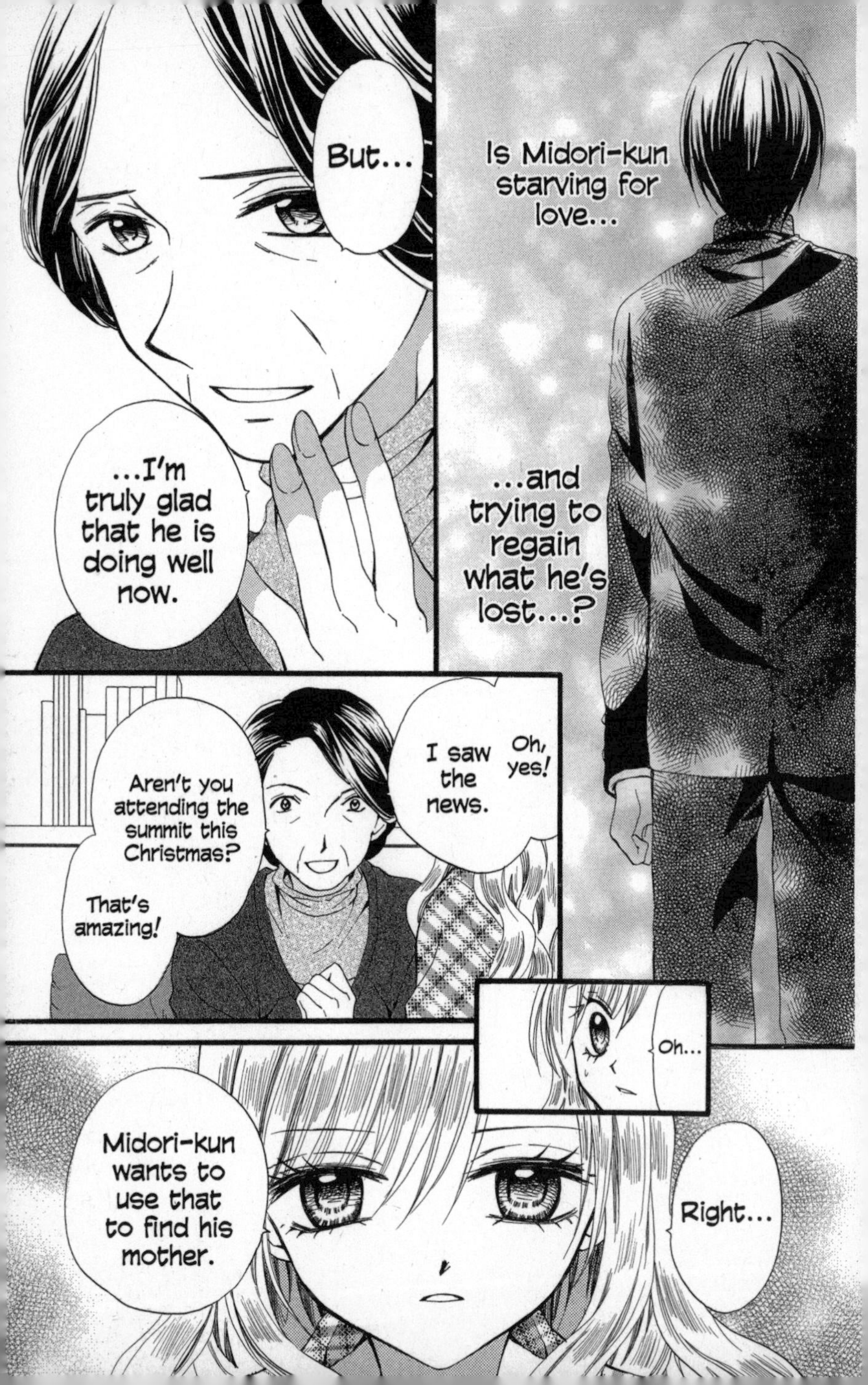
Is Midori-kun starving for love...
...and trying to regain what he's lost...?
But...
...I'm truly glad that he is doing well now.
Oh, yes!
I saw the news.
Aren't you attending the summit this Christmas?
That's amazing!
Oh...
Right...
Midori-kun wants to use that to find his mother.

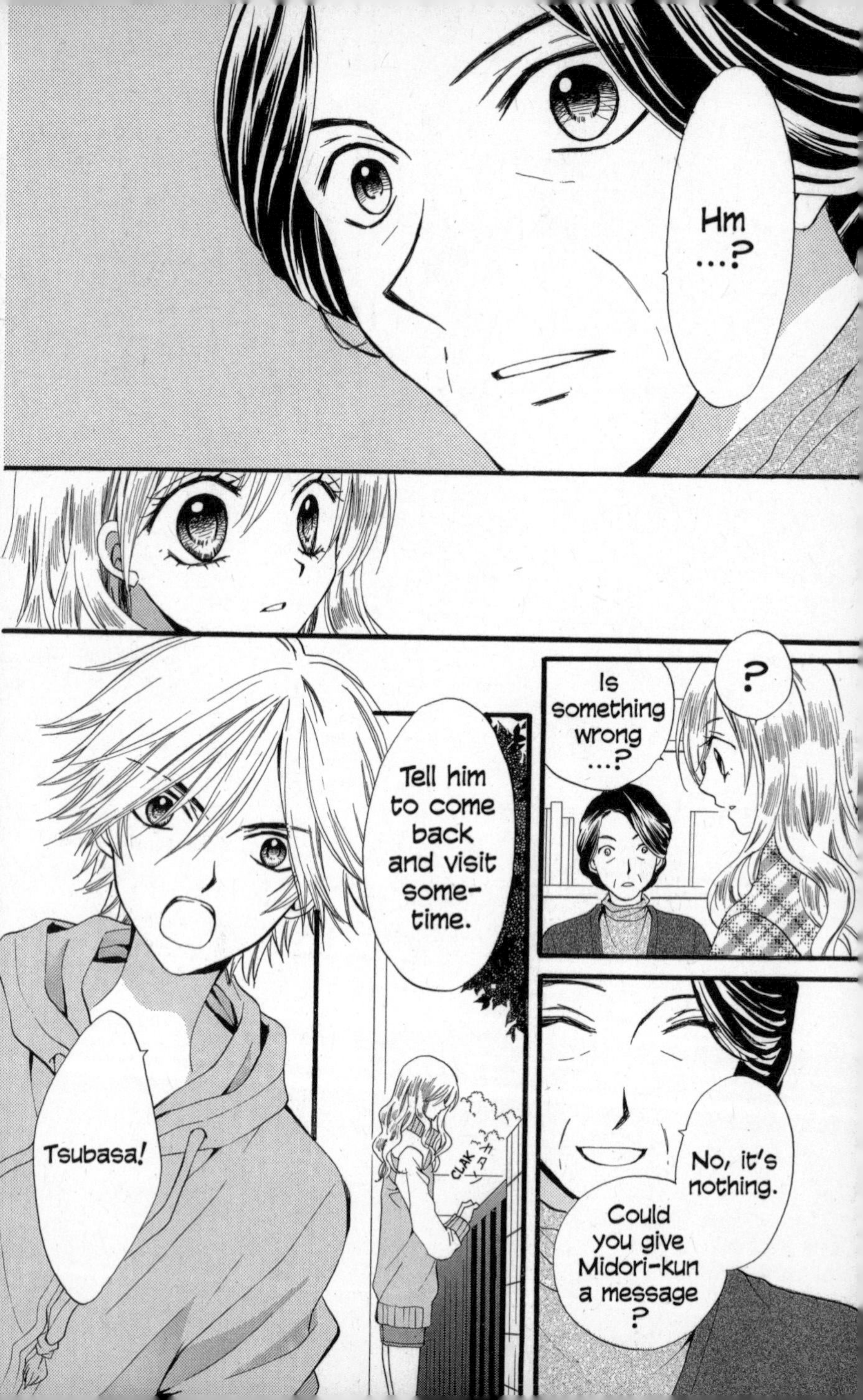
Hm ...?
?
Is something wrong ...?
No, it's nothing.
Could you give Midori-kun a message?
Tell him to come back and visit some-time.
CLAK
Tsubasa!

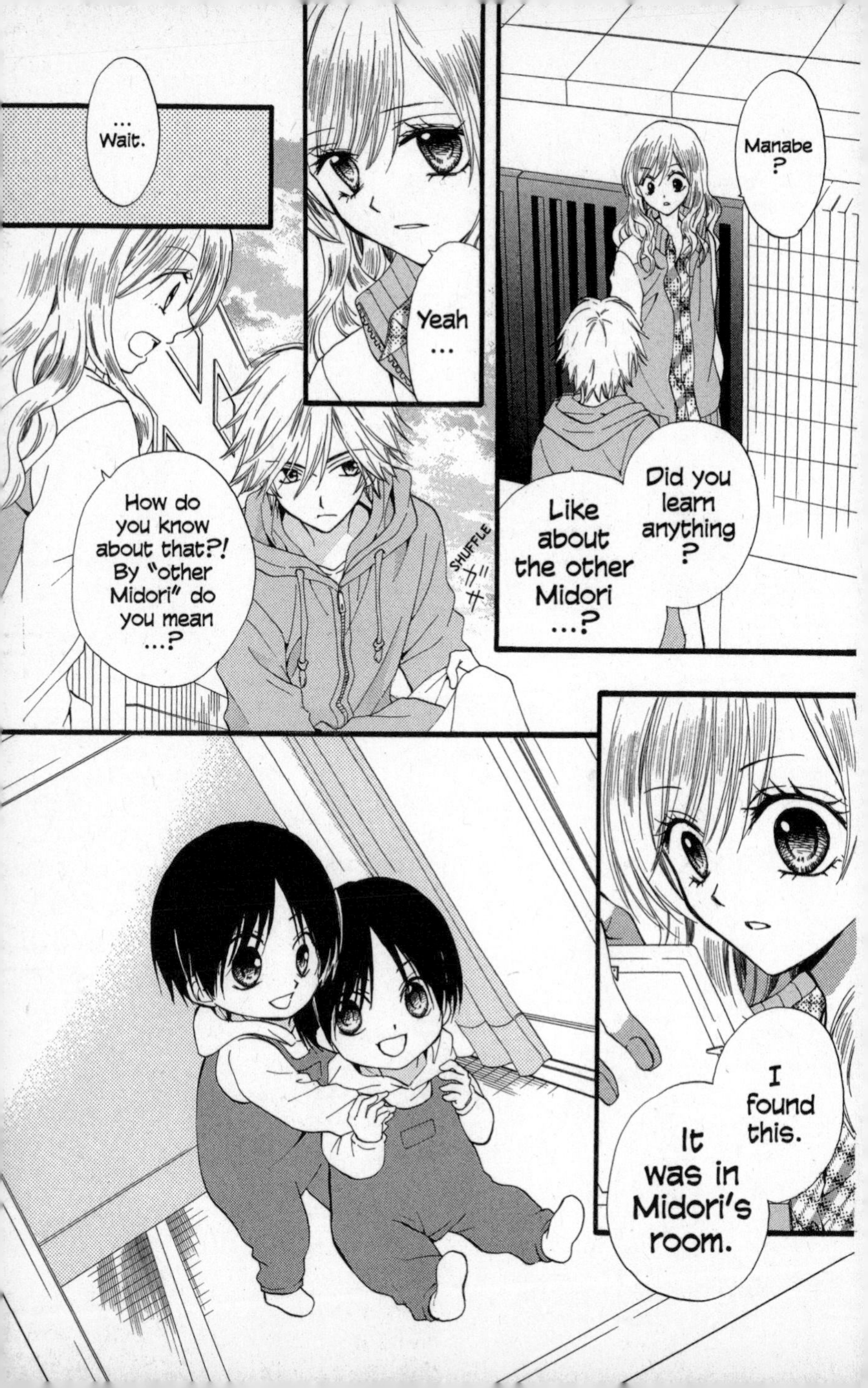
Manabe?
Did you learn anything?
Like about the other Midori ...?
Yeah ...
... Wait.
How do you know about that?! By "other Midori" do you mean ...?
SHUFFLE
I found this.
It was in Midori's room.

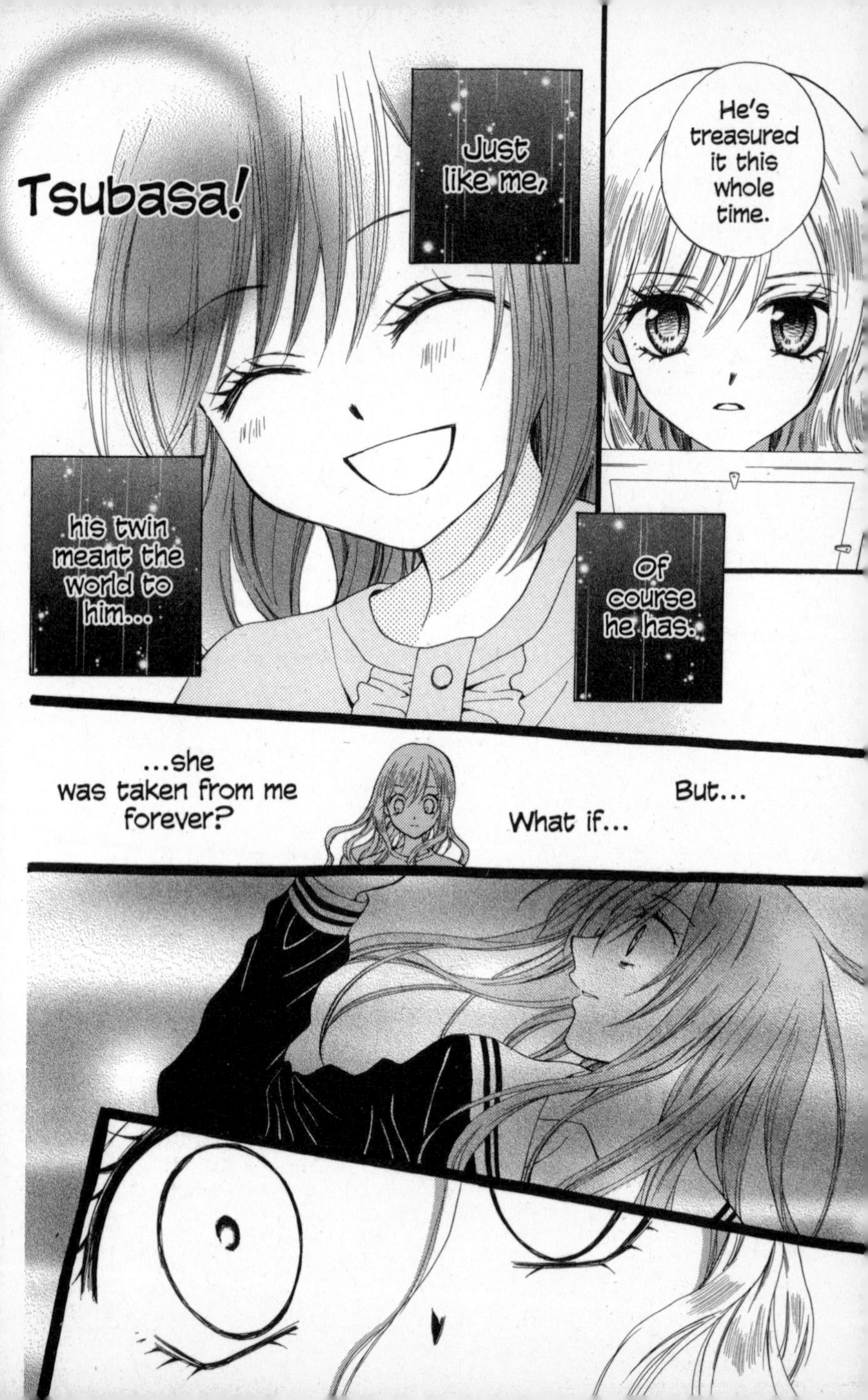
He's treasured it this whole time.
Of course he has.
Just like me,
Tsubasa!
his twin meant the world to him...
But...
What if...
...she was taken from me forever?

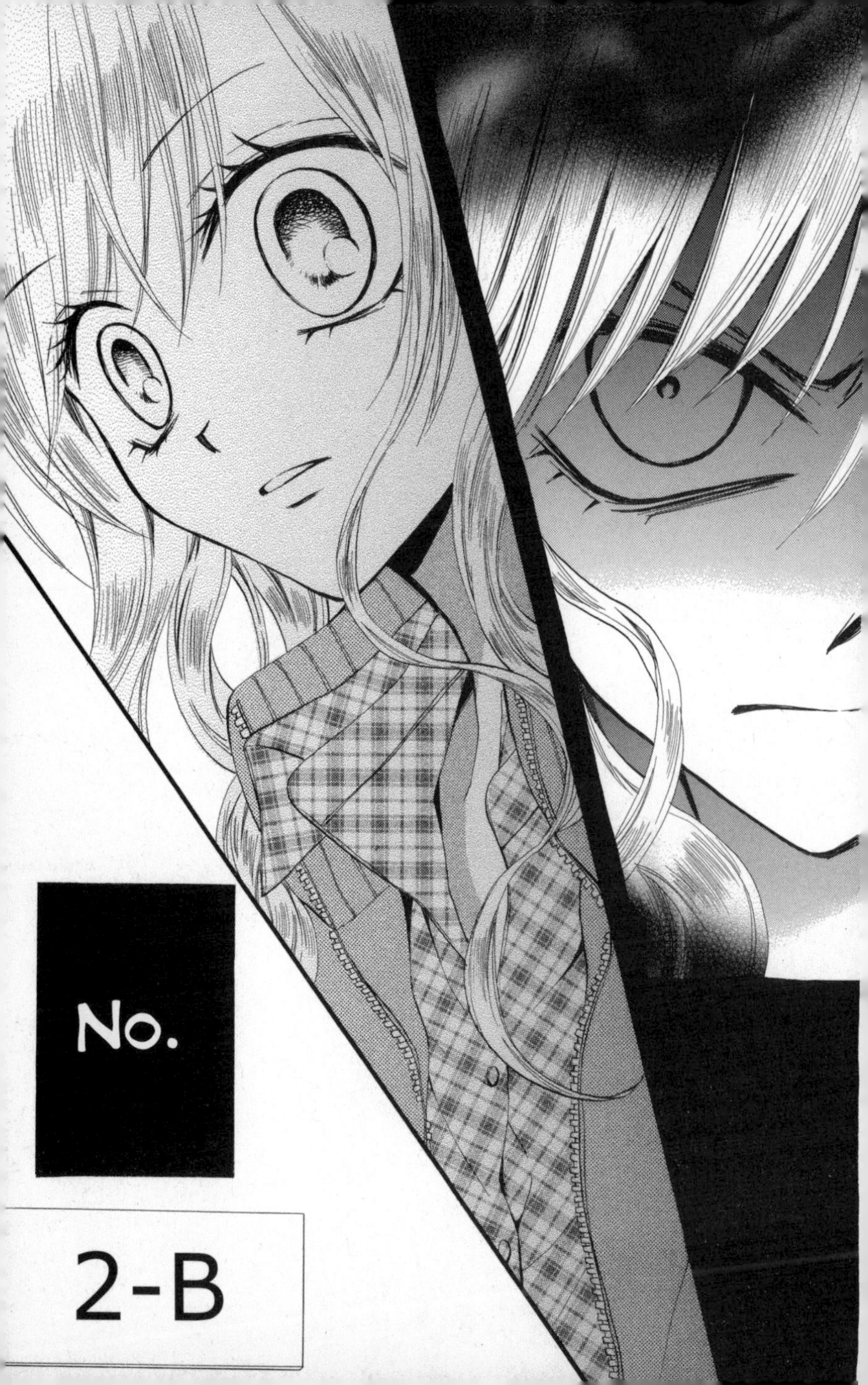
No.
2-B

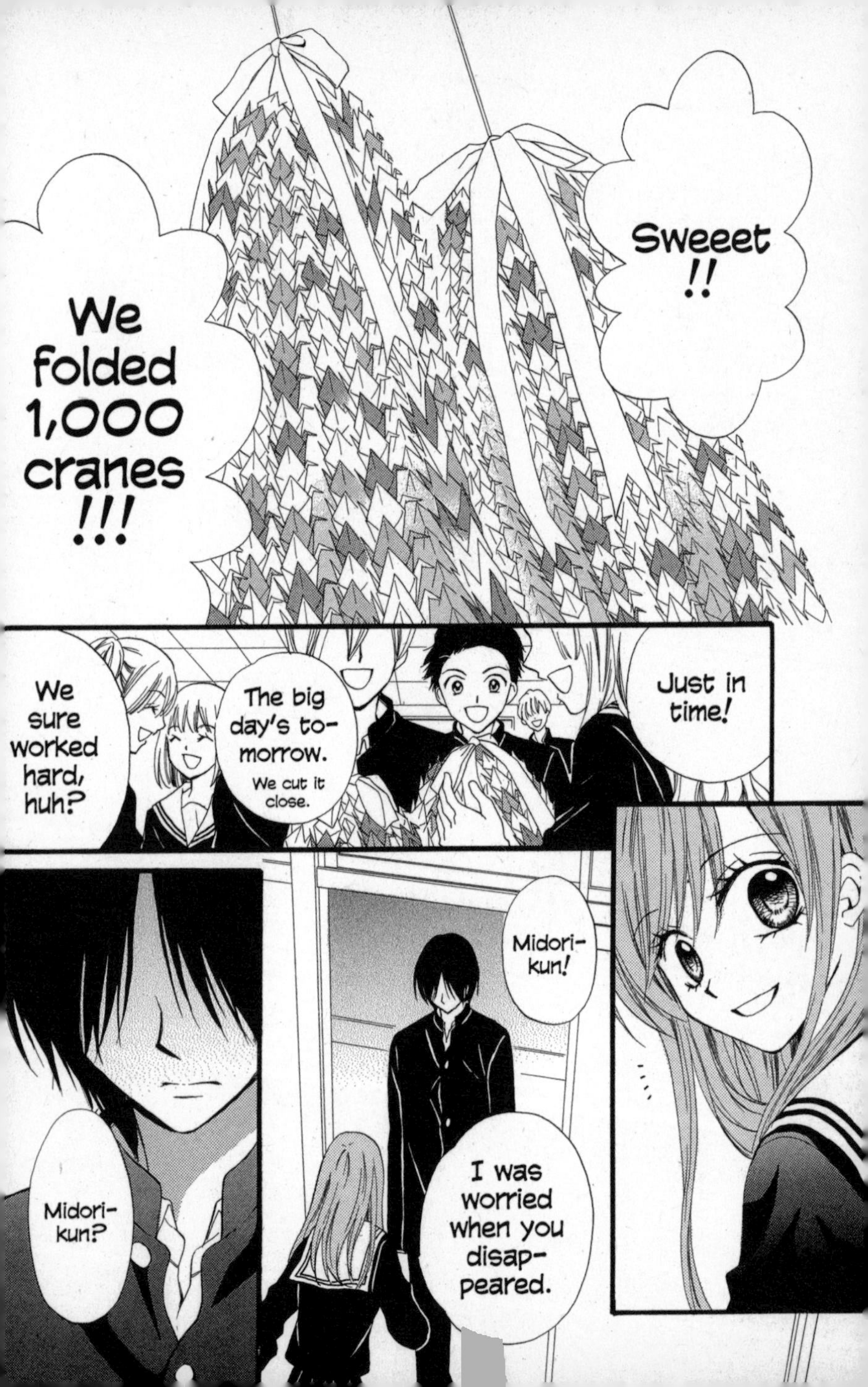
Sweeet!!
We folded 1,000 cranes!!!
Just in time!
The big day's tomorrow.
We cut it close.
We sure worked hard, huh?
...
Midori-kun!
I was worried when you disappeared.
Midori-kun?

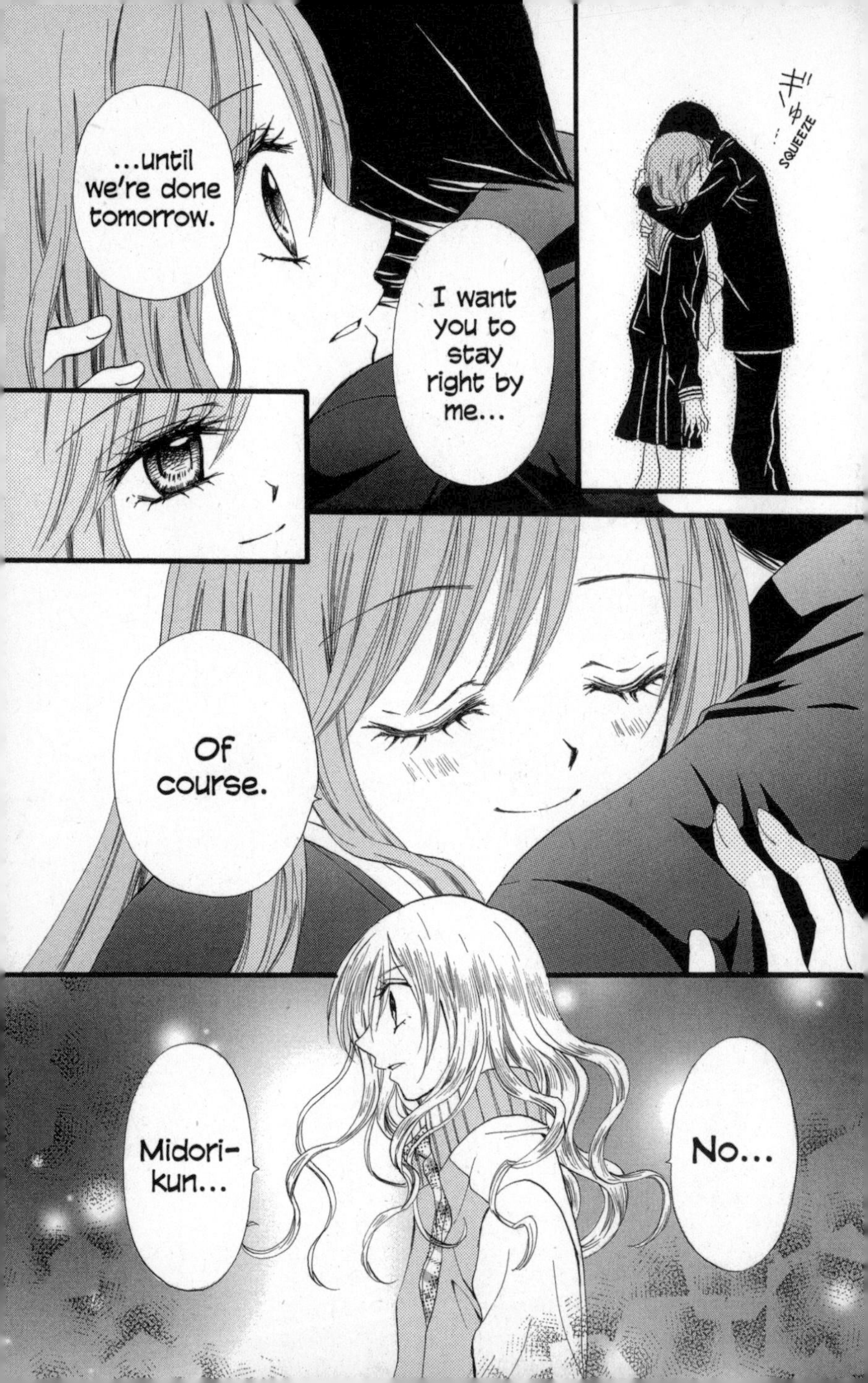
SQUEEZE
I want you to stay right by me...
...until we're done tomorrow.
Of course.
No...
Midori-kun...

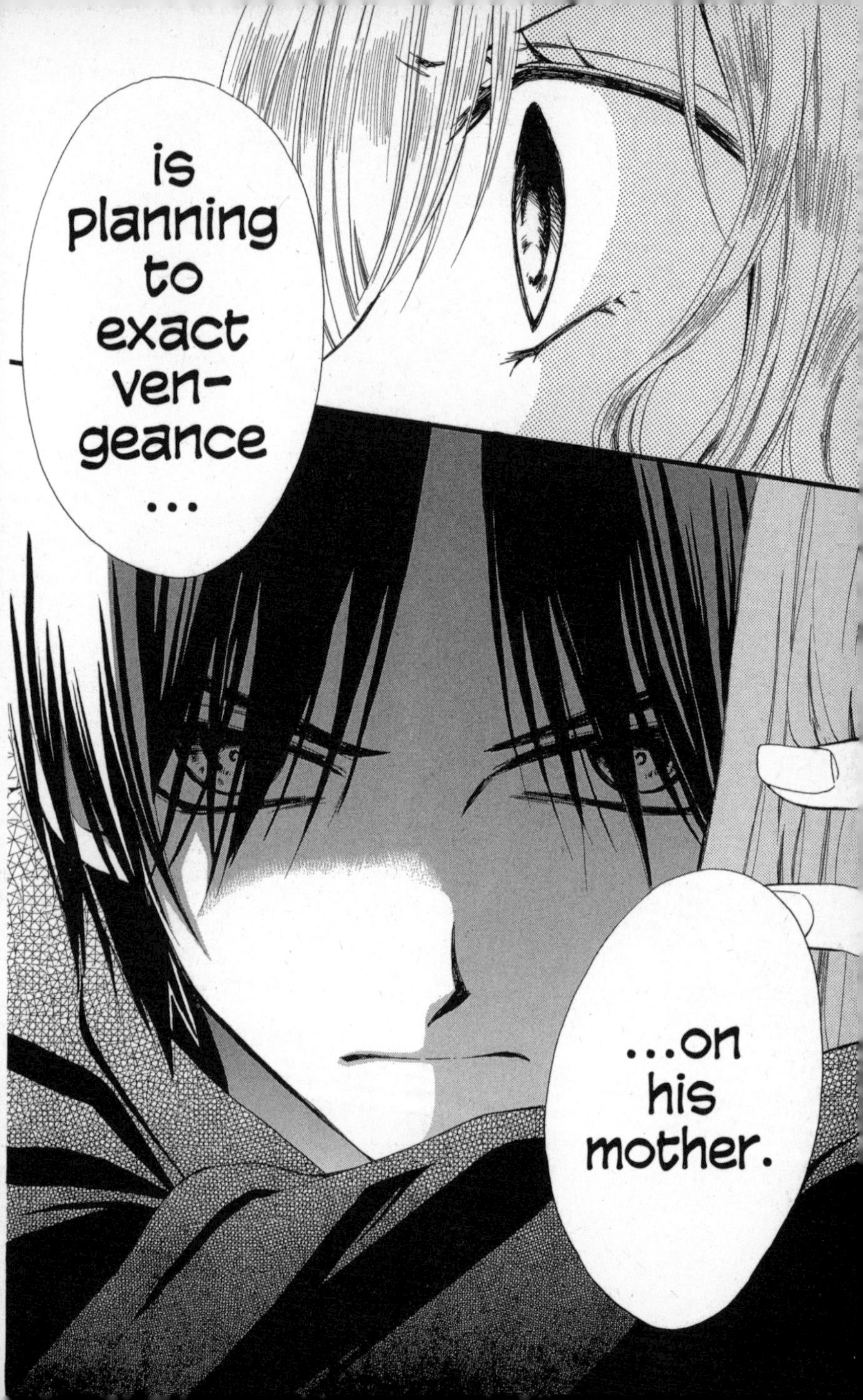
is planning to exact ven-geance ...
...on his mother.

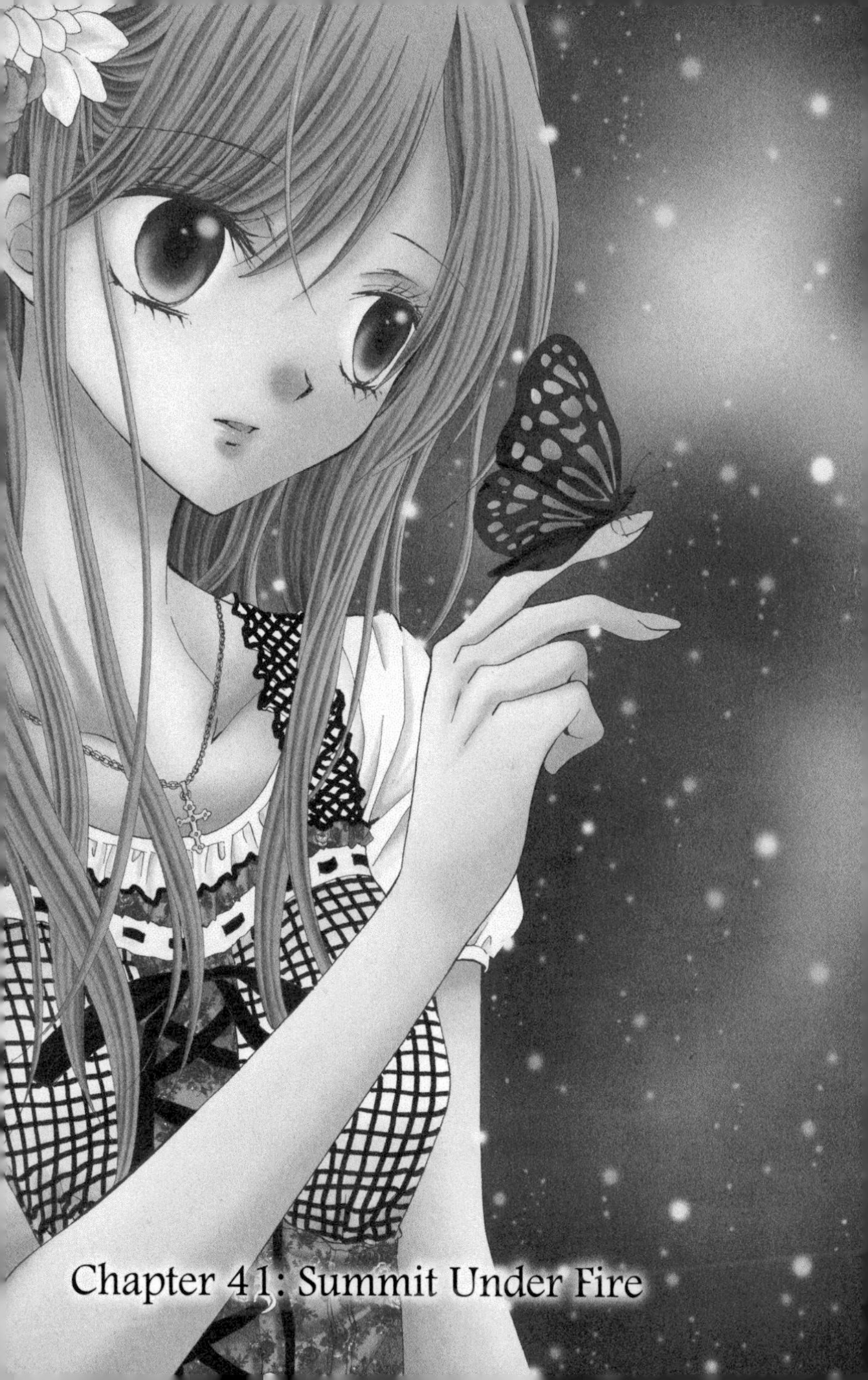
Chapter 41: Summit Under Fire

ARISA

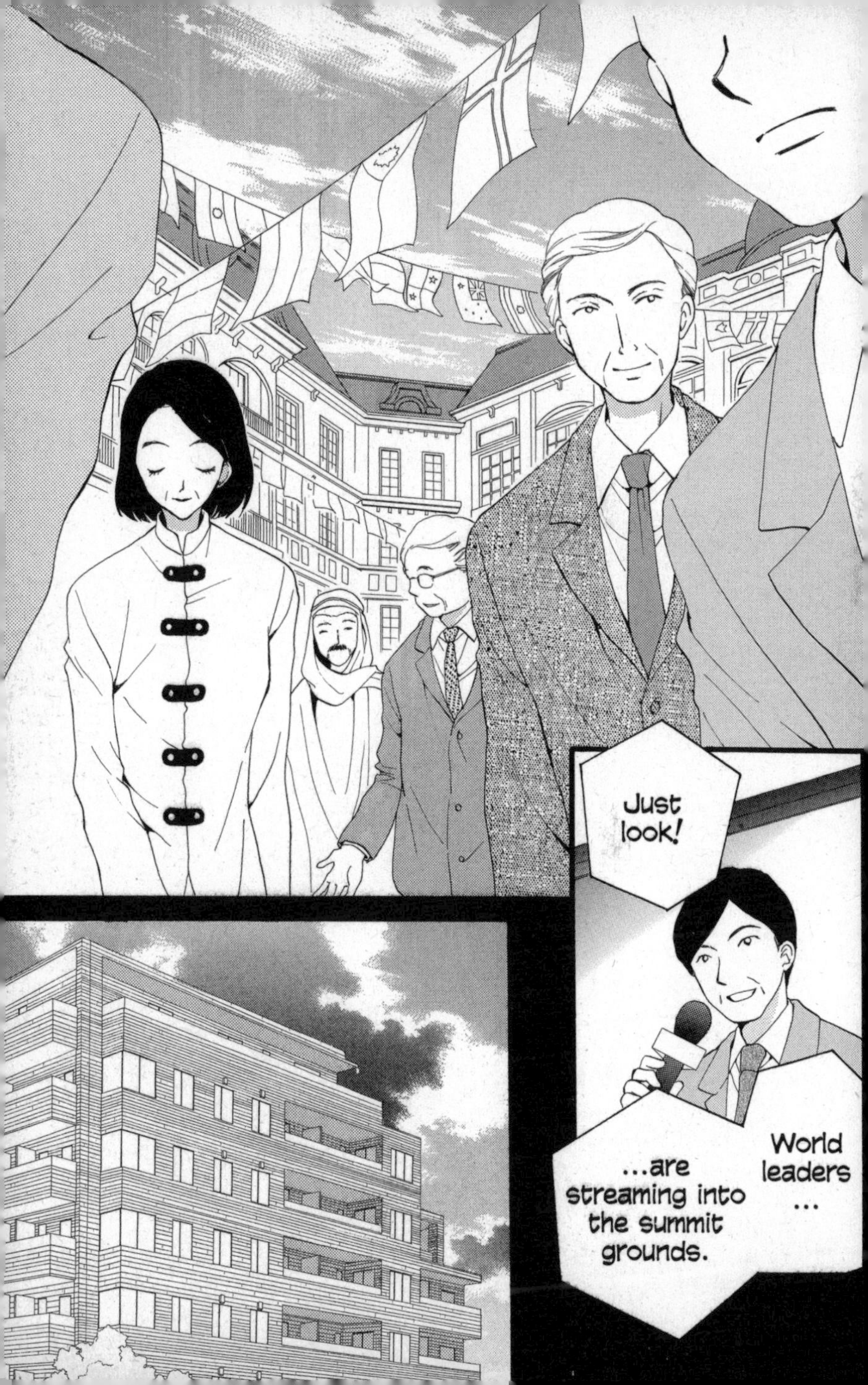
Just look!
World leaders ...
...are streaming into the summit grounds.

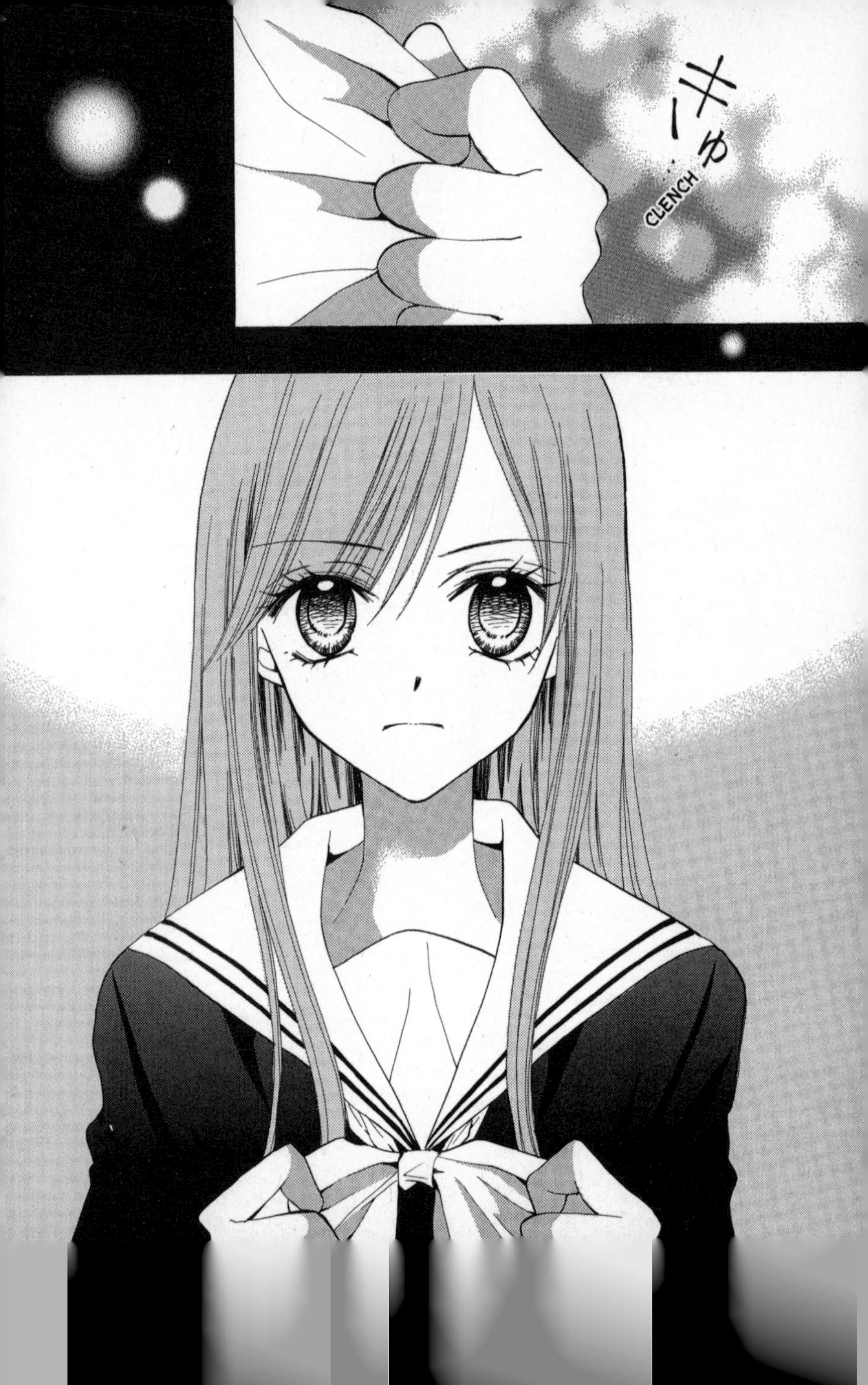
ギュ
CLENCH

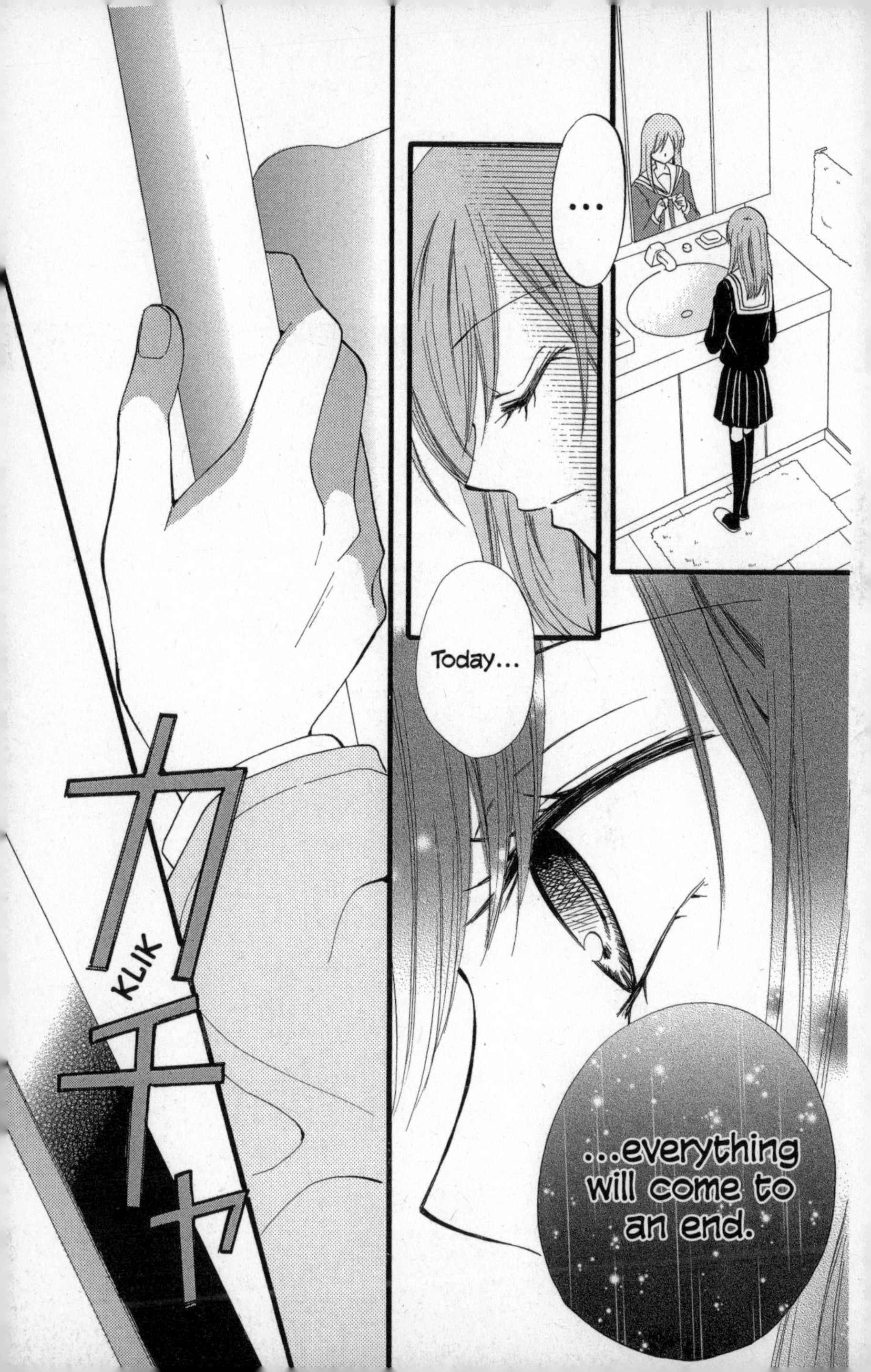
...
Today...
...everything will come to an end.
カチャ
KLIK

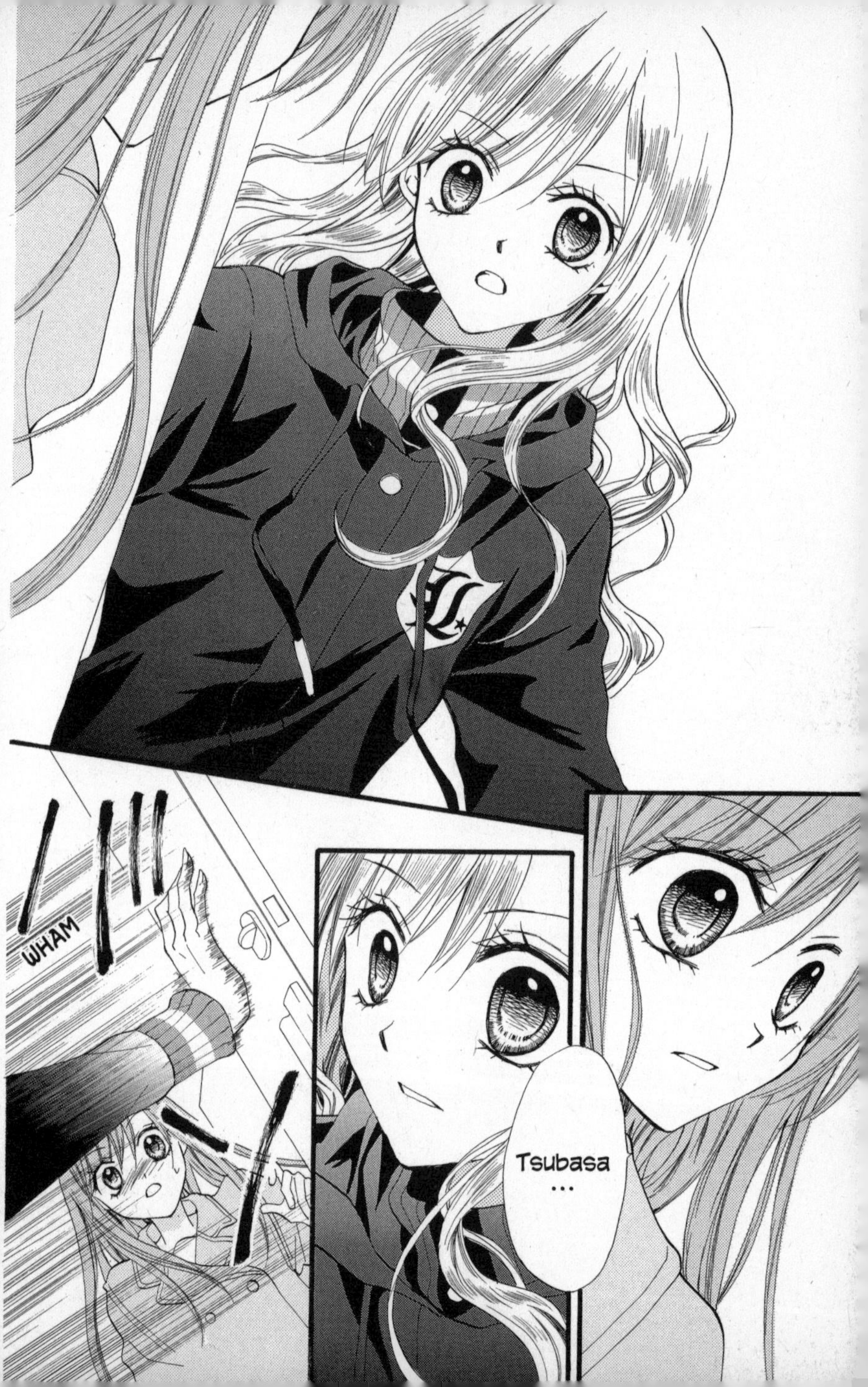
Tsubasa ...
WHAM

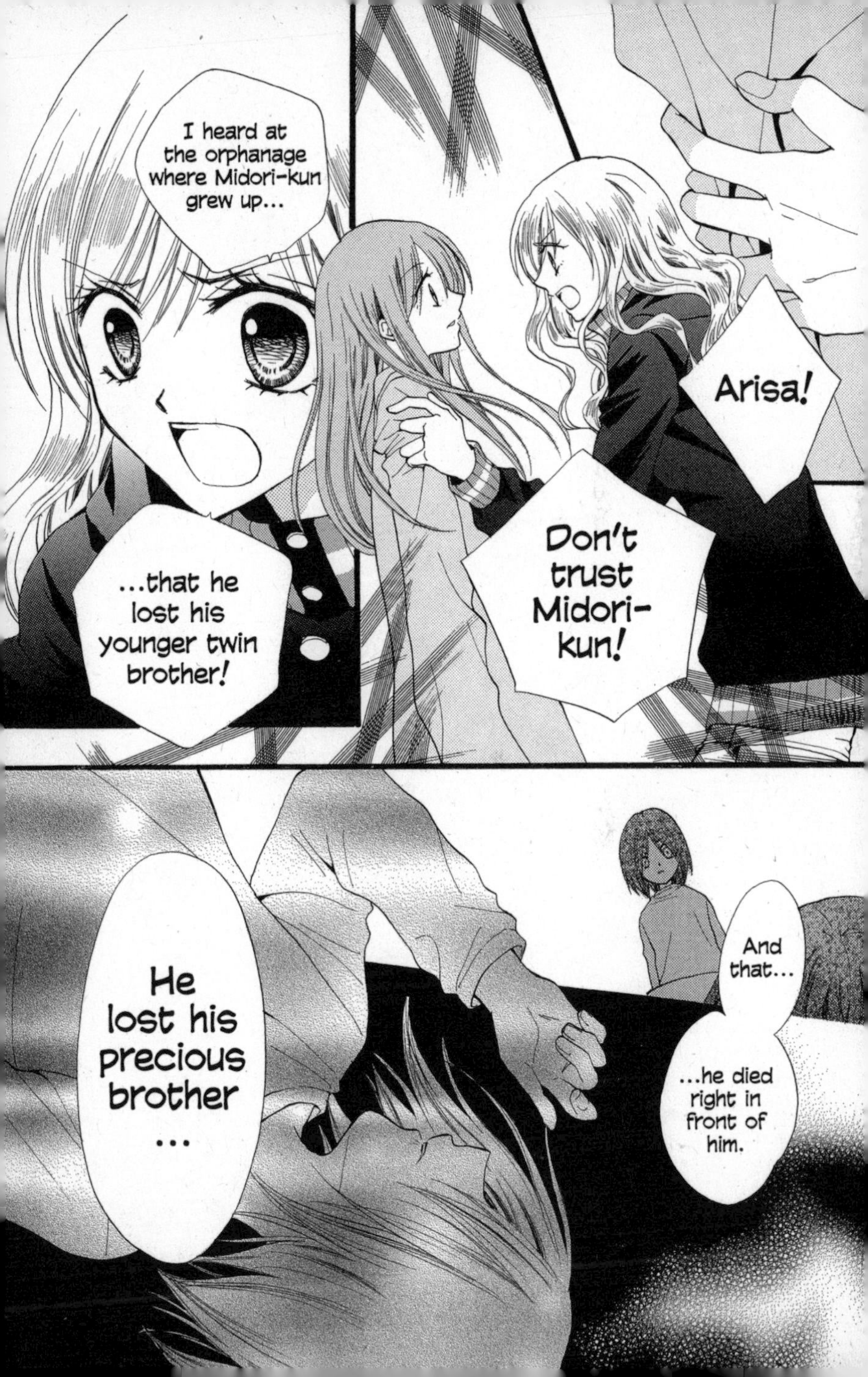

Arisa!
Don't trust Midori-kun!
I heard at the orphanage where Midori-kun grew up...
...that he lost his younger twin brother!
He lost his precious brother...
And that...
...he died right in front of him.

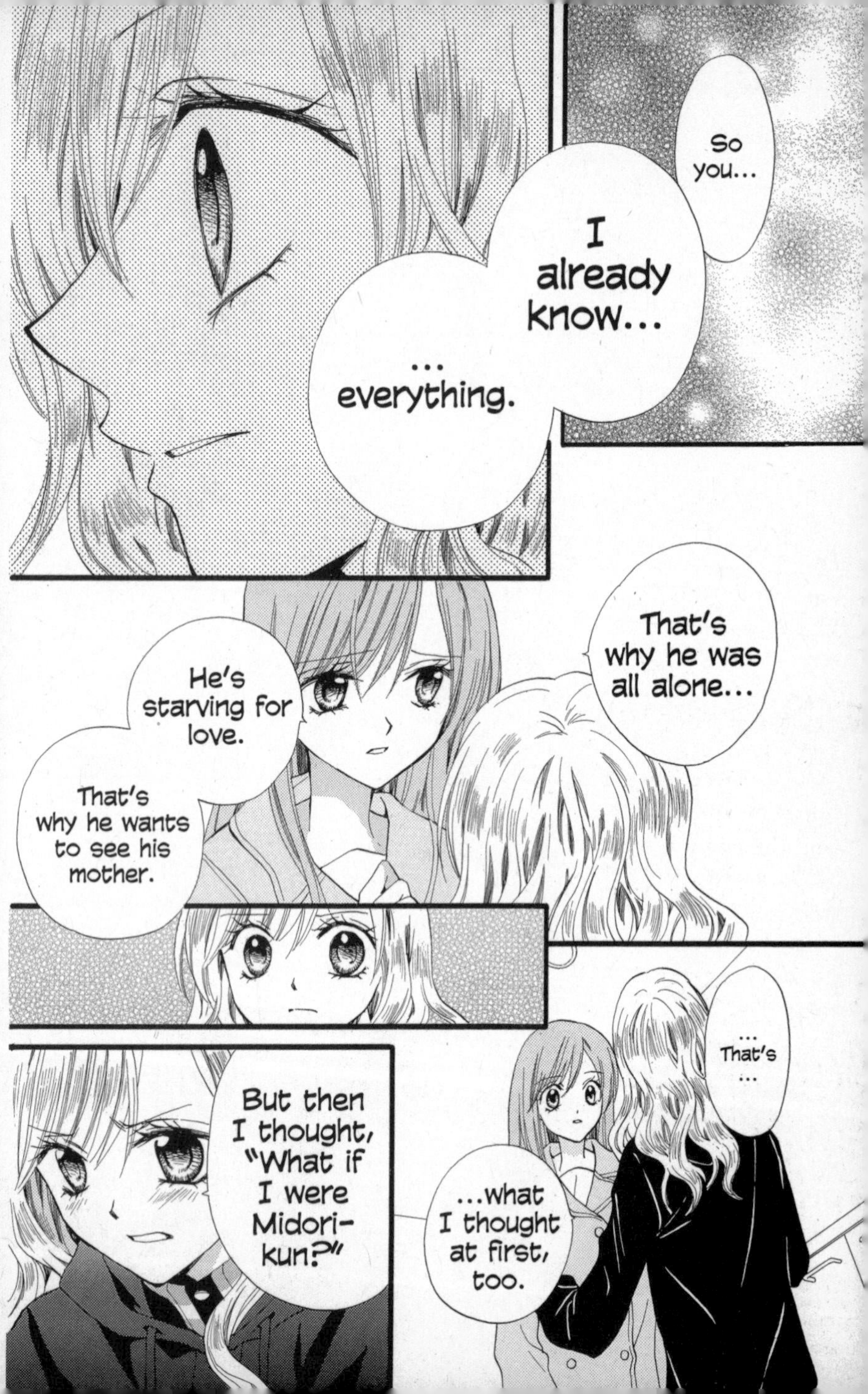
So you...
I already know...
... everything.
That's why he was all alone...
He's starving for love.
That's why he wants to see his mother.
... That's ...
...what I thought at first, too.
But then I thought, "What if I were Midori-kun?"

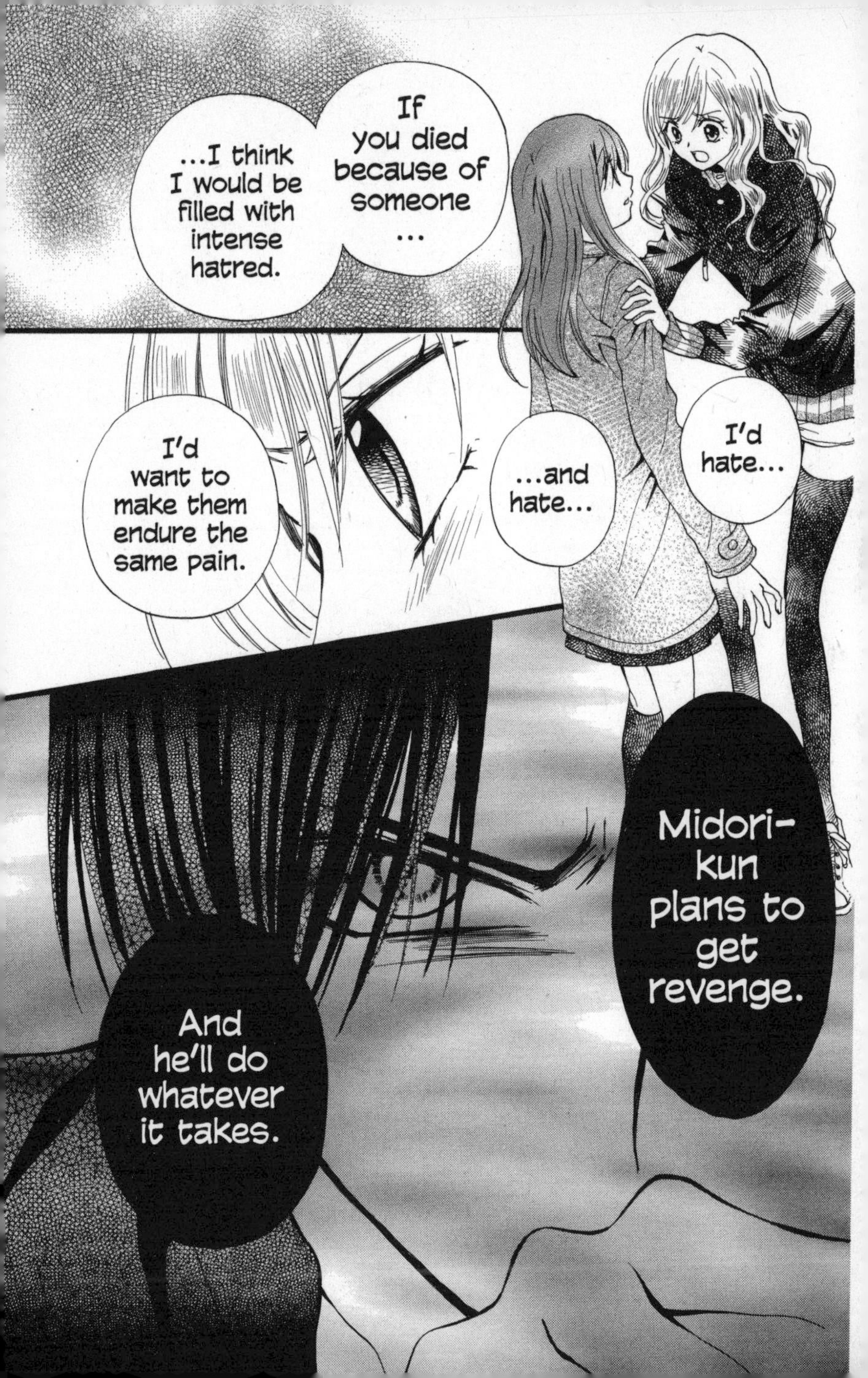
If you died because of someone ...
...I think I would be filled with intense hatred.
I'd hate...
...and hate...
I'd want to make them endure the same pain.
Midori-kun plans to get revenge.
And he'll do whatever it takes.

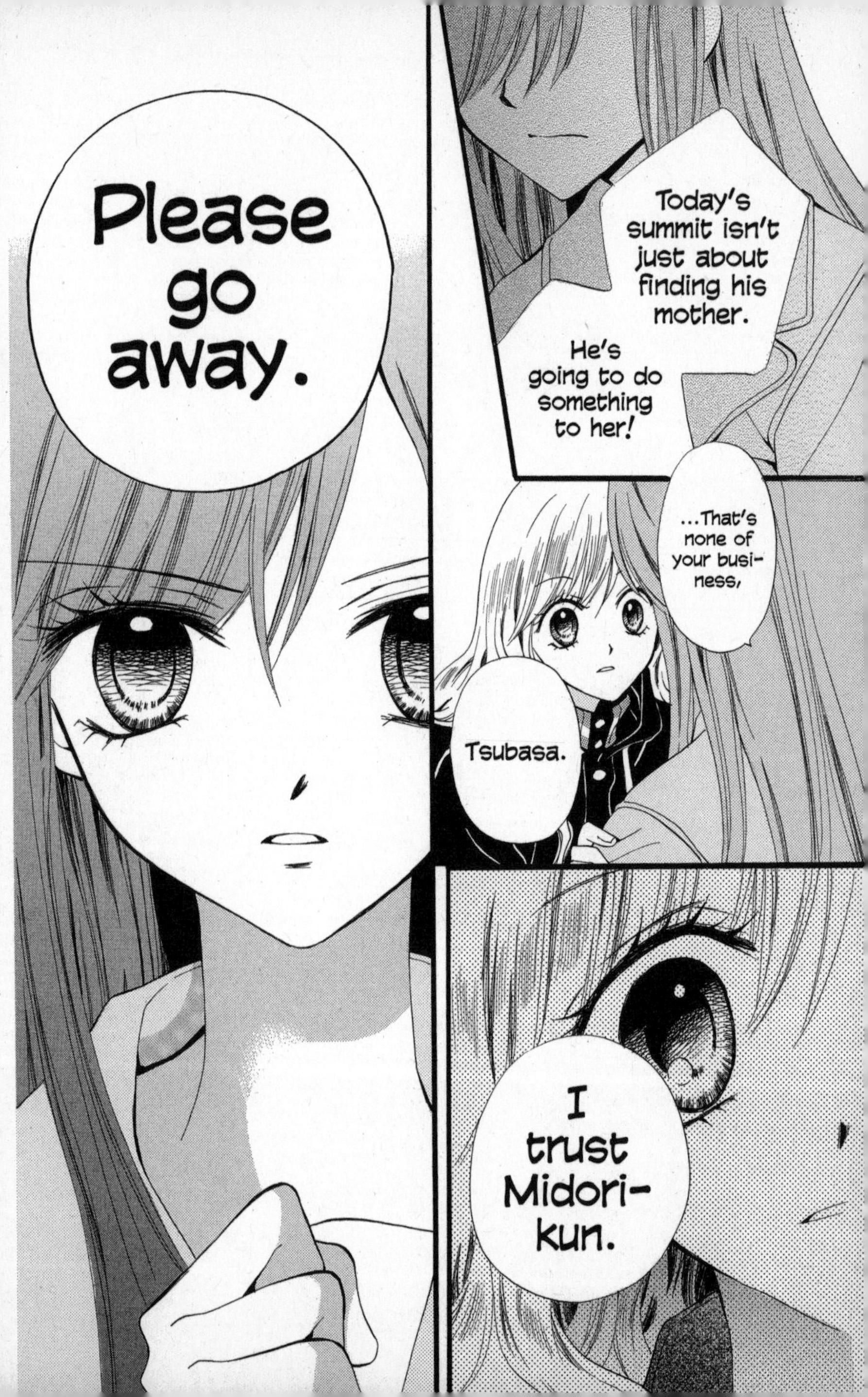
Today's summit isn't just about finding his mother.
He's going to do something to her!
...That's none of your business,
Tsubasa.
I trust Midori-kun.
Please go away.

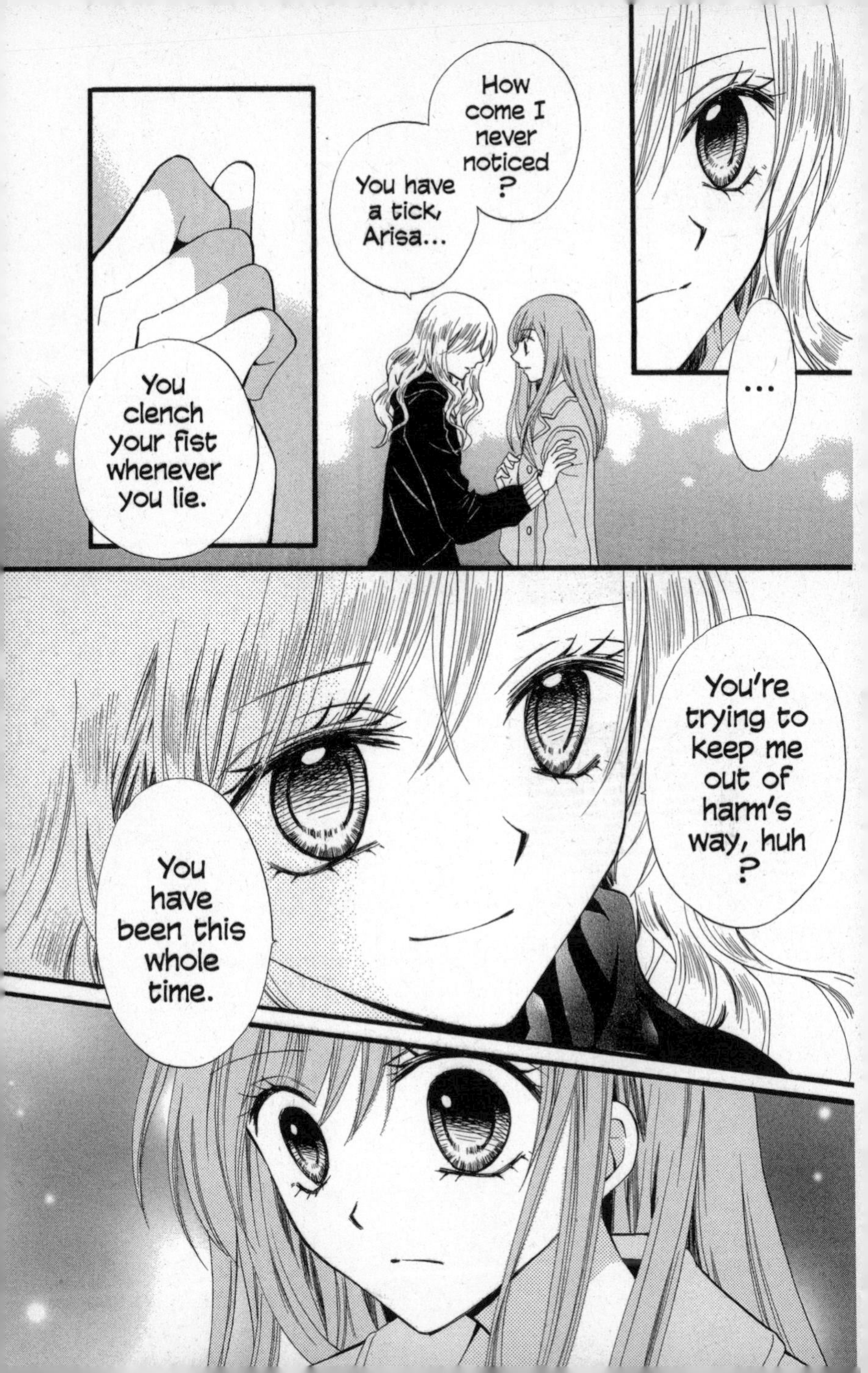
...
How come I never noticed?
You have a tick, Arisa...
You clench your fist whenever you lie.
You're trying to keep me out of harm's way, huh?
You have been this whole time.

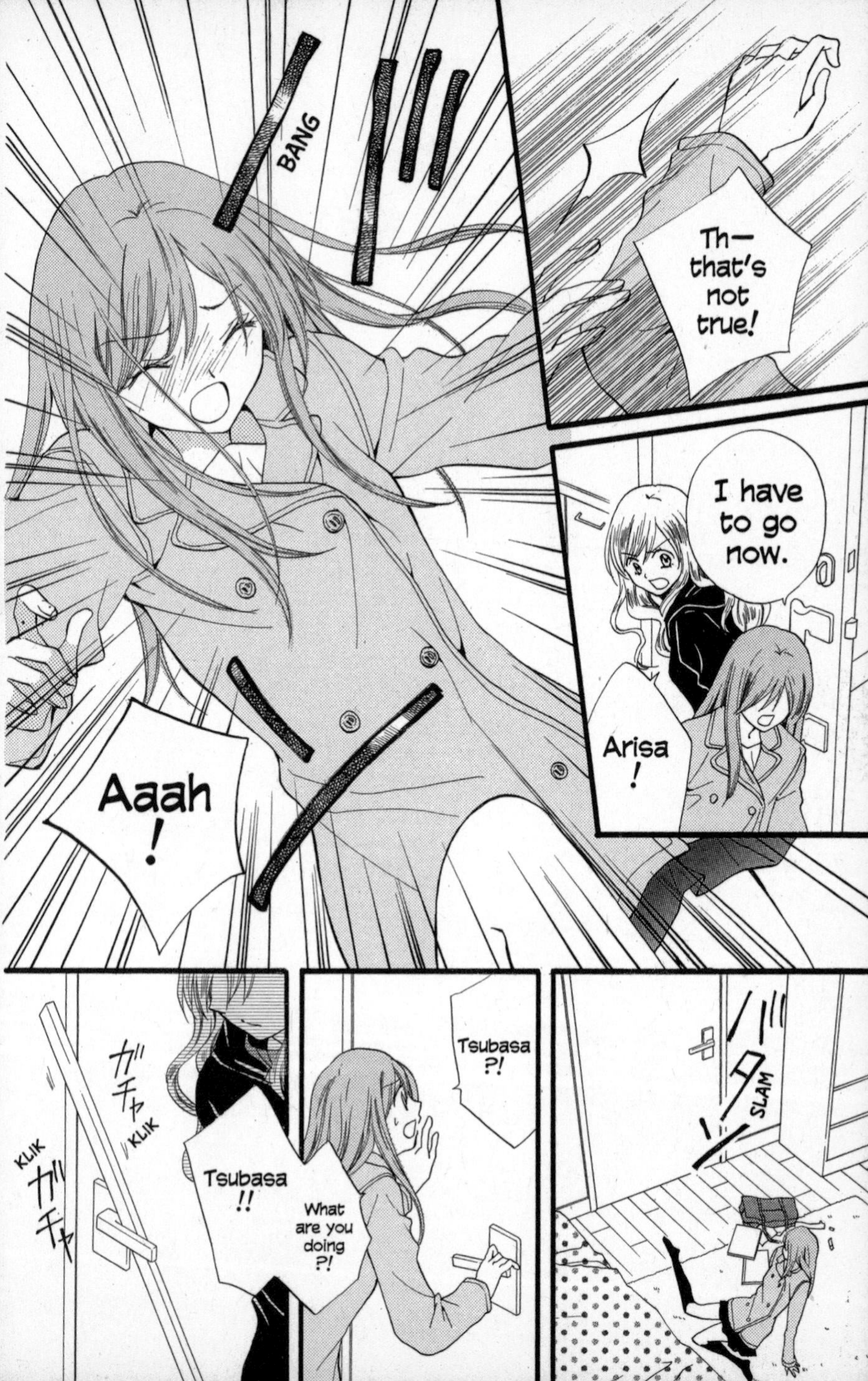
Th— that's not true!
I have to go now.
Arisa!
BANG
Aaah!
SLAM
Tsubasa?!
What are you doing?!
Tsubasa!!
ガチャ KLIK
KLIK ガチャ

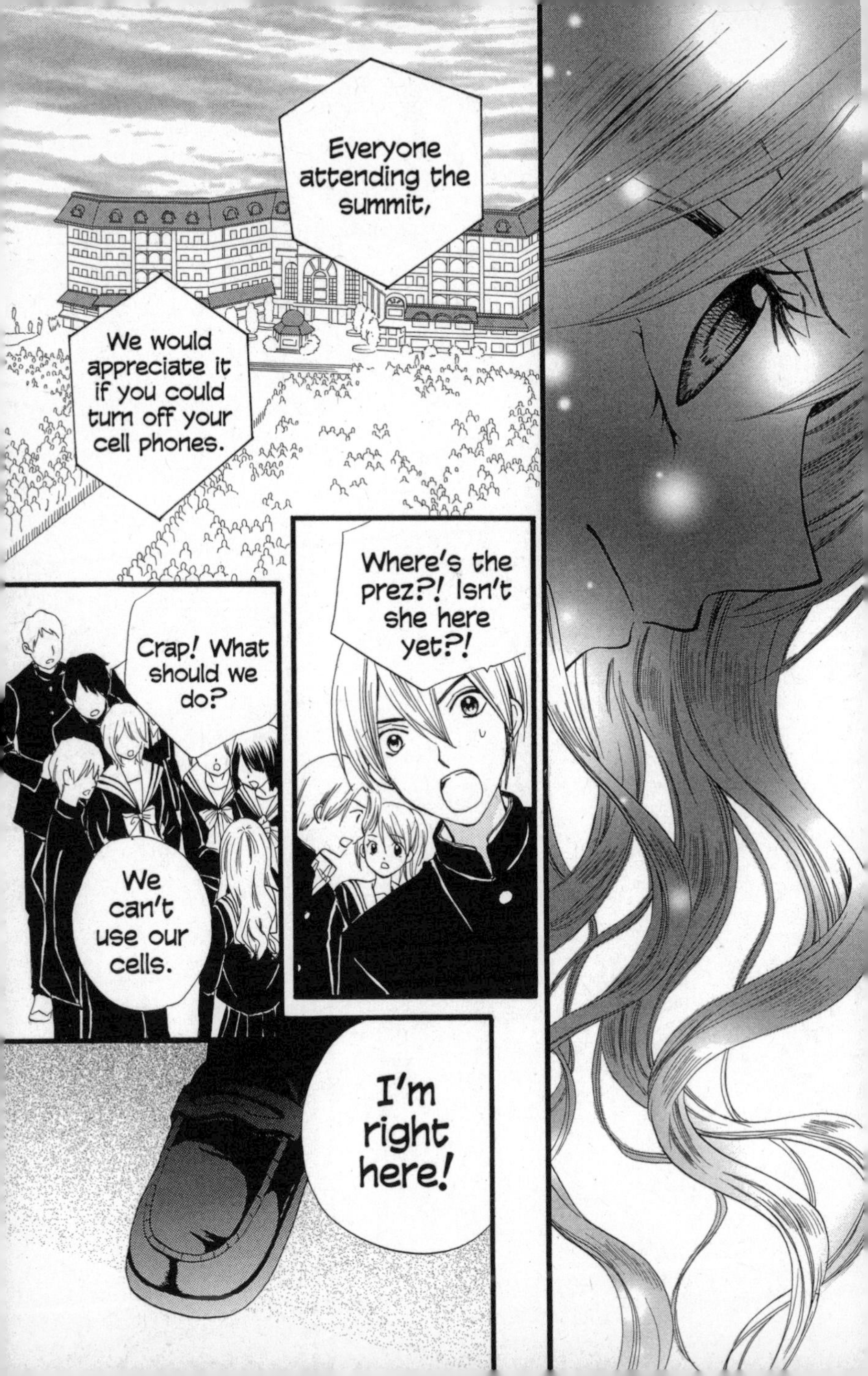
Everyone attending the summit,
We would appreciate it if you could turn off your cell phones.
Where's the prez?! Isn't she here yet?!
Crap! What should we do?
We can't use our cells.
I'm right here!

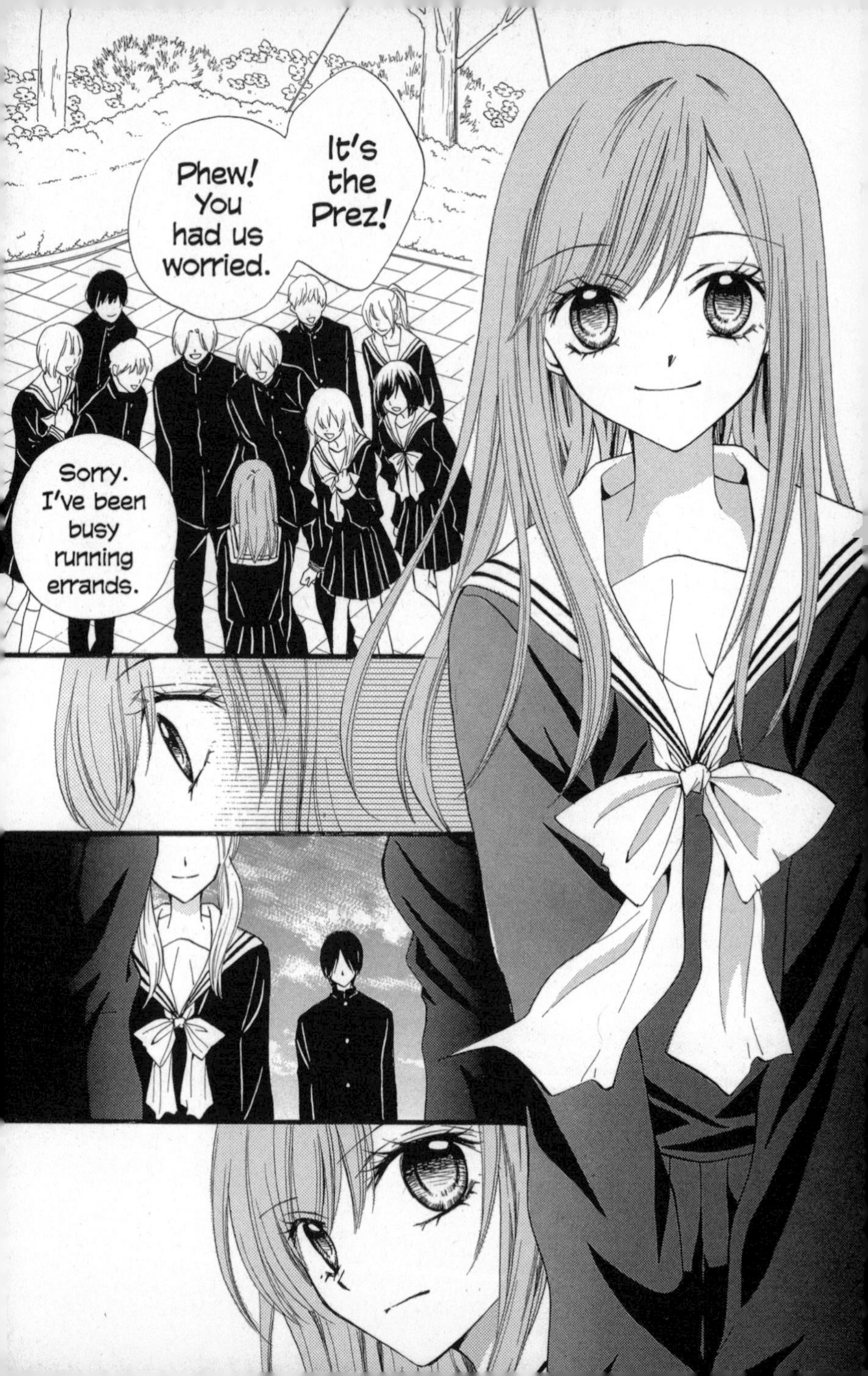
It's the Prez!
Phew! You had us worried.
Sorry. I've been busy running errands.

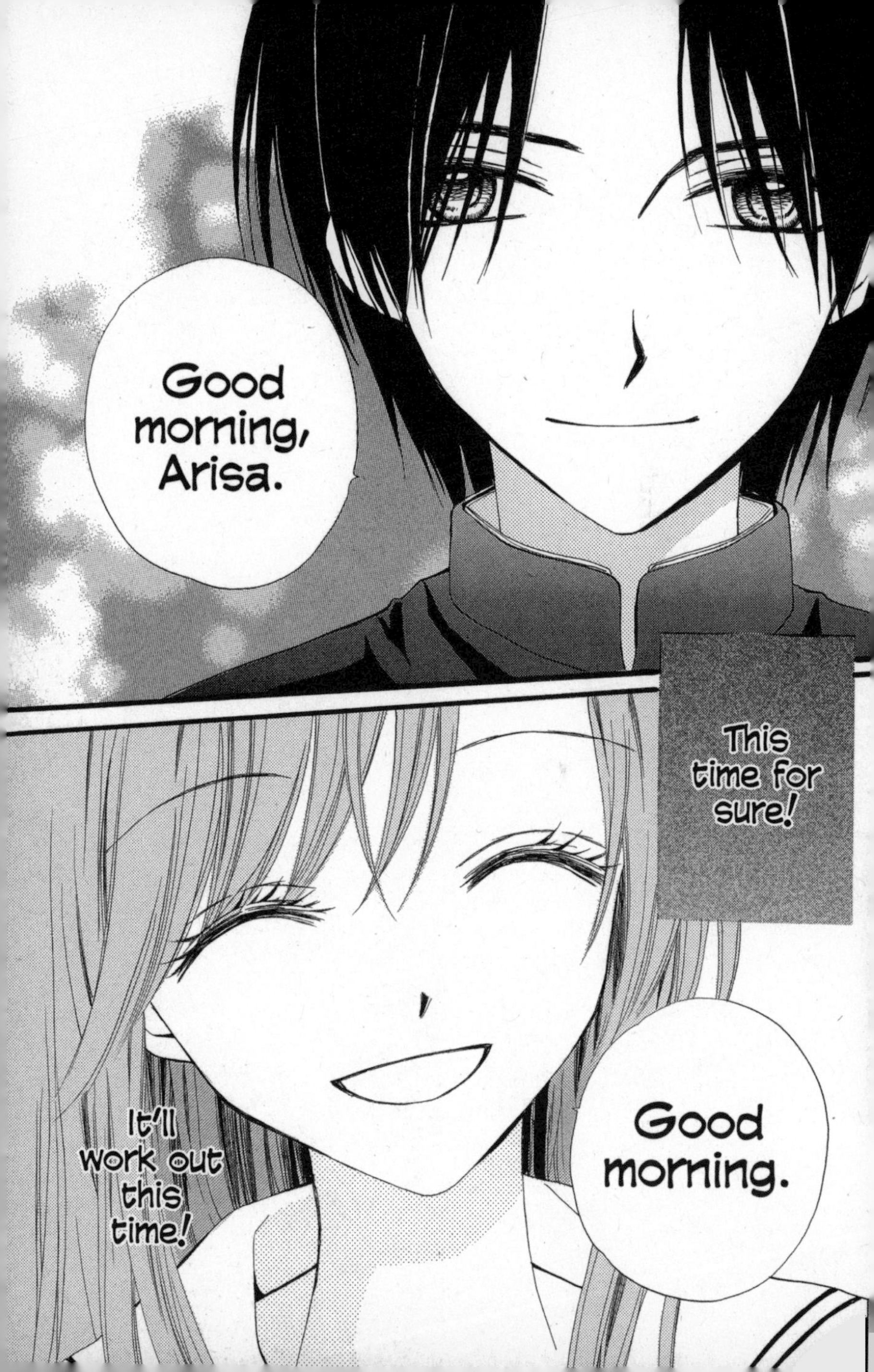
Good morning, Arisa.
This time for sure!
Good morning.
It'll work out this time!

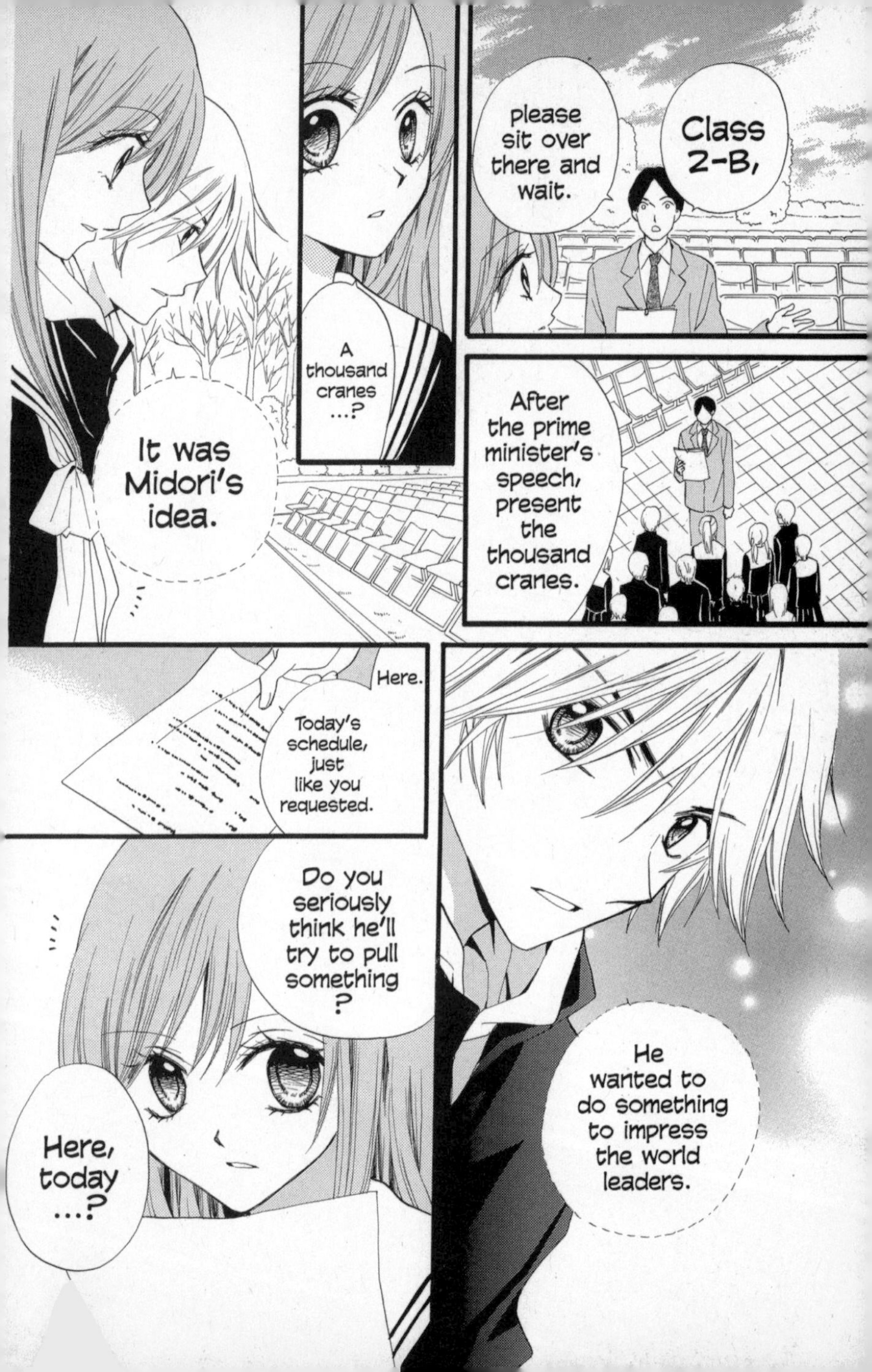
Class 2-B,
please sit over there and wait.
After the prime minister's speech, present the thousand cranes.
A thousand cranes ...?
It was Midori's idea.
He wanted to do something to impress the world leaders.
Here.
Today's schedule, just like you requested.
Do you seriously think he'll try to pull something?
Here, today ...?

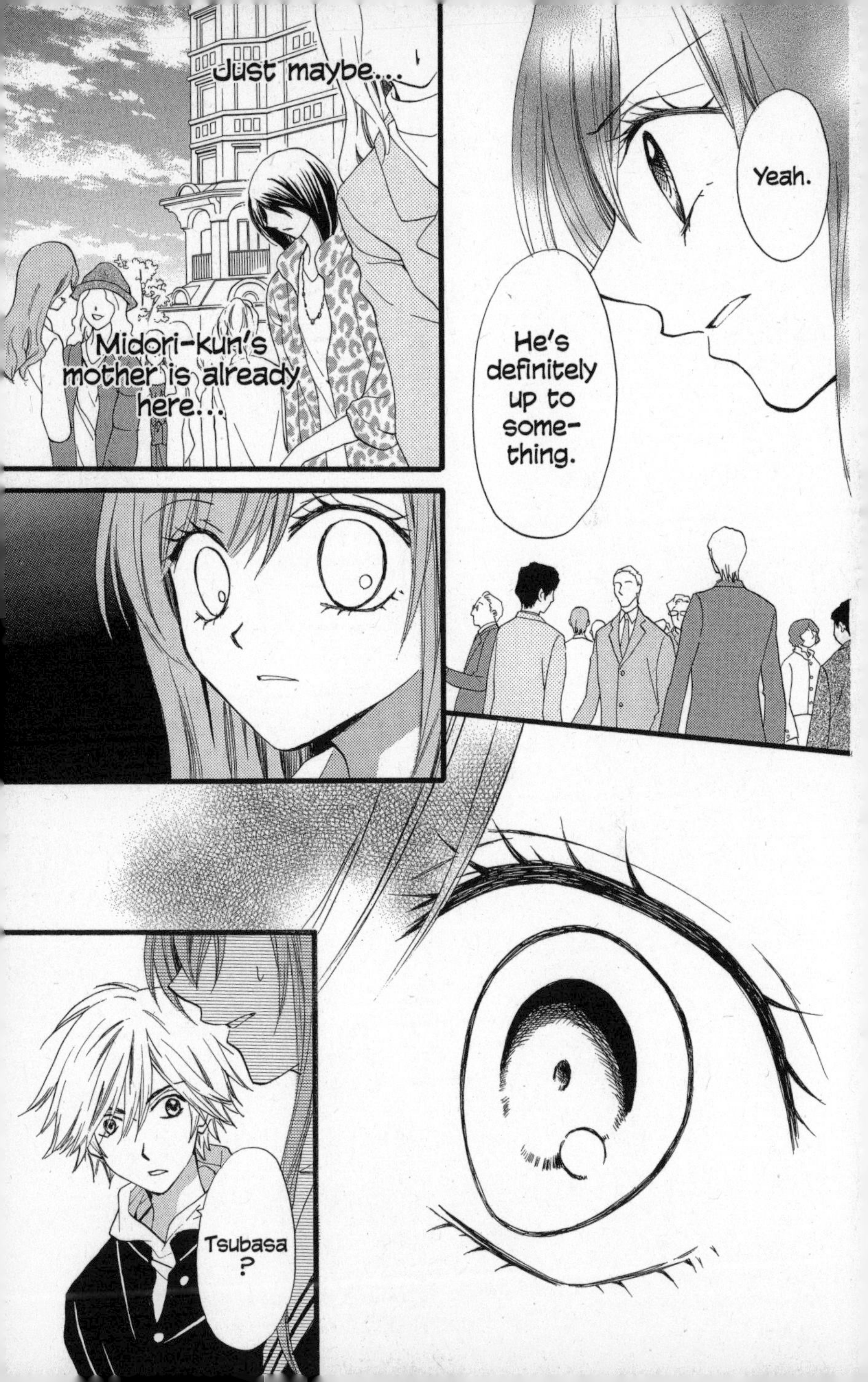
Yeah.
He's definitely up to some-thing.
Just maybe...
Midori-kun's mother is already here...
Tsubasa?

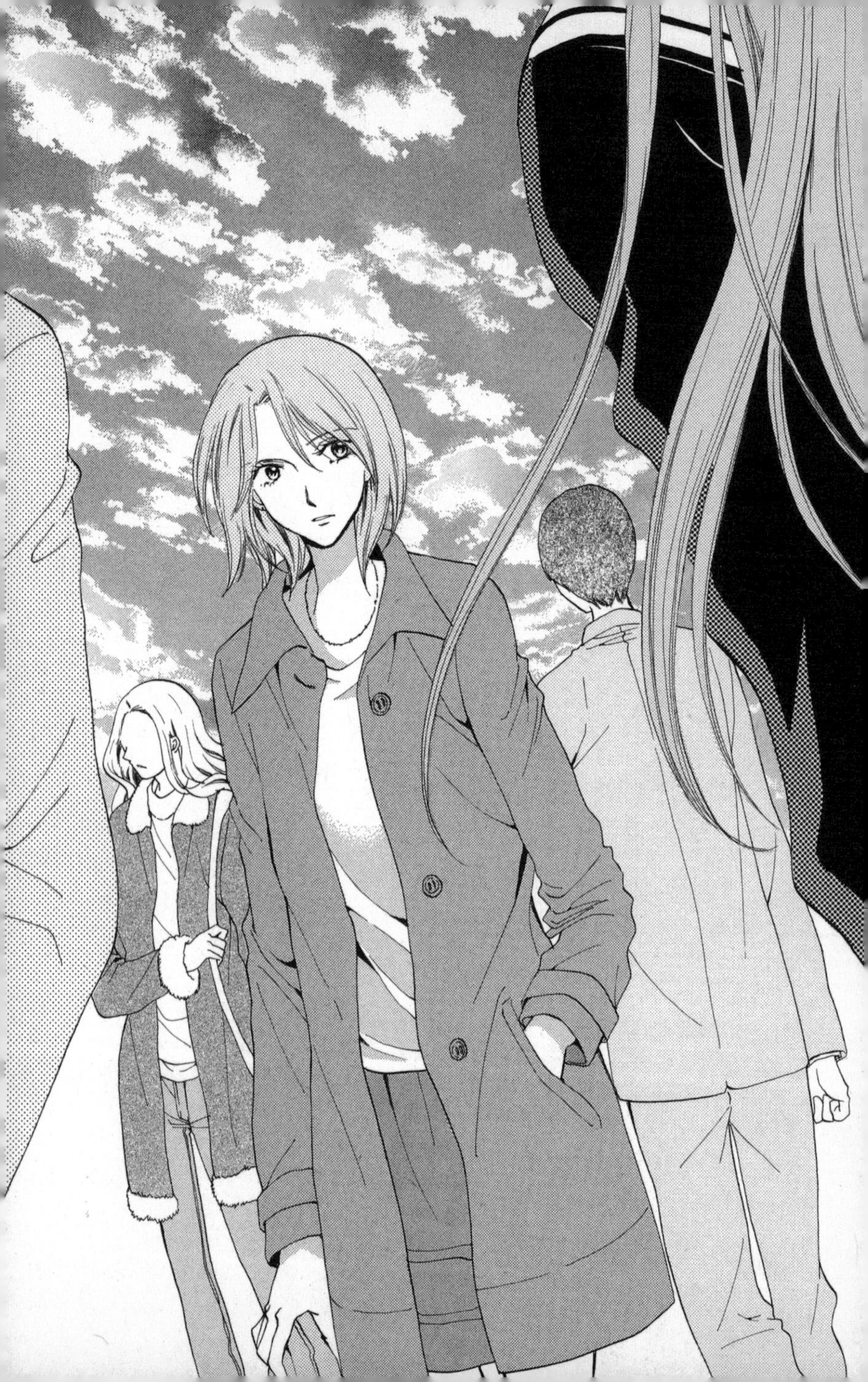

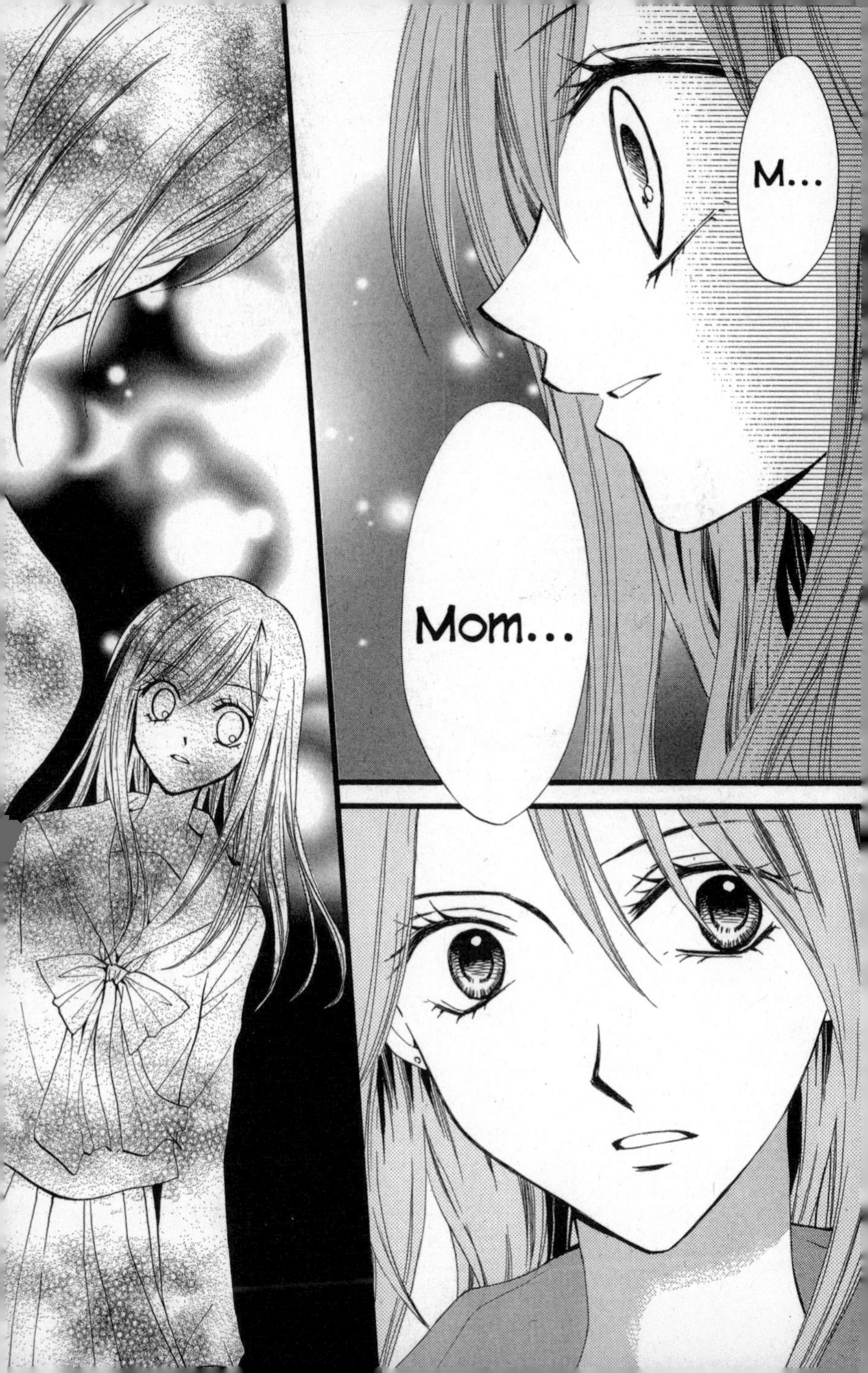
M...
Mom...

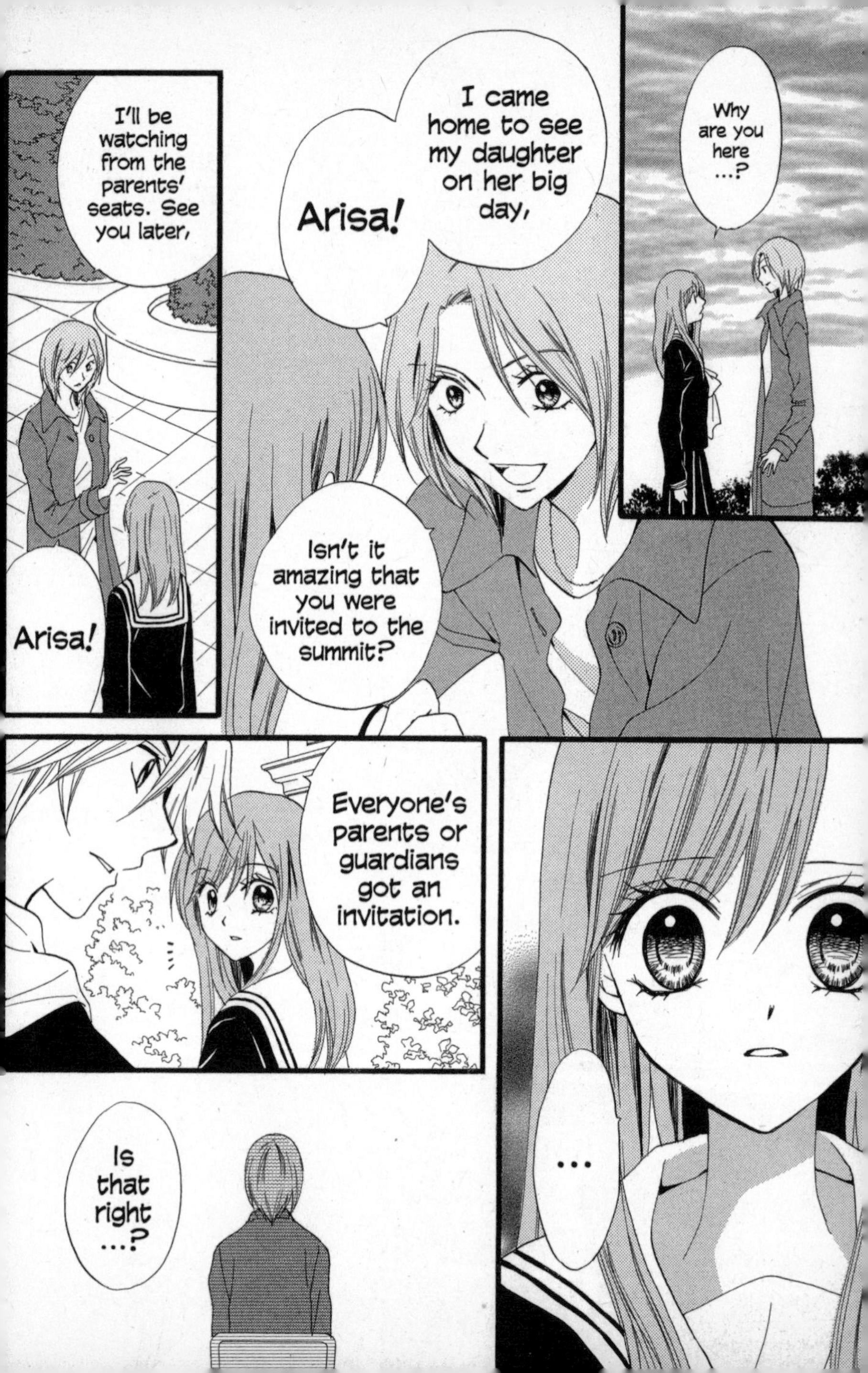
Why are you here ...?
I came home to see my daughter on her big day,
Arisa!
Isn't it amazing that you were invited to the summit?
I'll be watching from the parents' seats. See you later,
Arisa!
...
Everyone's parents or guardians got an invitation.
Is that right ...?

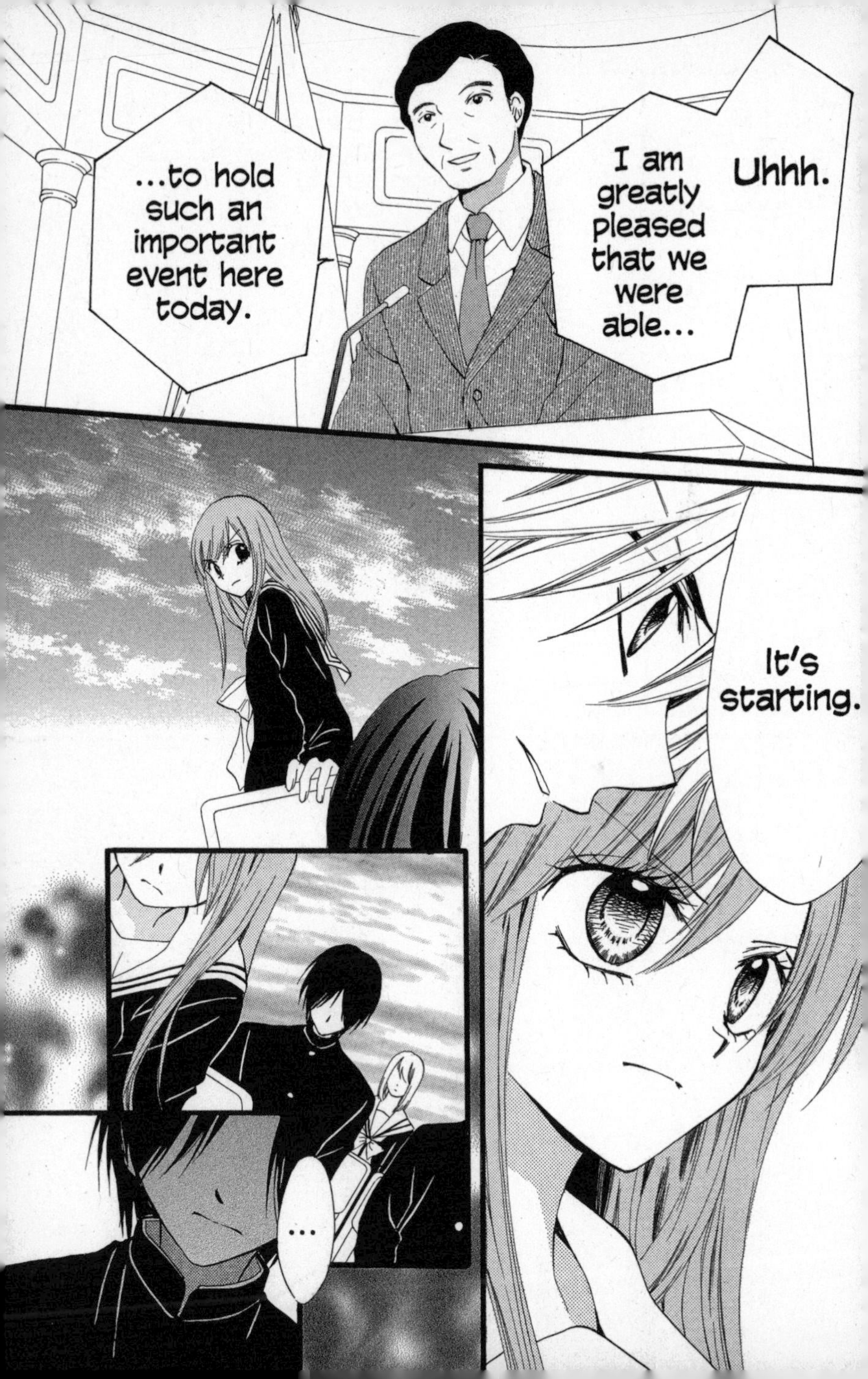
Uhhh.
I am greatly pleased that we were able...
...to hold such an important event here today.
It's starting.
...

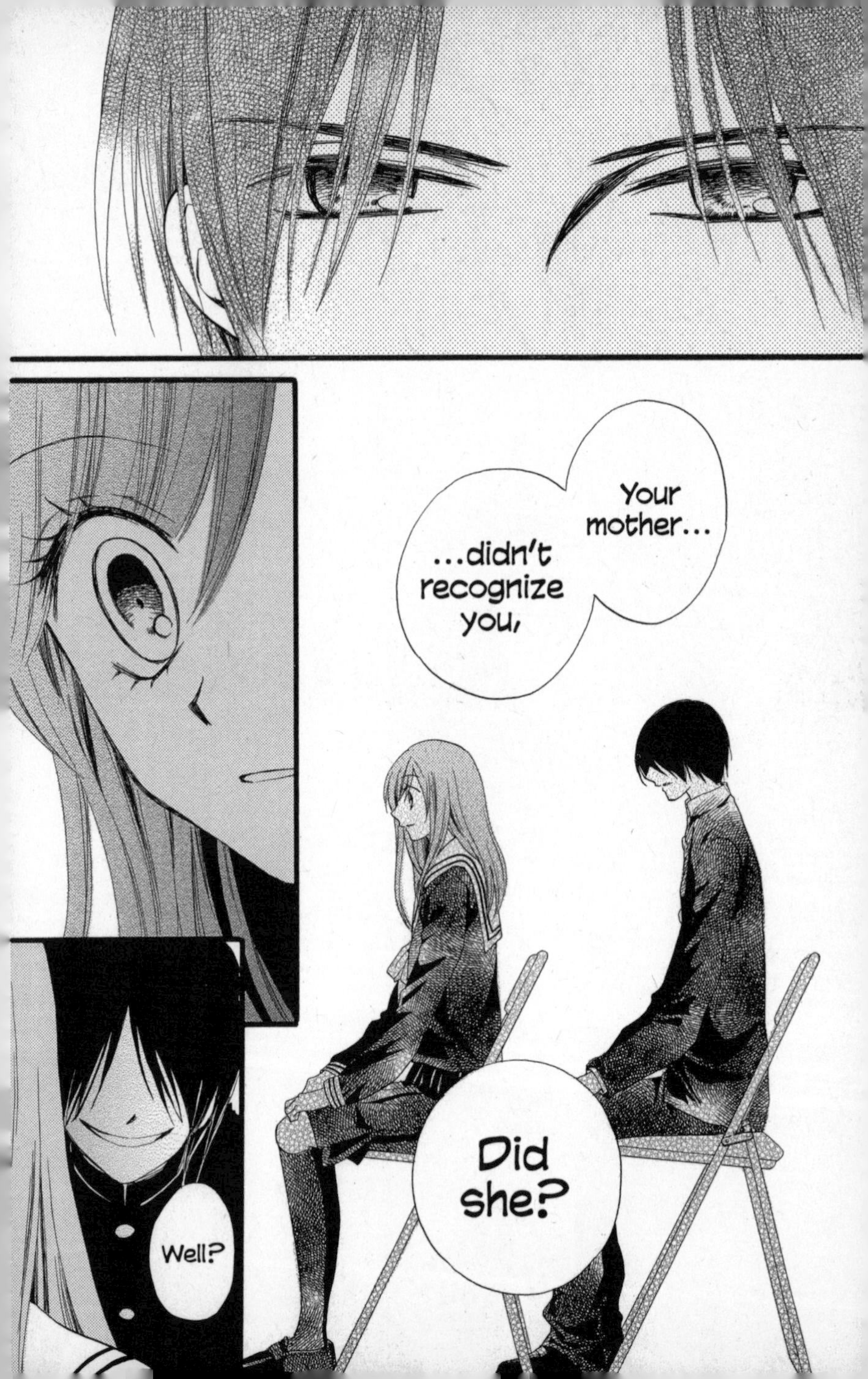
Your mother...
...didn't recognize you,
Did she?
Well?

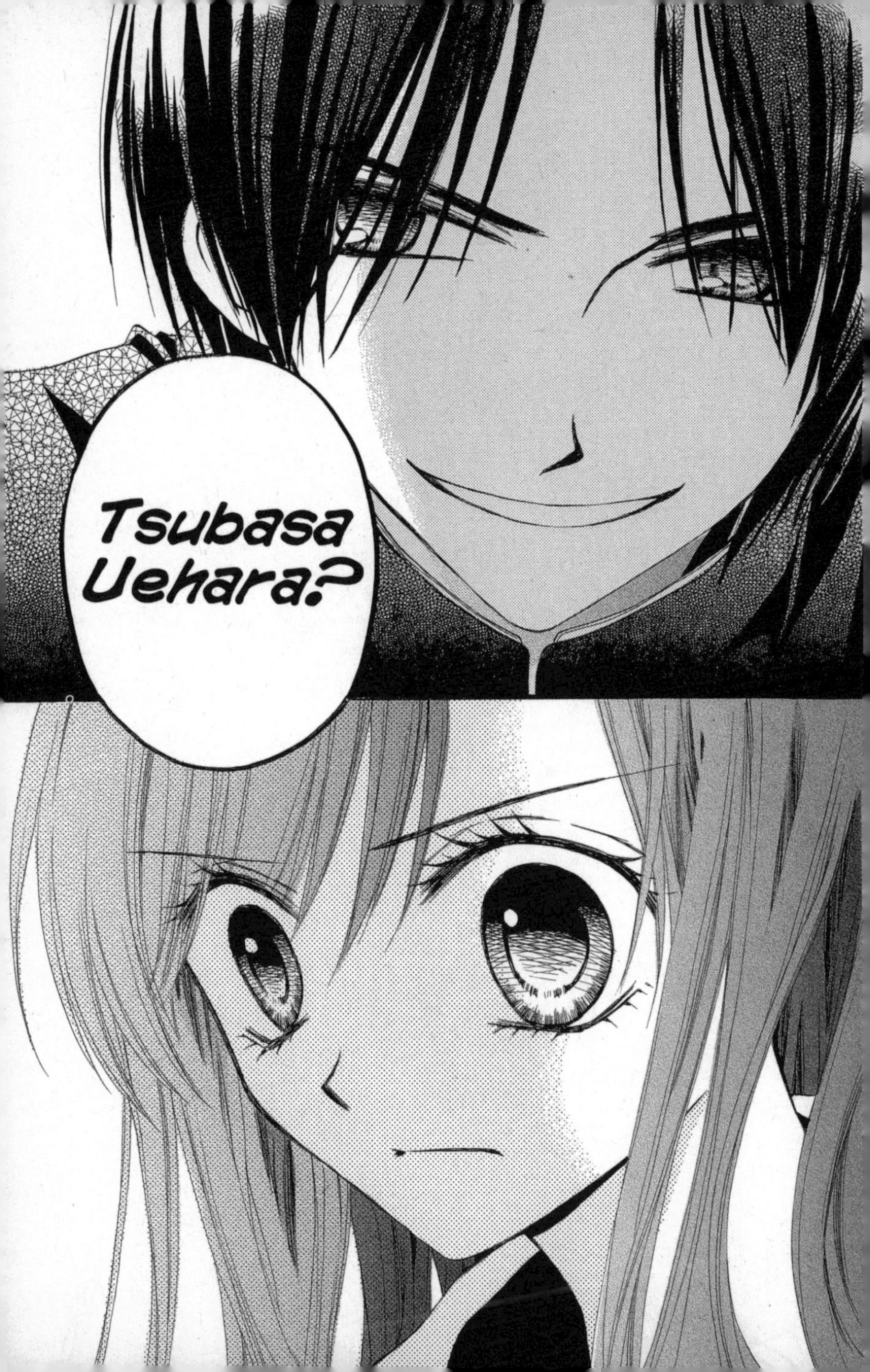
Tsubasa Uehara?

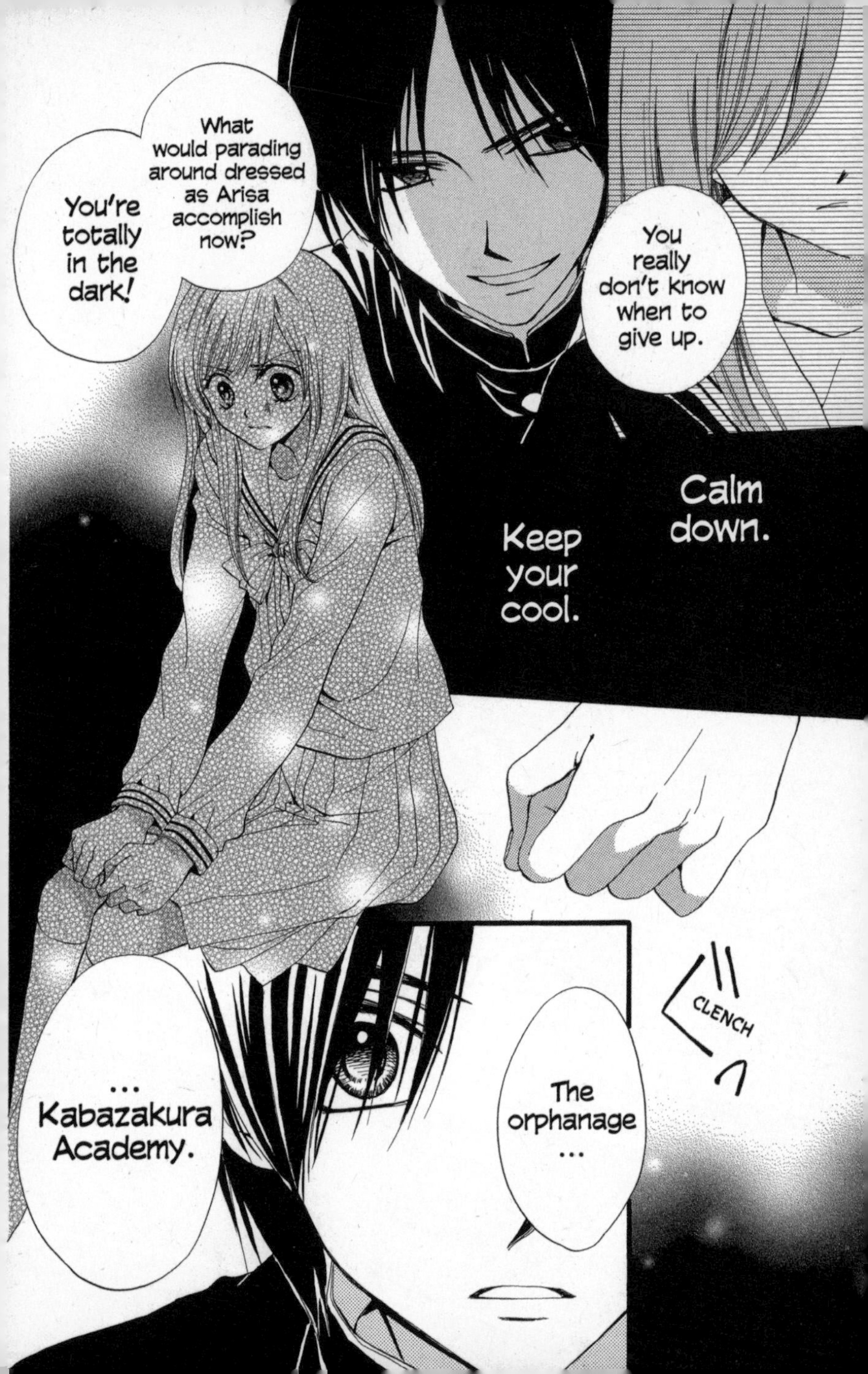

You really don't know when to give up.
What would parading around dressed as Arisa accomplish now?
You're totally in the dark!
Calm down.
Keep your cool.
CLENCH
The orphanage ...
... Kabazakura Academy.

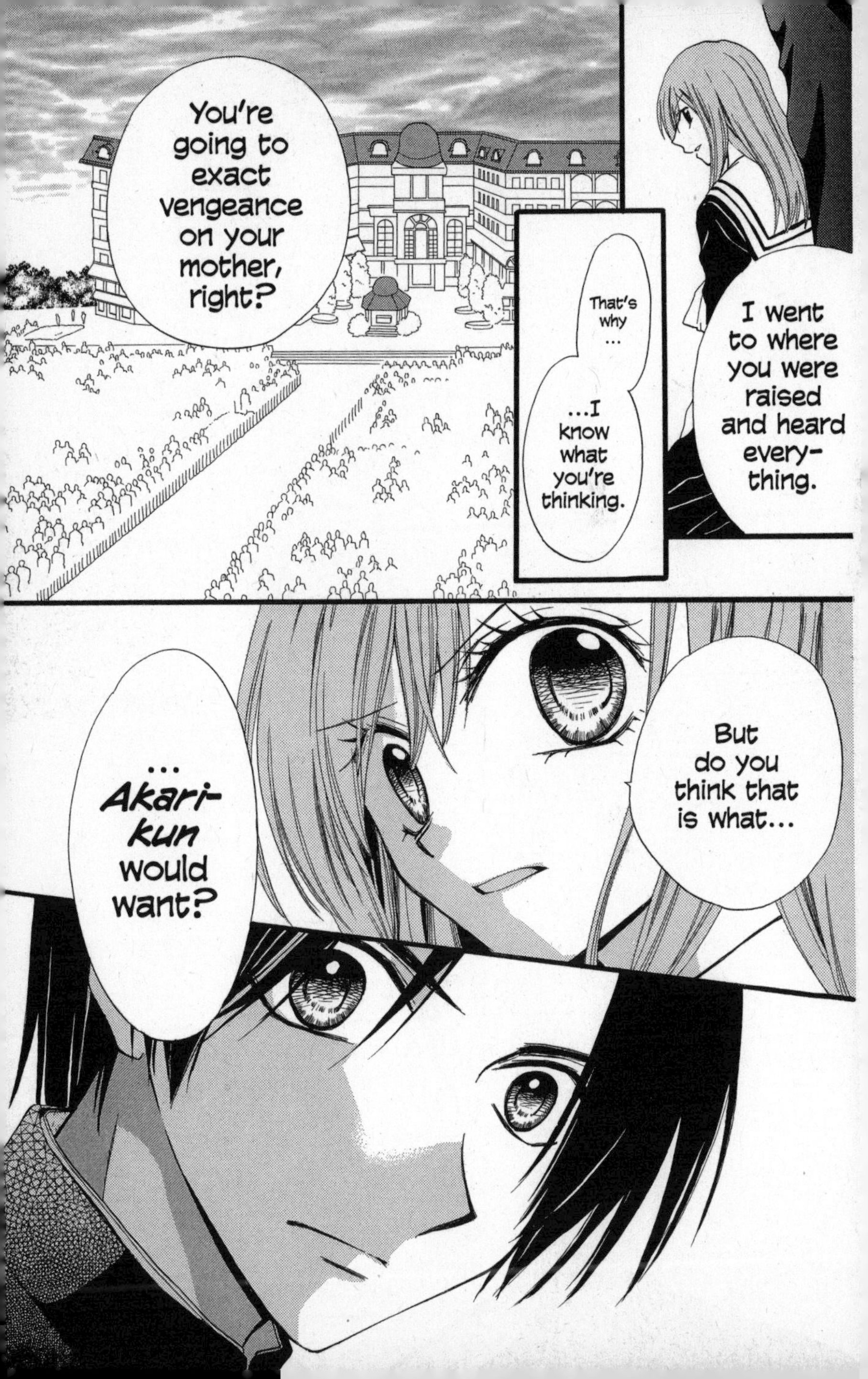
I went to where you were raised and heard every-thing.
That's why ...
...I know what you're thinking.
You're going to exact vengeance on your mother, right?
But do you think that is what...
... *Akari-kun* would want?

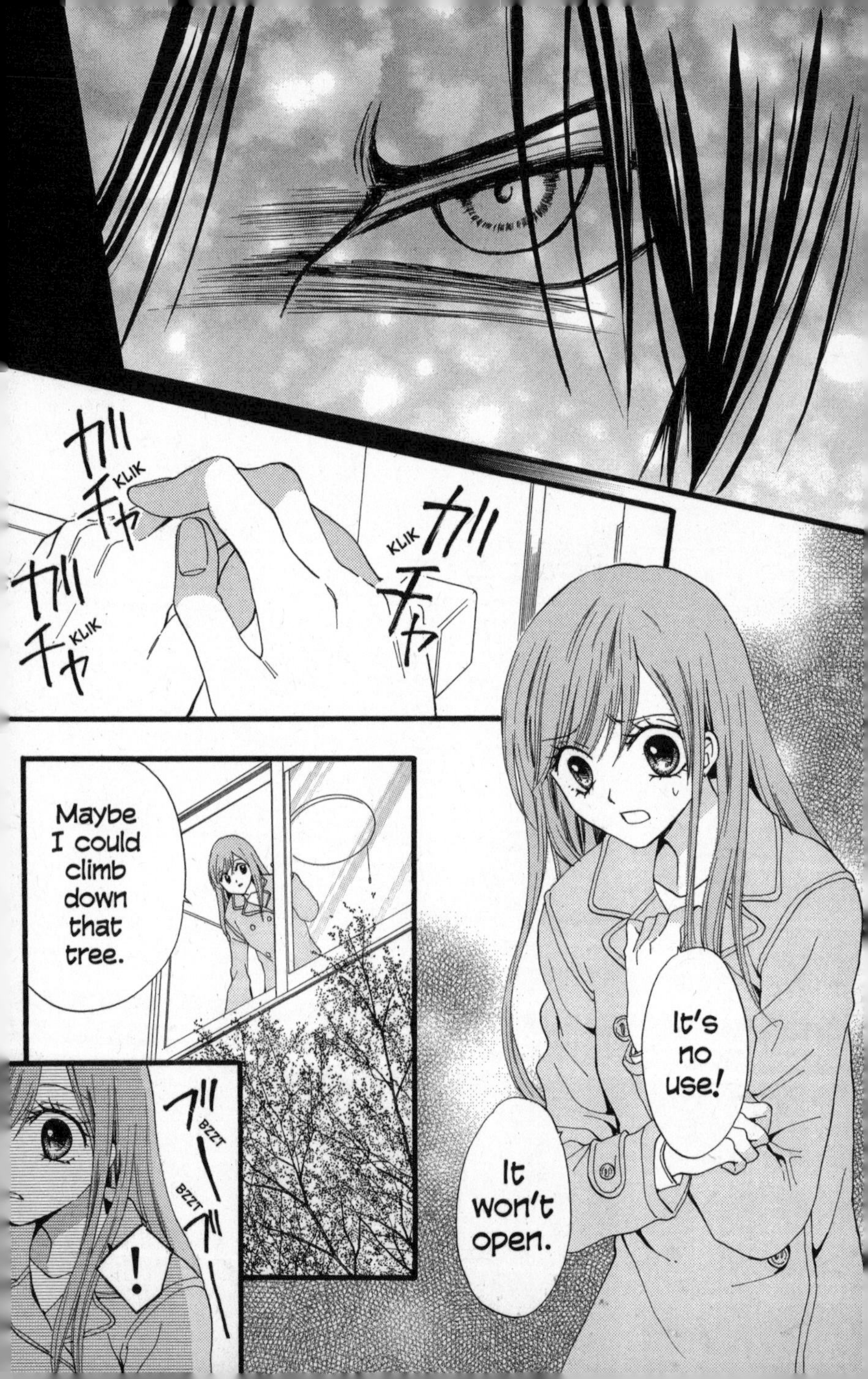
It's no use!
It won't open.
ガチャ
KLIK
ガチャ
KLIK
ガチャ
KLIK
Maybe I could climb down that tree.
ブー
BZZT
ブー
BZZT
!

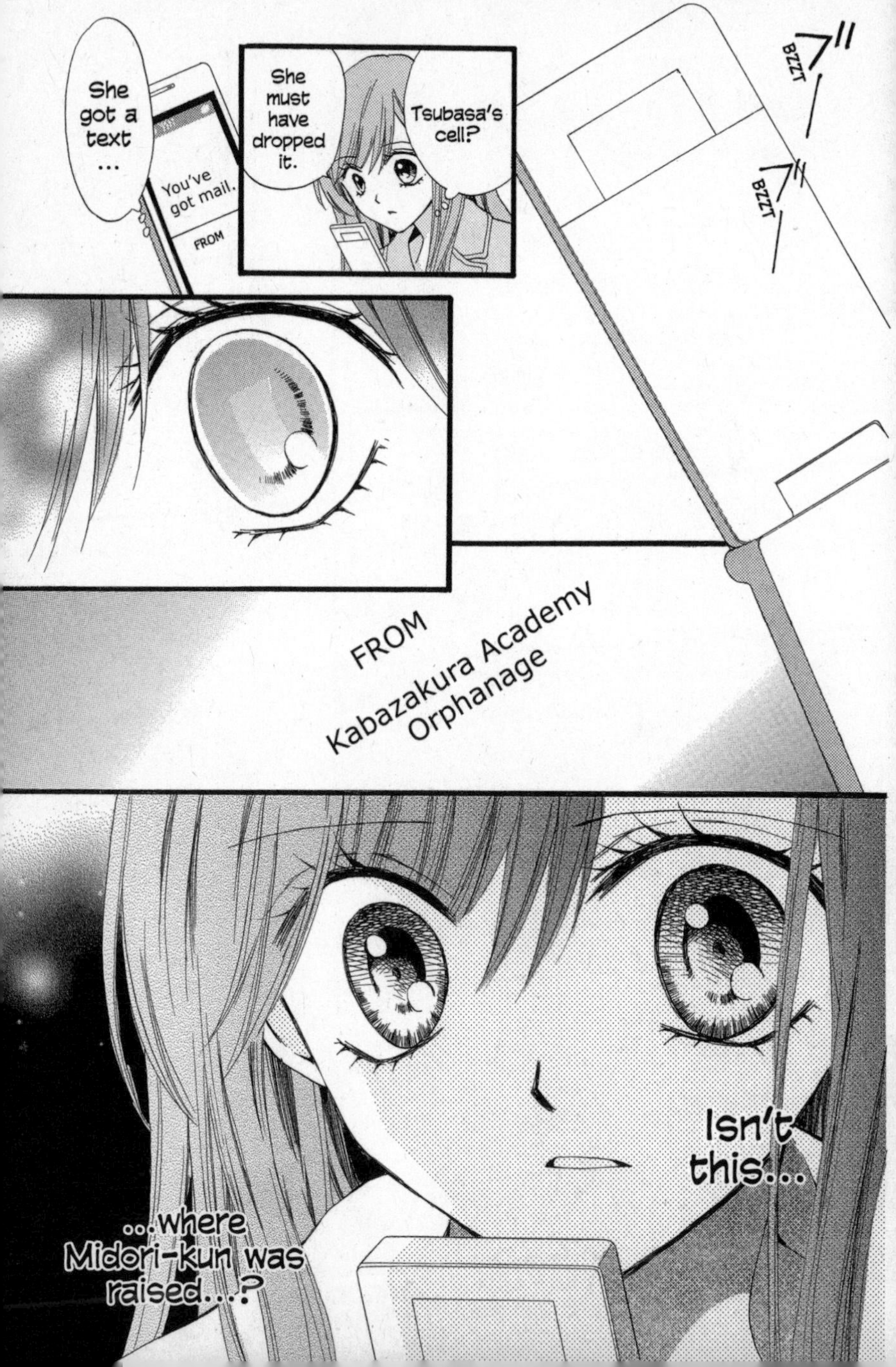
BZZT
BZZT
Tsubasa's cell?
She must have dropped it.
She got a text ...
You've got mail.
FROM
FROM
Kabazakura Academy Orphanage
Isn't this...
...where Midori-kun was raised...?

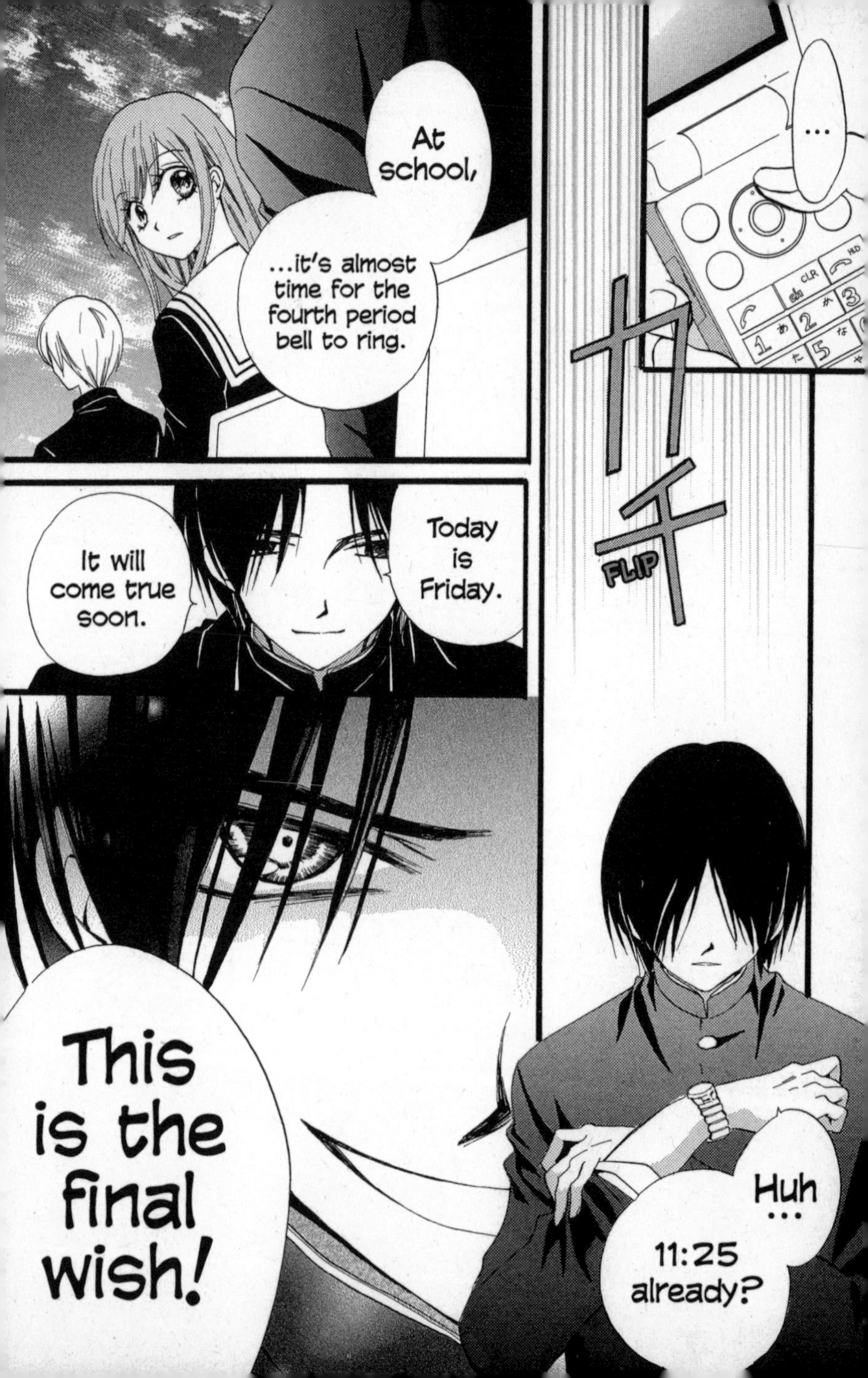
...
FLIP
At school,
...it's almost time for the fourth period bell to ring.
Today is Friday.
It will come true soon.
This is the final wish!
Huh... 11:25 already?

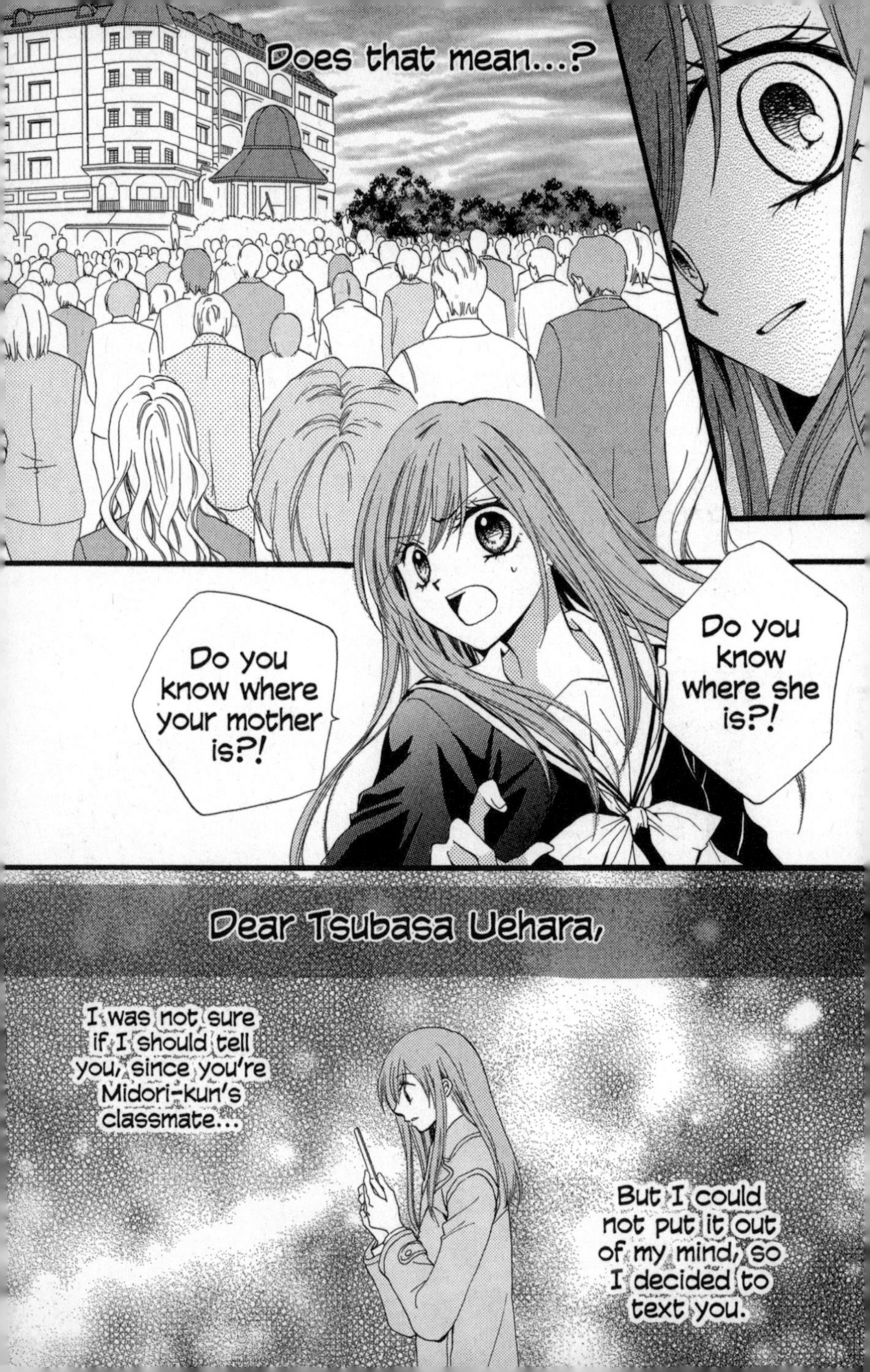
Does that mean...?
Do you know where she is?!
Do you know where your mother is?!
Dear Tsubasa Uehara,
I was not sure if I should tell you, since you're Midori-kun's classmate...
But I could not put it out of my mind, so I decided to text you.

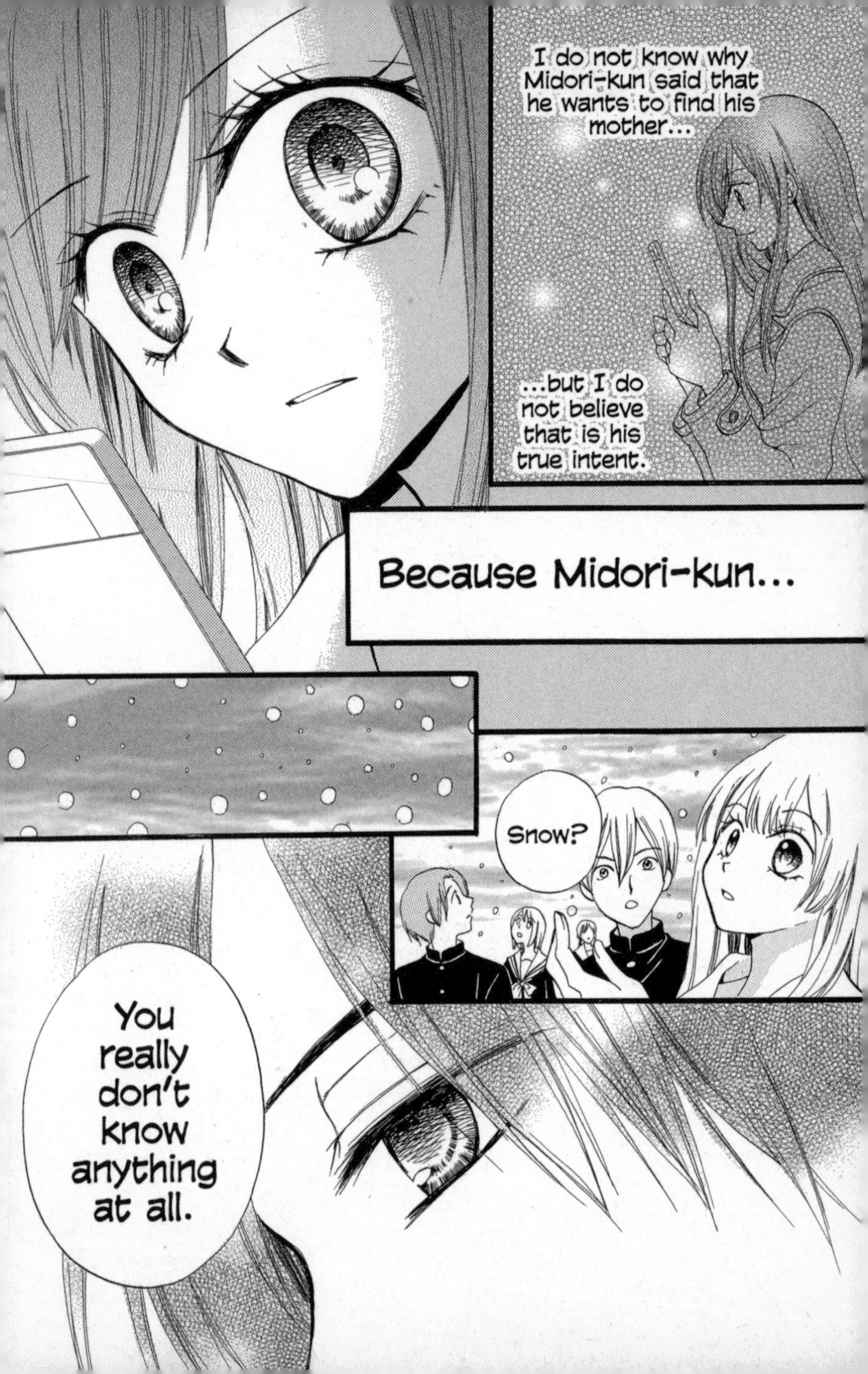
I do not know why Midori-kun said that he wants to find his mother...
...but I do not believe that is his true intent.
Because Midori-kun...
Snow?
You really don't know anything at all.

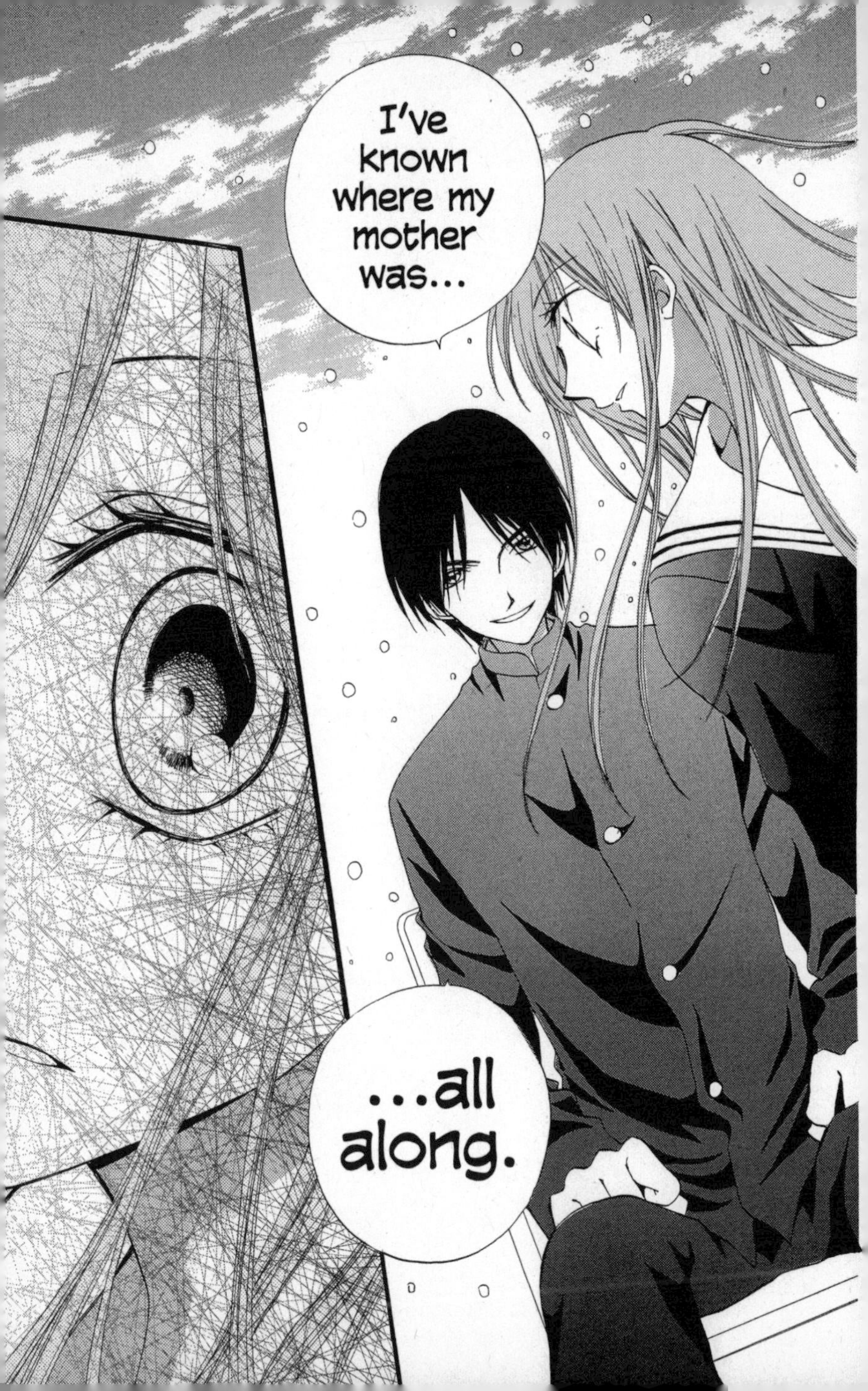

I've known where my mother was...
...all along.

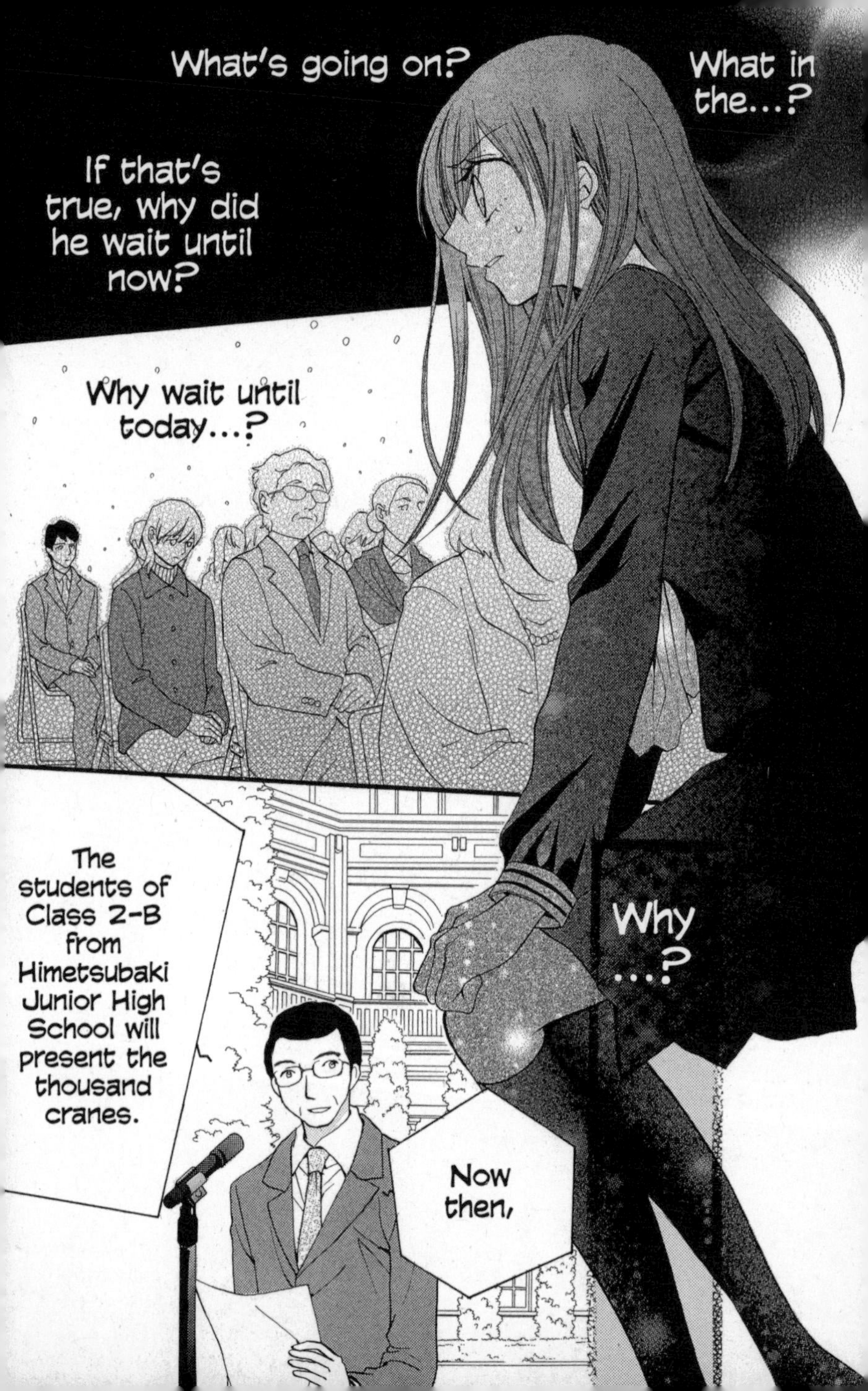
What in the...?
What's going on?
If that's true, why did he wait until now?
Why wait until today...?
Why...?
Now then,
The students of Class 2-B from Himetsubaki Junior High School will present the thousand cranes.

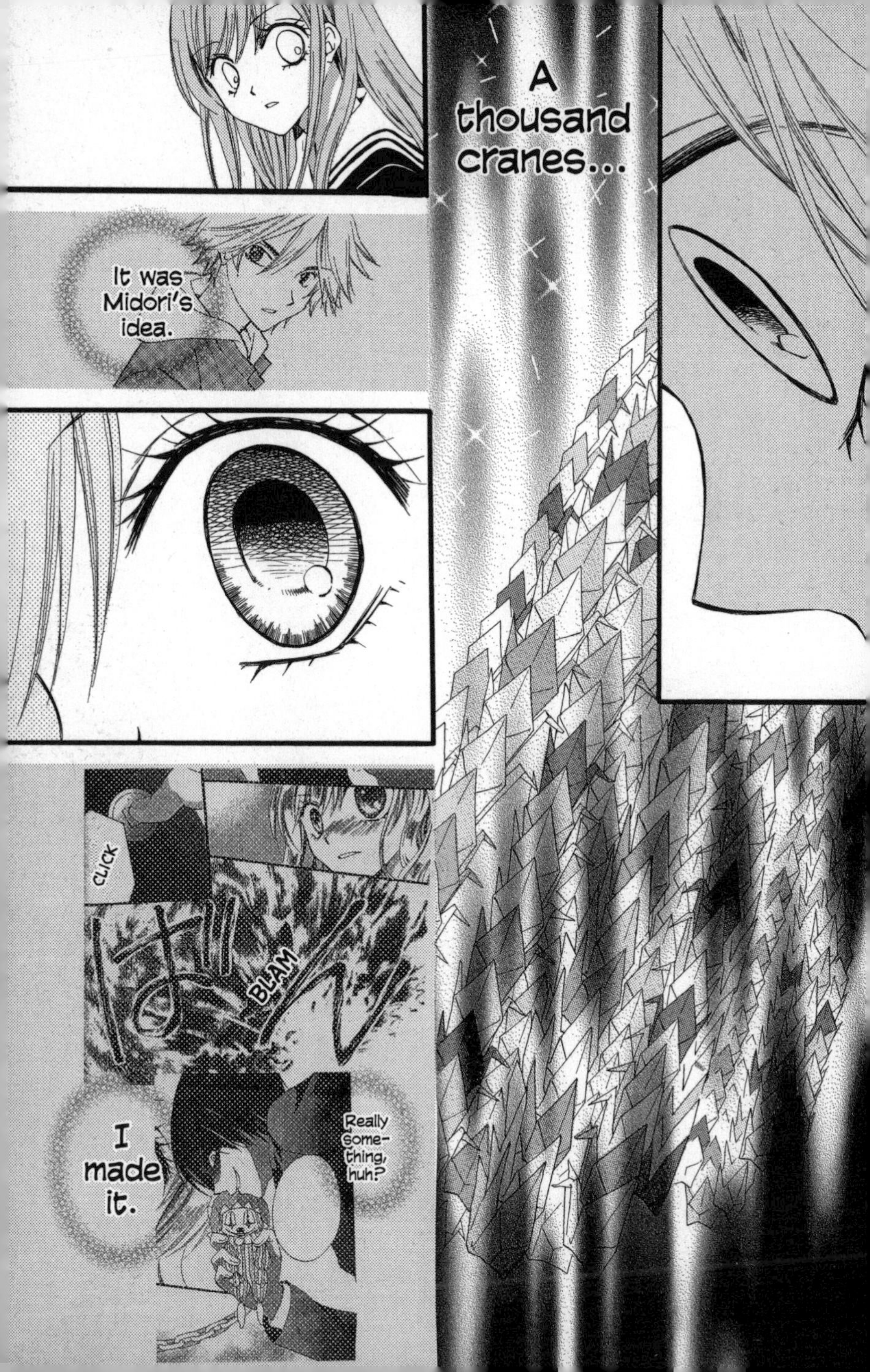
A thousand cranes...
It was Midori's idea.
CLICK
BLAM
Really something, huh?
I made it.

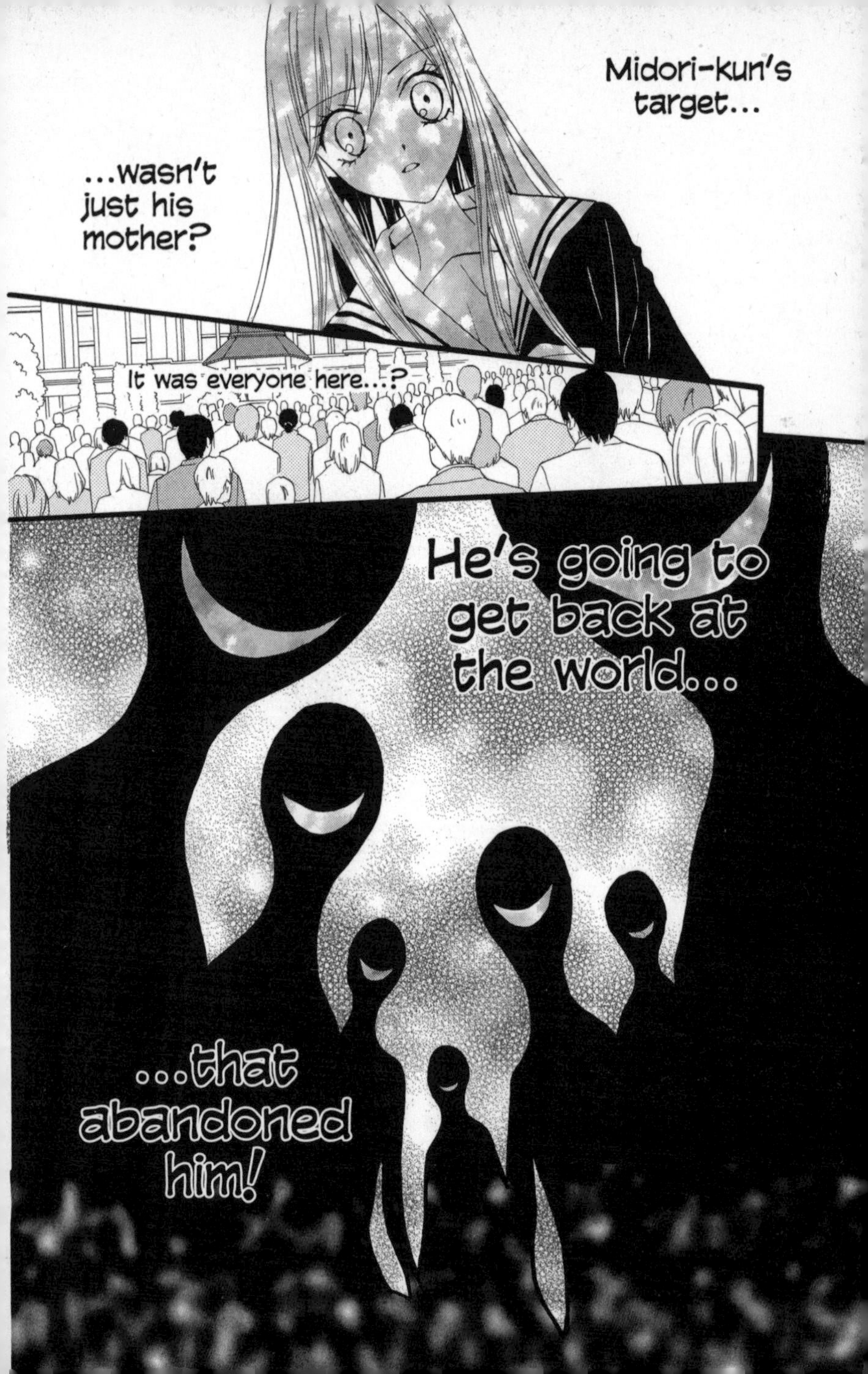
Midori-kun's target...
...wasn't just his mother?
It was everyone here...?
He's going to get back at the world...
...that abandoned him!

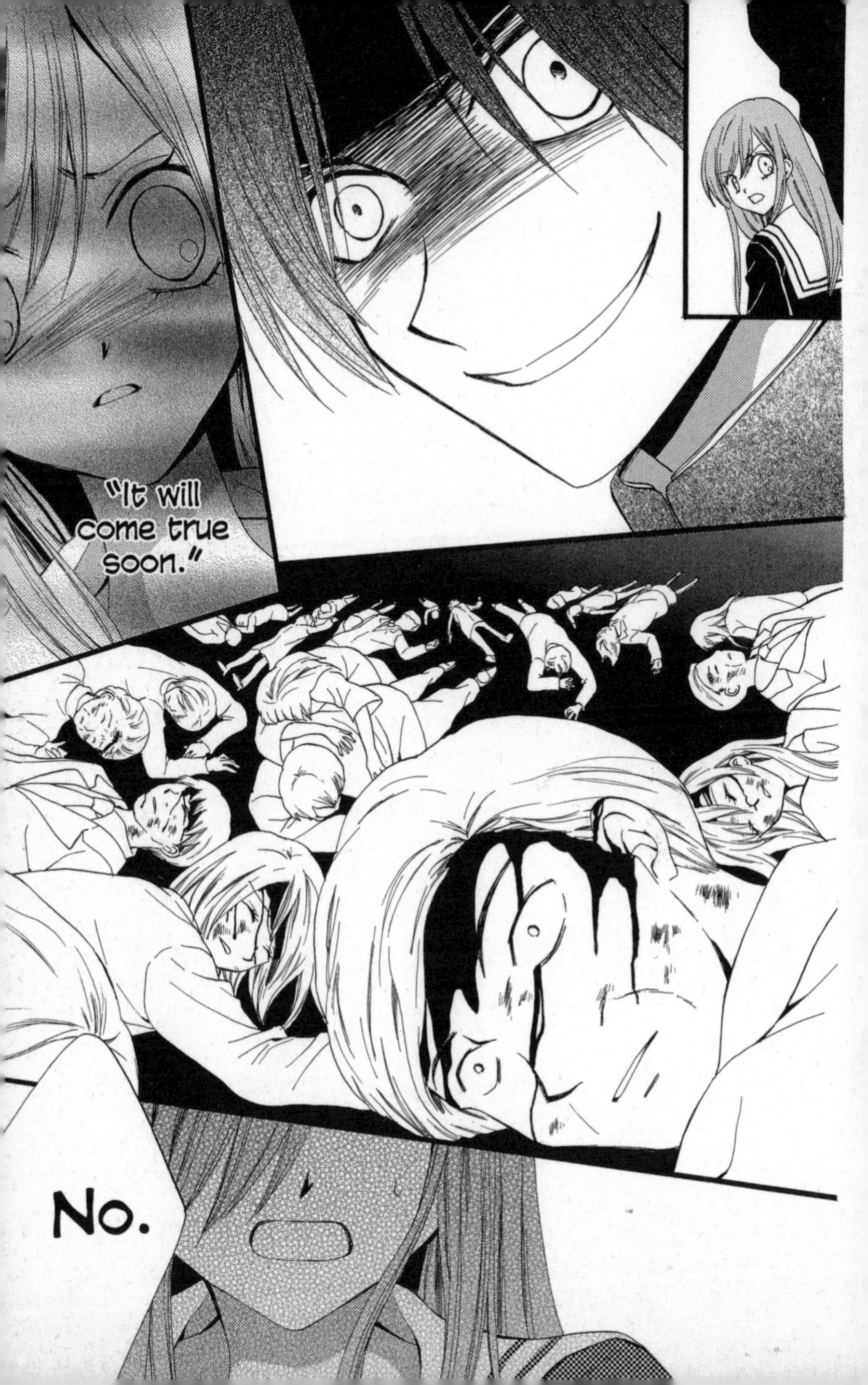
"It will come true soon."
No.

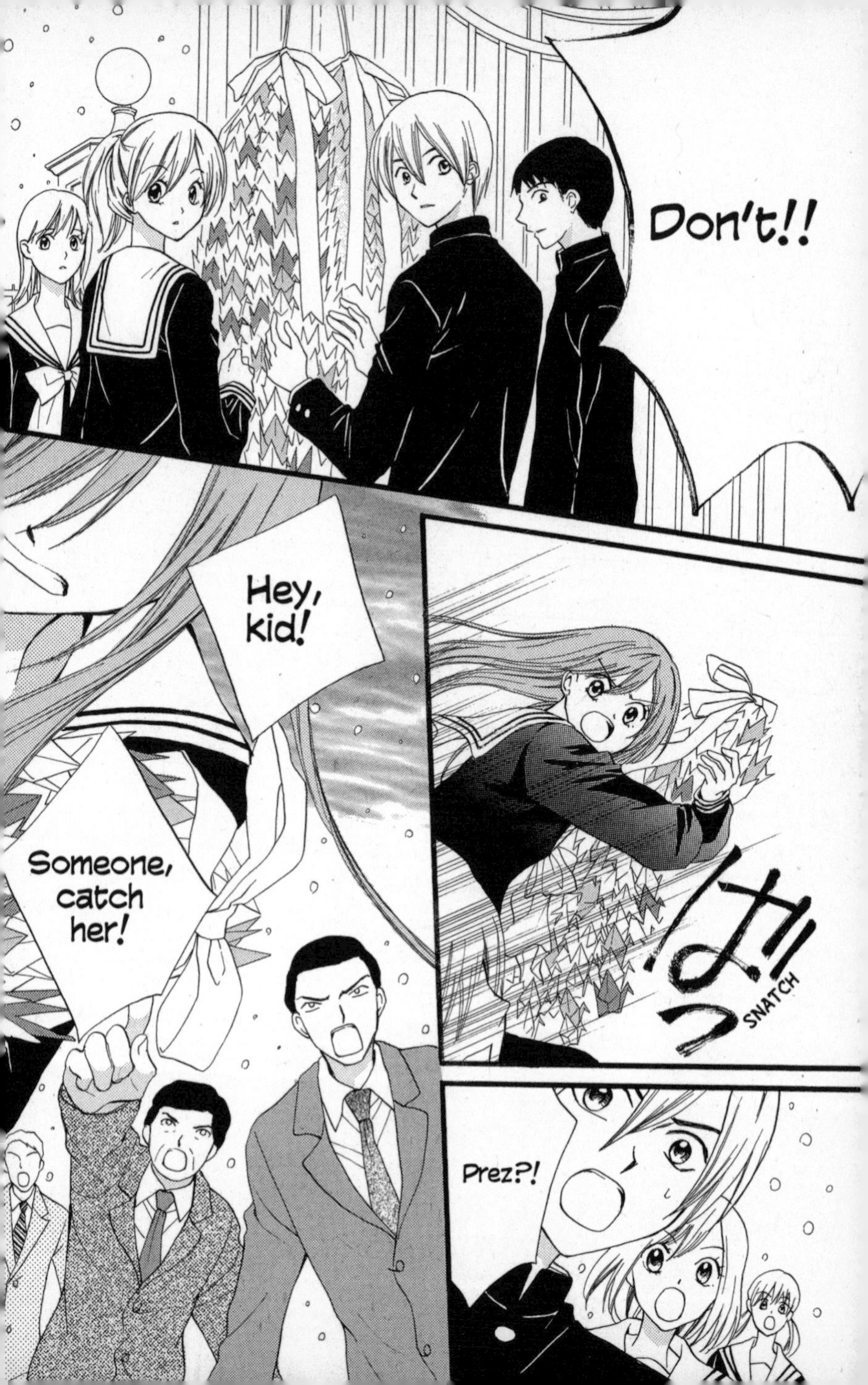
Don't!!
SNATCH
Prez?!
Hey, kid!
Someone, catch her!

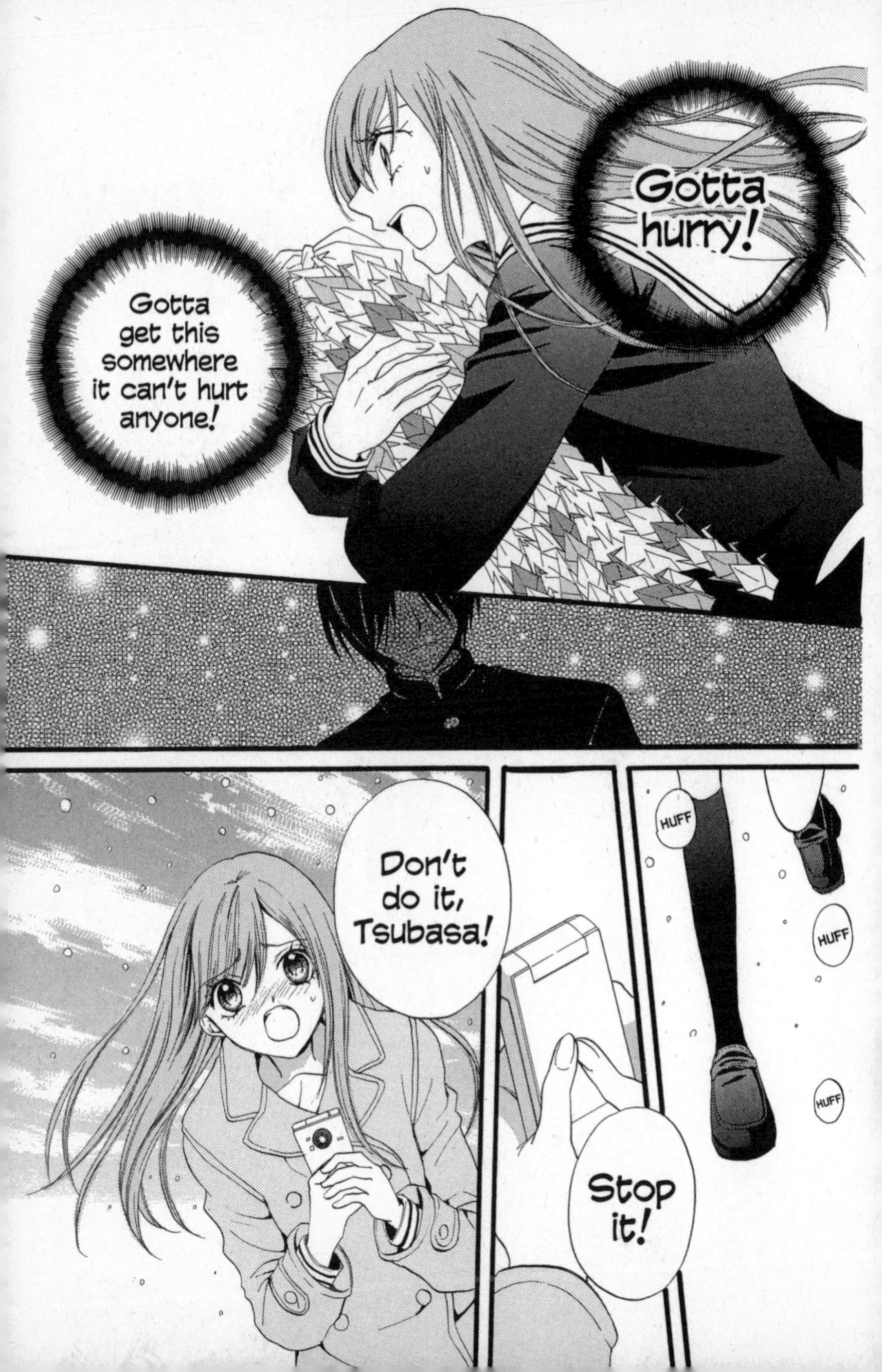
Gotta hurry!
Gotta get this somewhere it can't hurt anyone!
HUFF
HUFF
HUFF
Stop it!
Don't do it, Tsubasa!

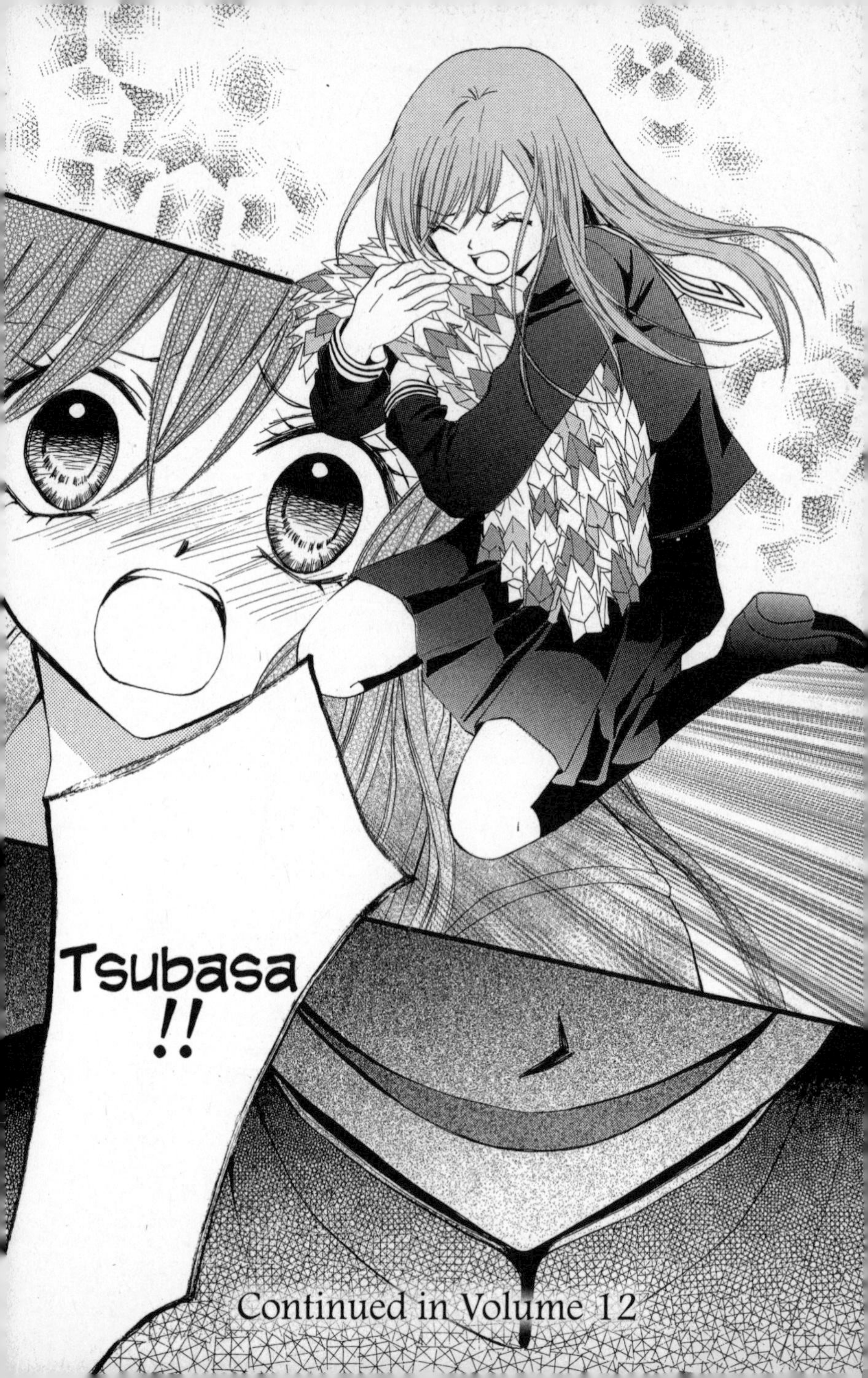
Tsubasa !!
Continued in Volume 12

Special Thanks

T. Nakamura
H. Kishimoto
M.Nakata
&
Kawamoto-sama
and
Yonemura-sama
of the Nakayoshi
editorial dept.
&
"Red rooster"
Takashi Shimoyama-sama
&
Ginnansha-sama

Send Letters To:
Natsumi Ando
c/o Kodansha Comics
451 Park Ave. South, 7th floor
New York, NY 10016

Illustration Gallery No. 1

Every month, I draw a bunch of pictures of Tsubasa for the next issue's preview. I've never had a chance to show them all off, so I'm doing it now!! Please enjoy Tsubasa's wardrobe! ♥

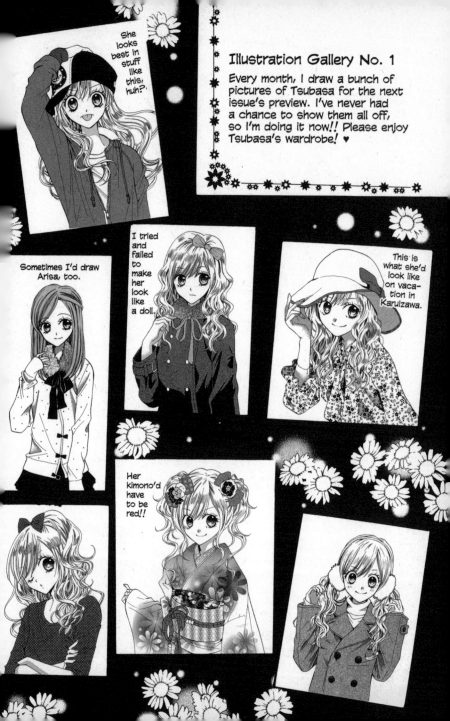

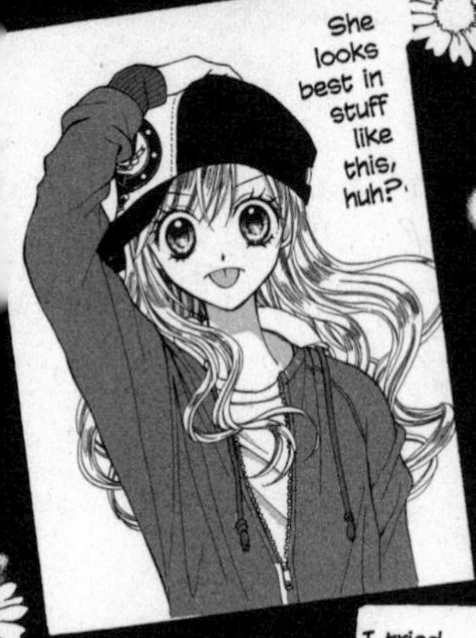
She looks best in stuff like this, huh?

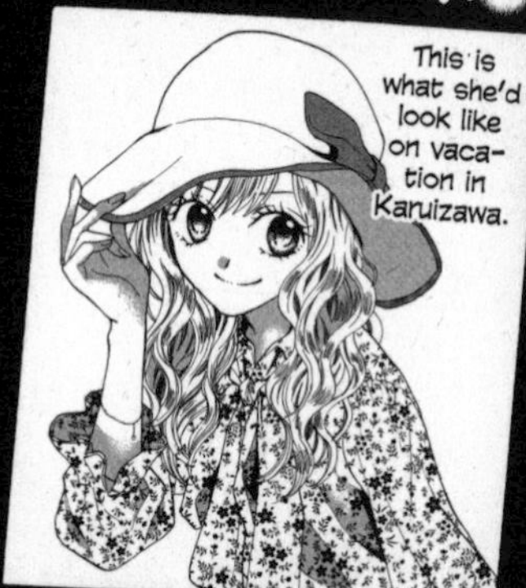
This is what she'd look like on vacation in Karuizawa.

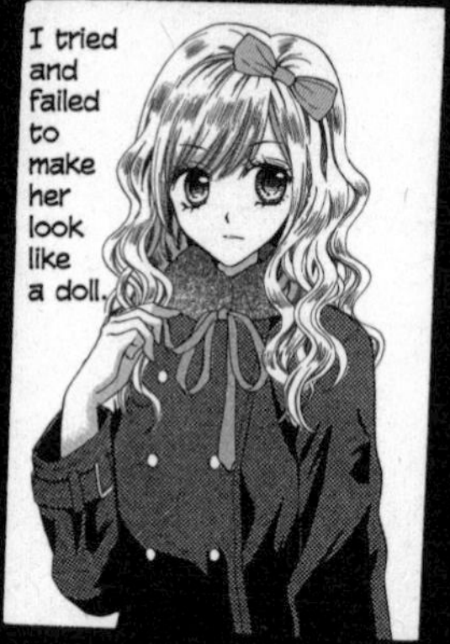
I tried and failed to make her look like a doll.

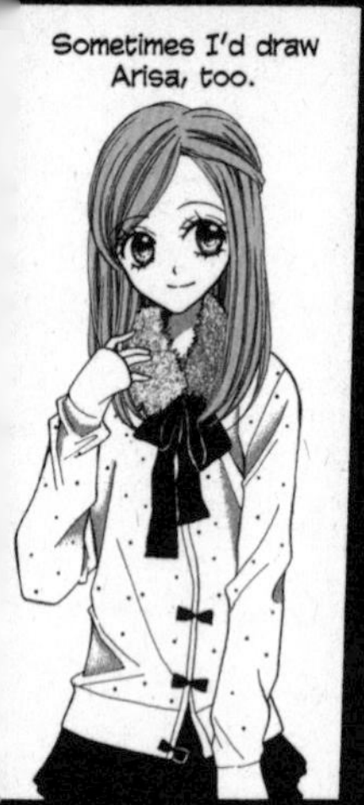
Sometimes I'd draw Arisa, too.

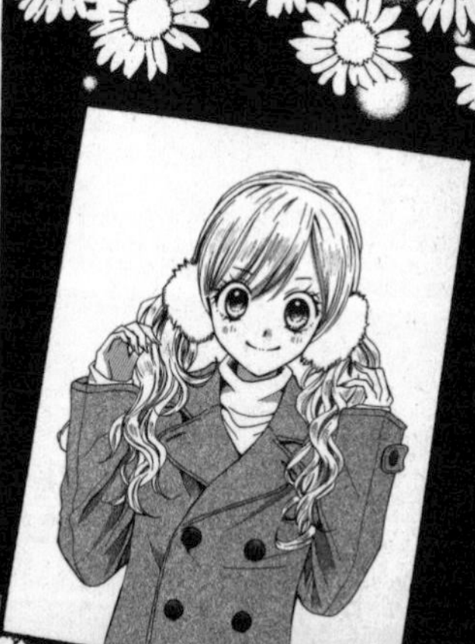

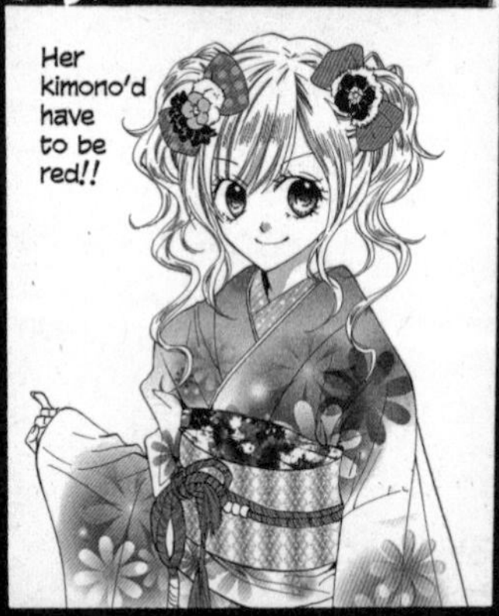
Her kimono'd have to be red!!

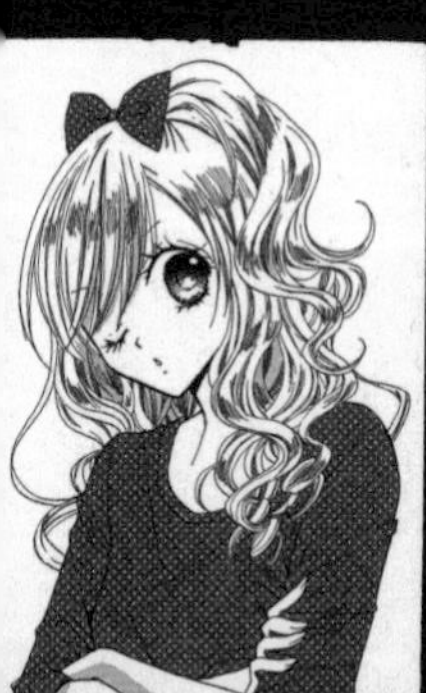

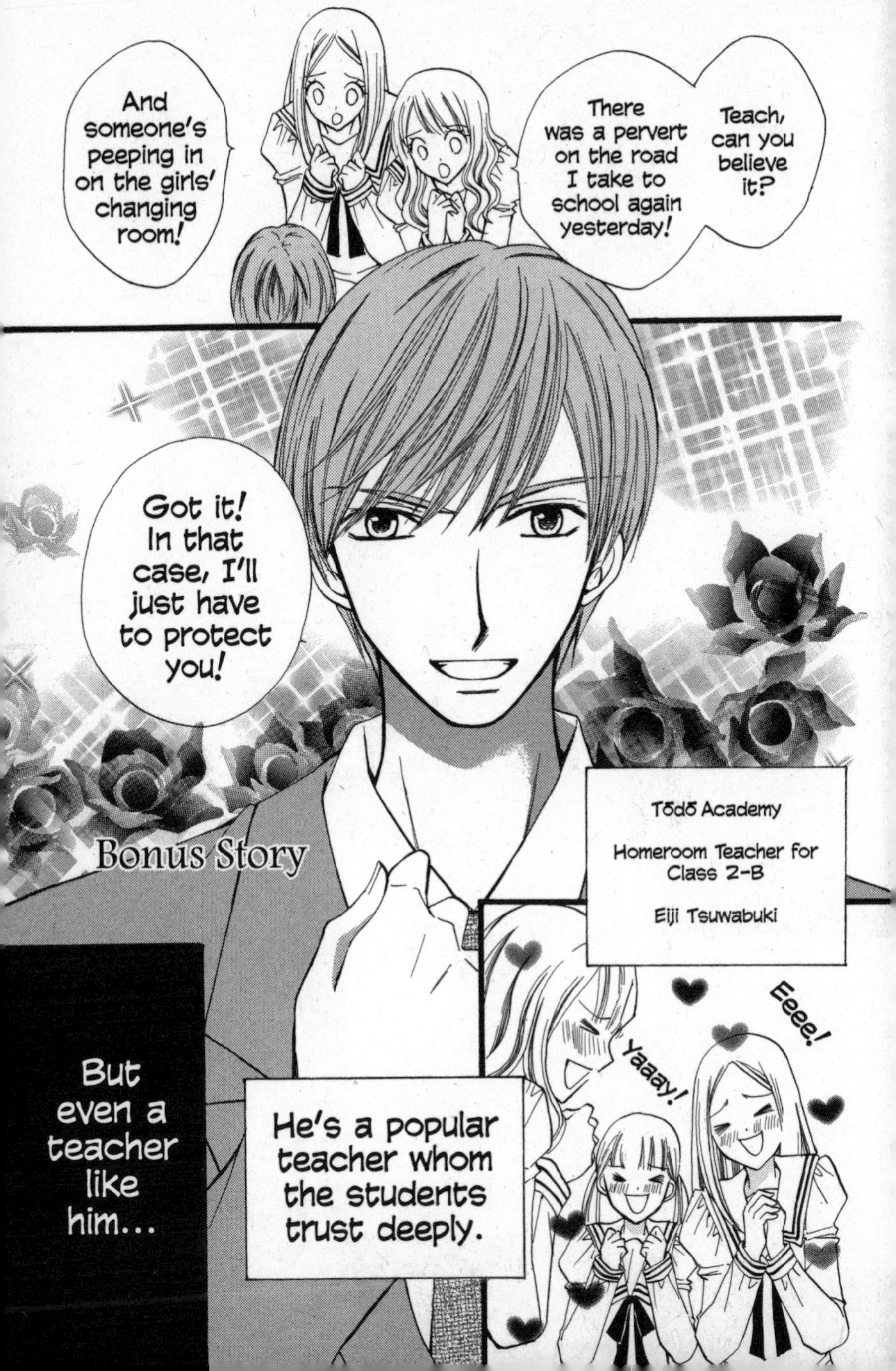
Teach, can you believe it?
There was a pervert on the road I take to school again yesterday!
And someone's peeping in on the girls' changing room!
Got it! In that case, I'll just have to protect you!
Tōdō Academy
Homeroom Teacher for Class 2-B
Eiji Tsuwabuki
Bonus Story
Eeee!
Yaaay!
He's a popular teacher whom the students trust deeply.
But even a teacher like him...

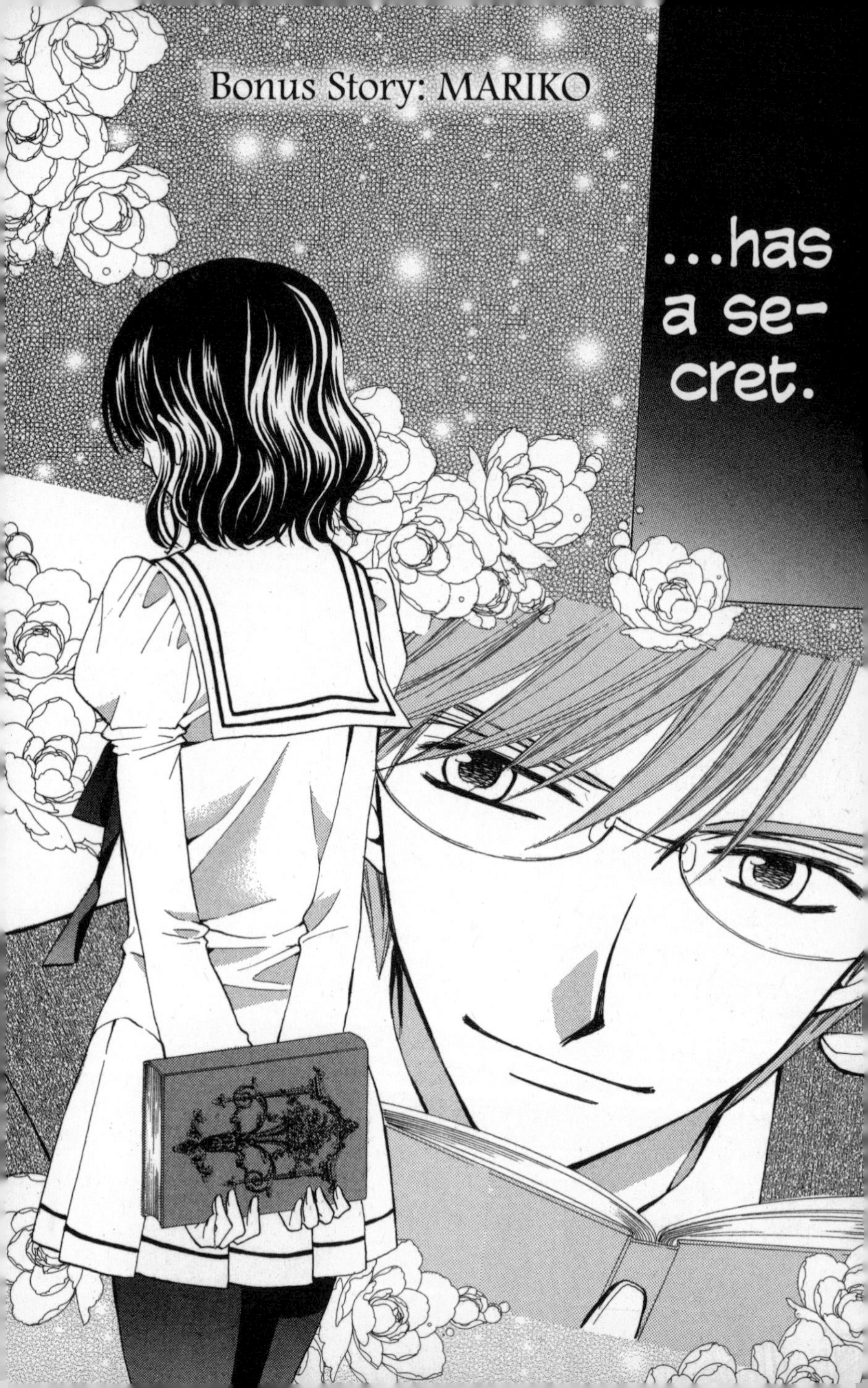
Bonus Story: MARIKO
...has a se-cret.

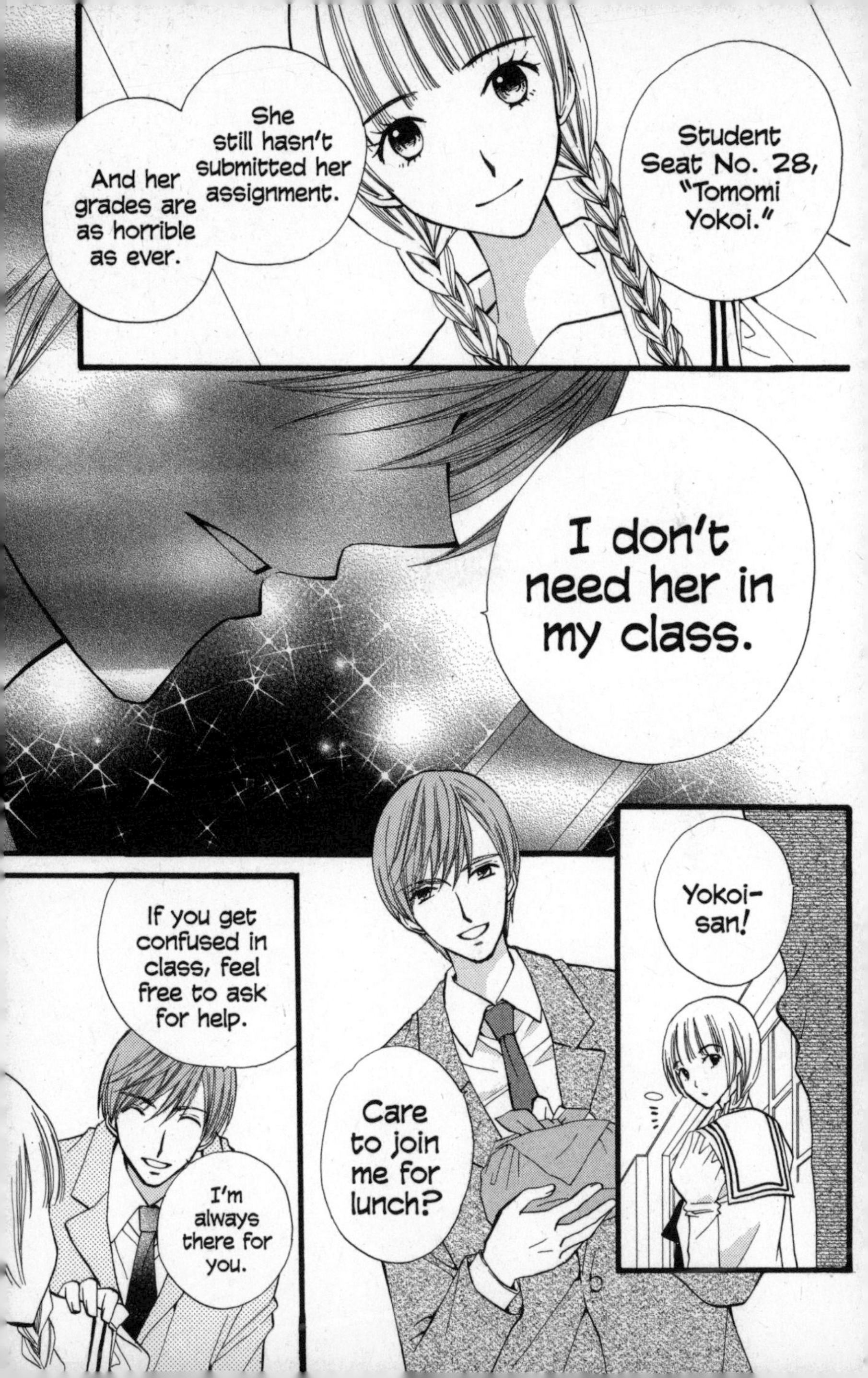
Student Seat No. 28, "Tomomi Yokoi."
She still hasn't submitted her assignment.
And her grades are as horrible as ever.
I don't need her in my class.
Yokoi-san!
Care to join me for lunch?
If you get confused in class, feel free to ask for help.
I'm always there for you.

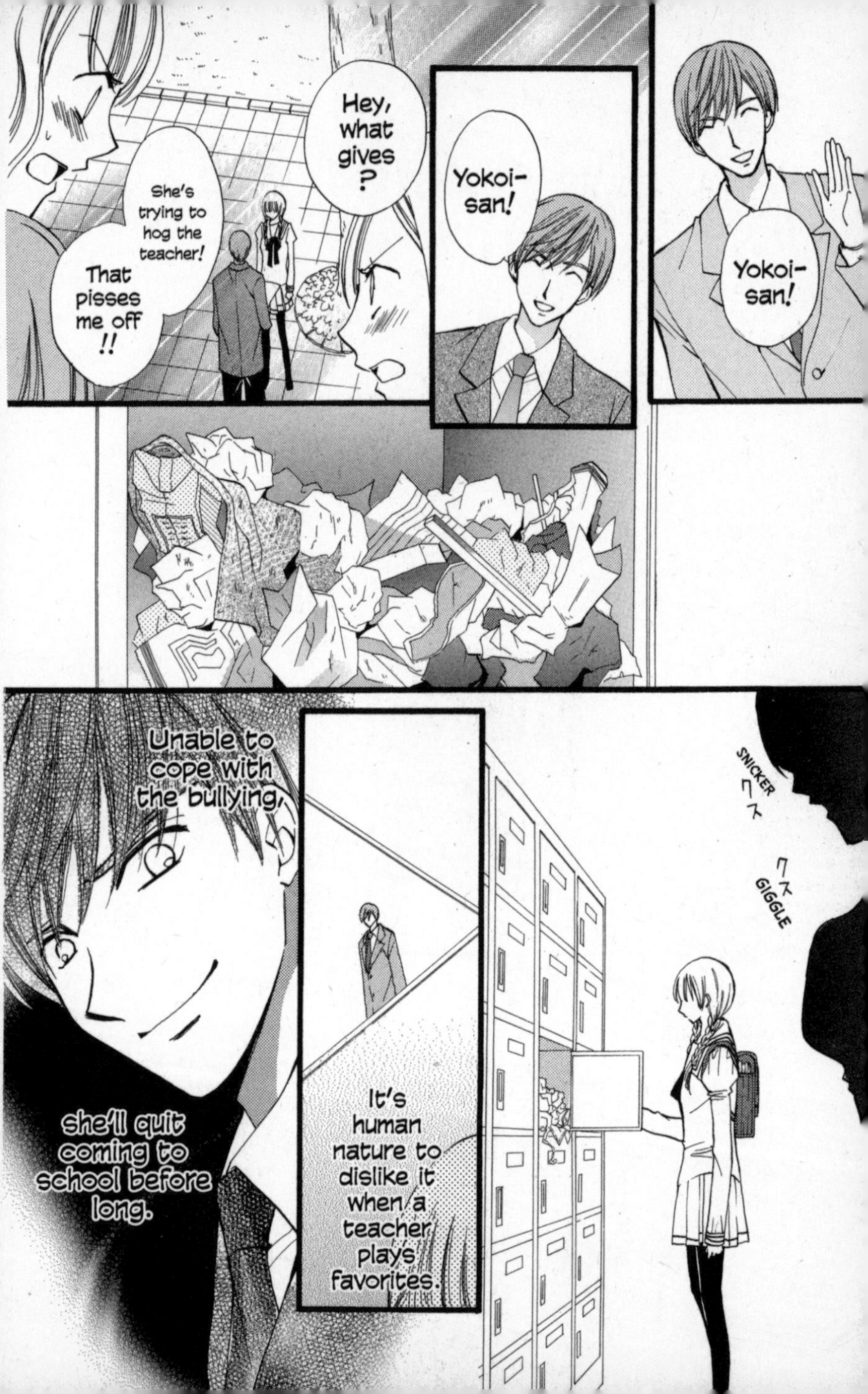
Yokoi-san!
Yokoi-san!
Hey, what gives?
She's trying to hog the teacher!
That pisses me off!!
SNICKER クス
クス GIGGLE
It's human nature to dislike it when a teacher plays favorites.
Unable to cope with the bullying,
she'll quit coming to school before long.

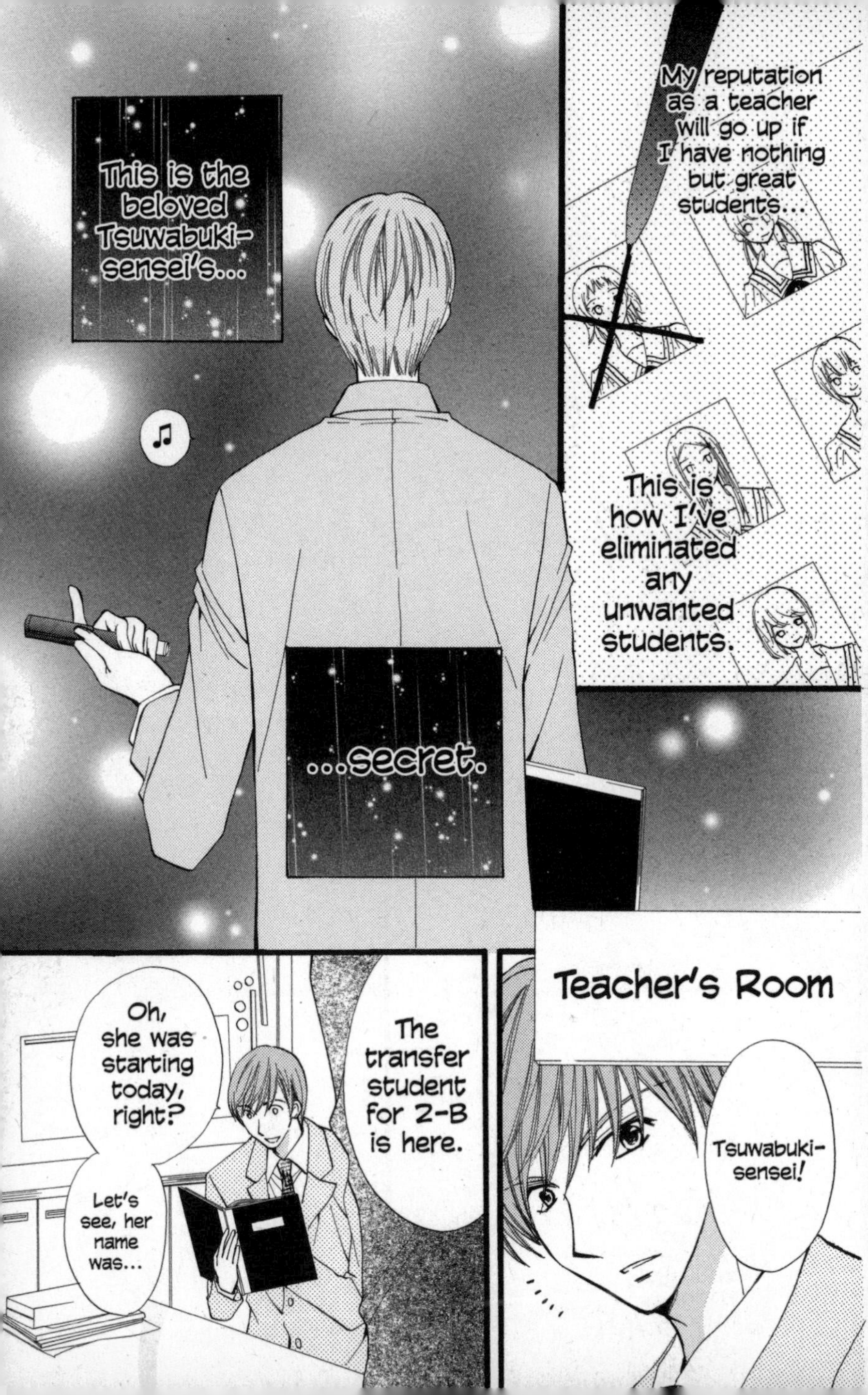
My reputation as a teacher will go up if I have nothing but great students...
This is how I've eliminated any unwanted students.
This is the beloved Tsuwabuki-sensei's...
♫
...secret.
Teacher's Room
Tsuwabuki-sensei!
The transfer student for 2-B is here.
Oh, she was starting today, right?
Let's see, her name was...

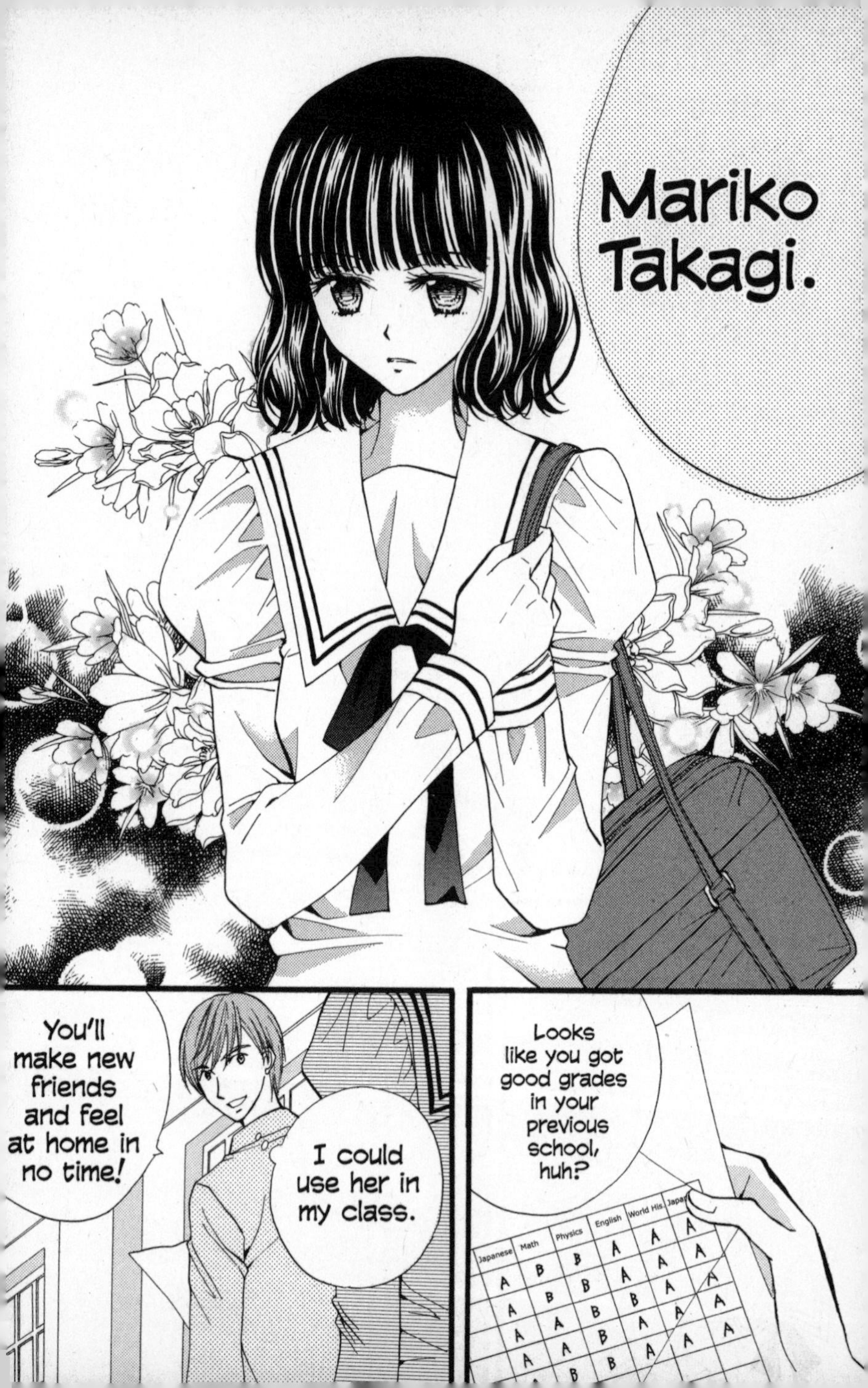

Mariko Takagi.
Looks like you got good grades in your previous school, huh?
Japanese
Math
Physics
English
World His.
I could use her in my class.
You'll make new friends and feel at home in no time!

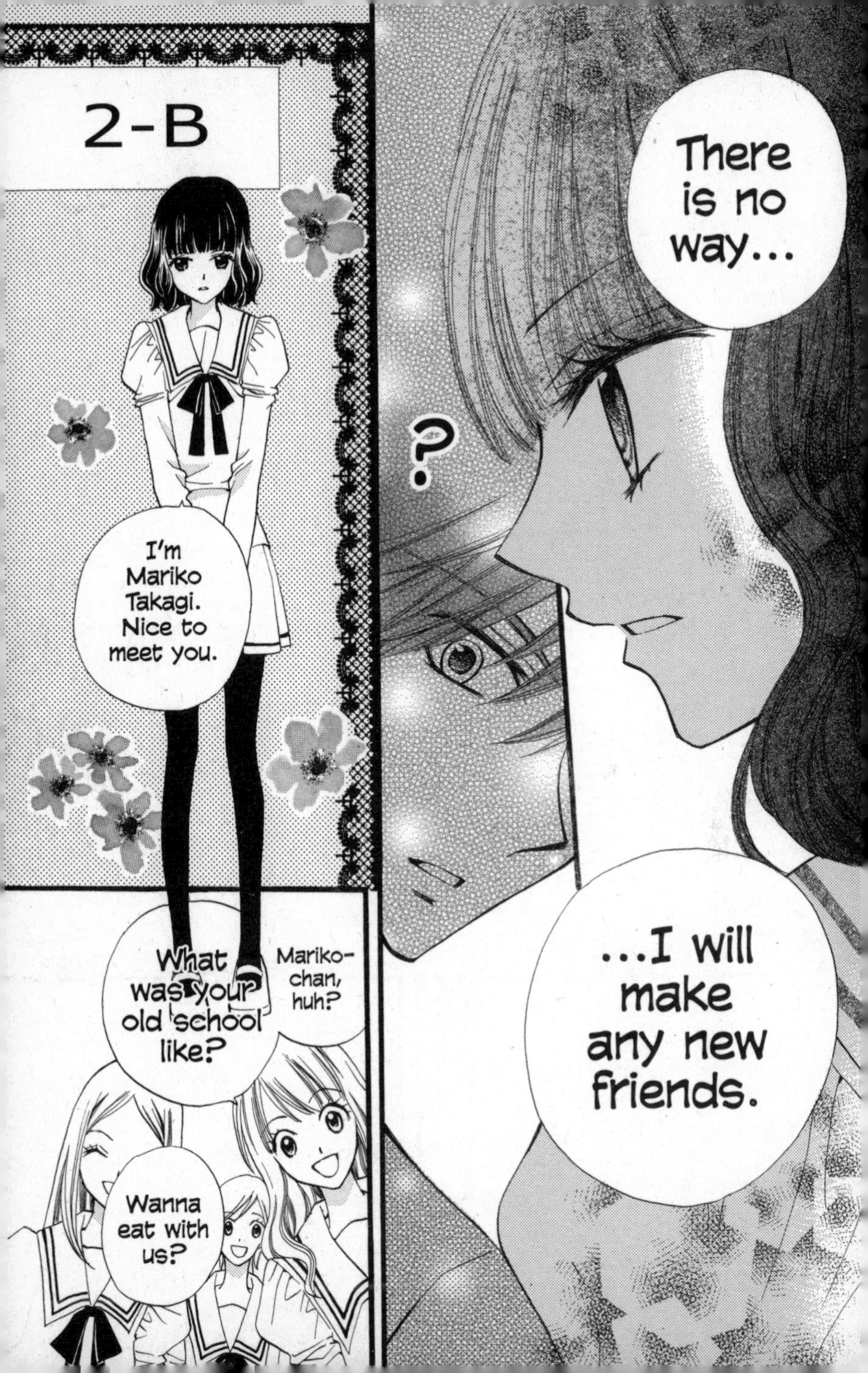
There is no way...
?
...I will make any new friends.
2-B
I'm Mariko Takagi. Nice to meet you.
Mariko-chan, huh?
What was your old school like?
Wanna eat with us?

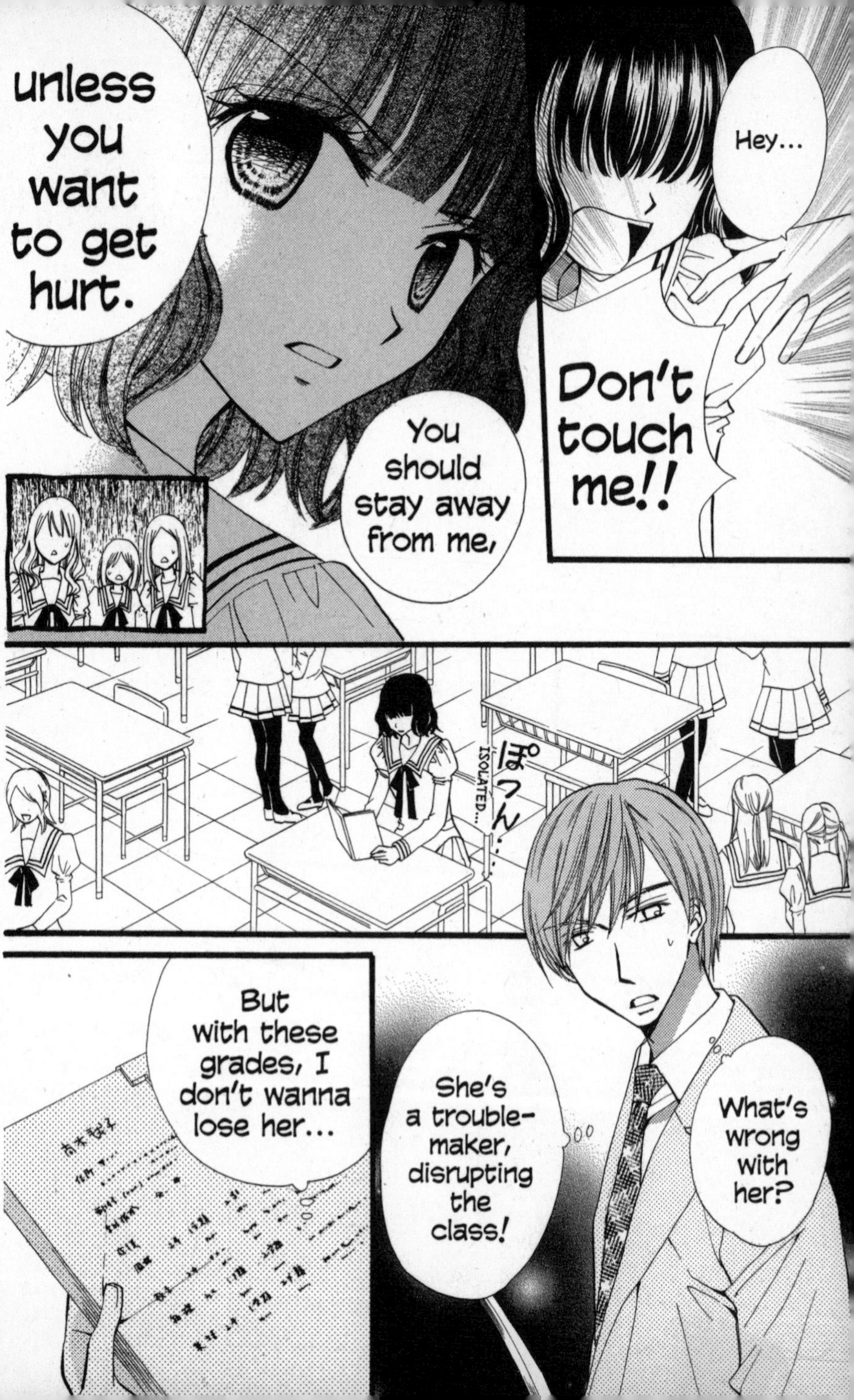
Hey...
Don't touch me!!
You should stay away from me,
unless you want to get hurt.
ぽつん...
ISOLATED...
What's wrong with her?
She's a trouble-maker, disrupting the class!
But with these grades, I don't wanna lose her...

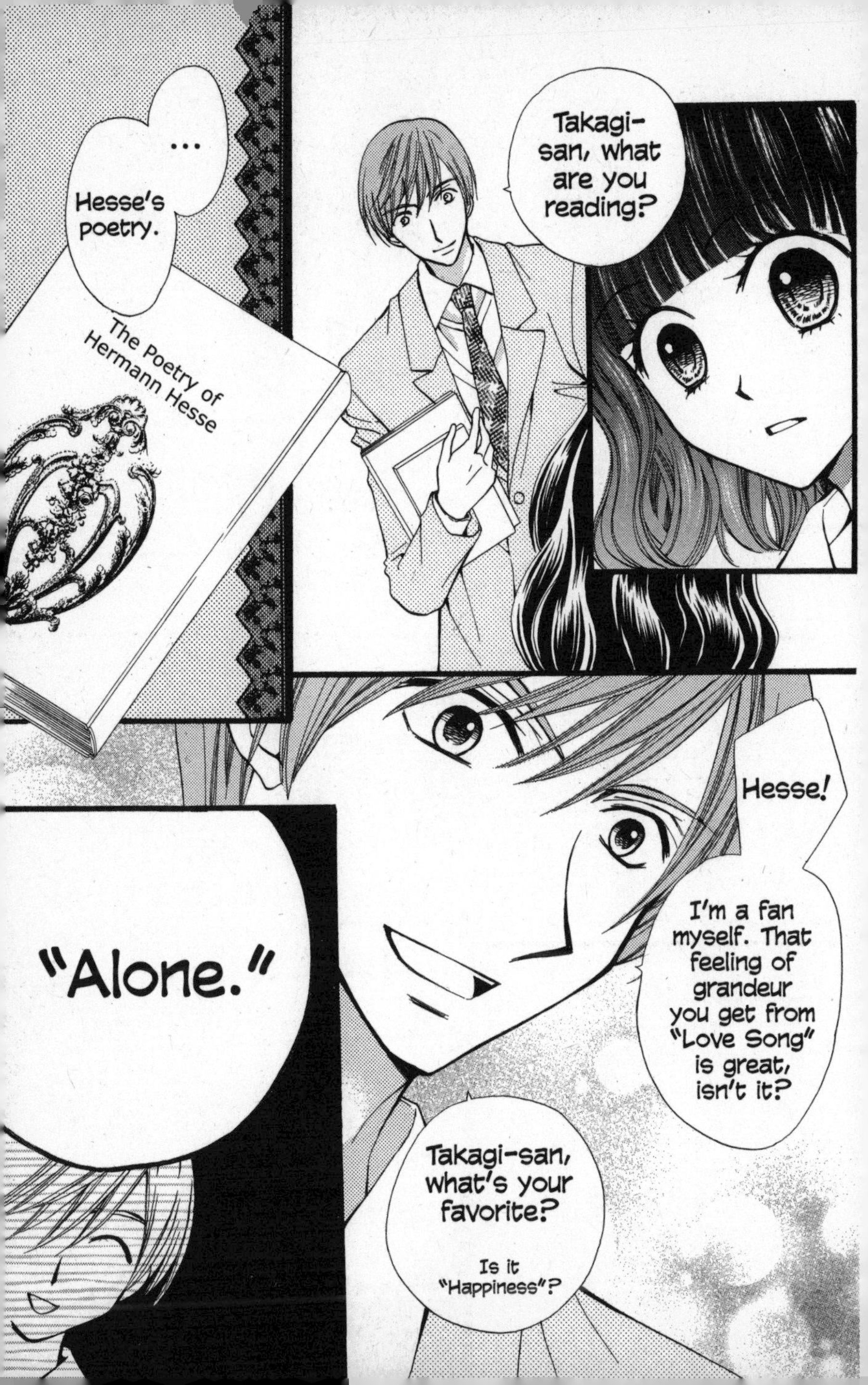
Takagi-san, what are you reading?
...
Hesse's poetry.
The Poetry of Hermann Hesse
Hesse!
I'm a fan myself. That feeling of grandeur you get from "Love Song" is great, isn't it?
Takagi-san, what's your favorite?
Is it "Happiness"?
"Alone."

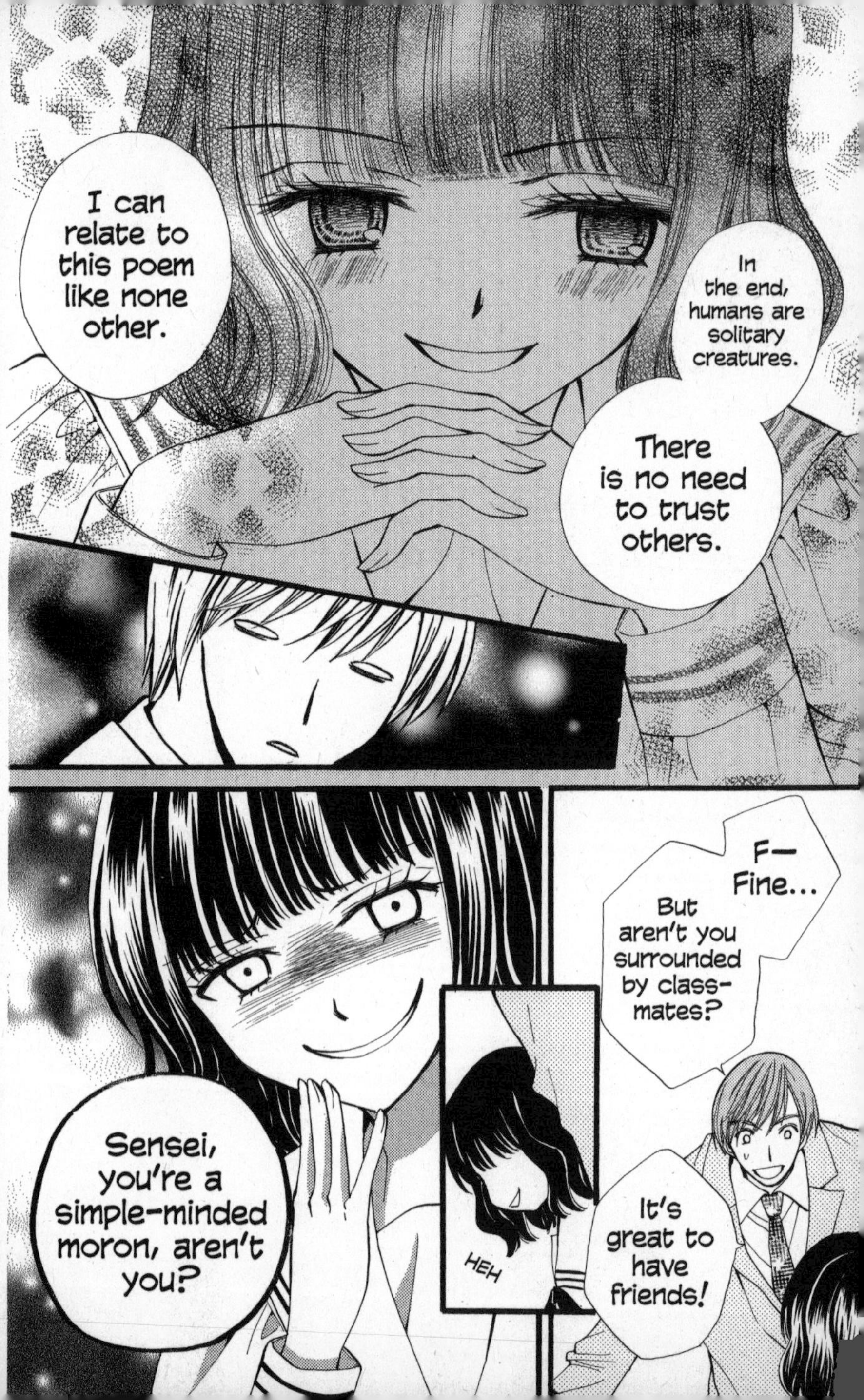
In the end, humans are solitary creatures.
There is no need to trust others.
I can relate to this poem like none other.
F— Fine...
But aren't you surrounded by class-mates?
It's great to have friends!
HEH
Sensei, you're a simple-minded moron, aren't you?

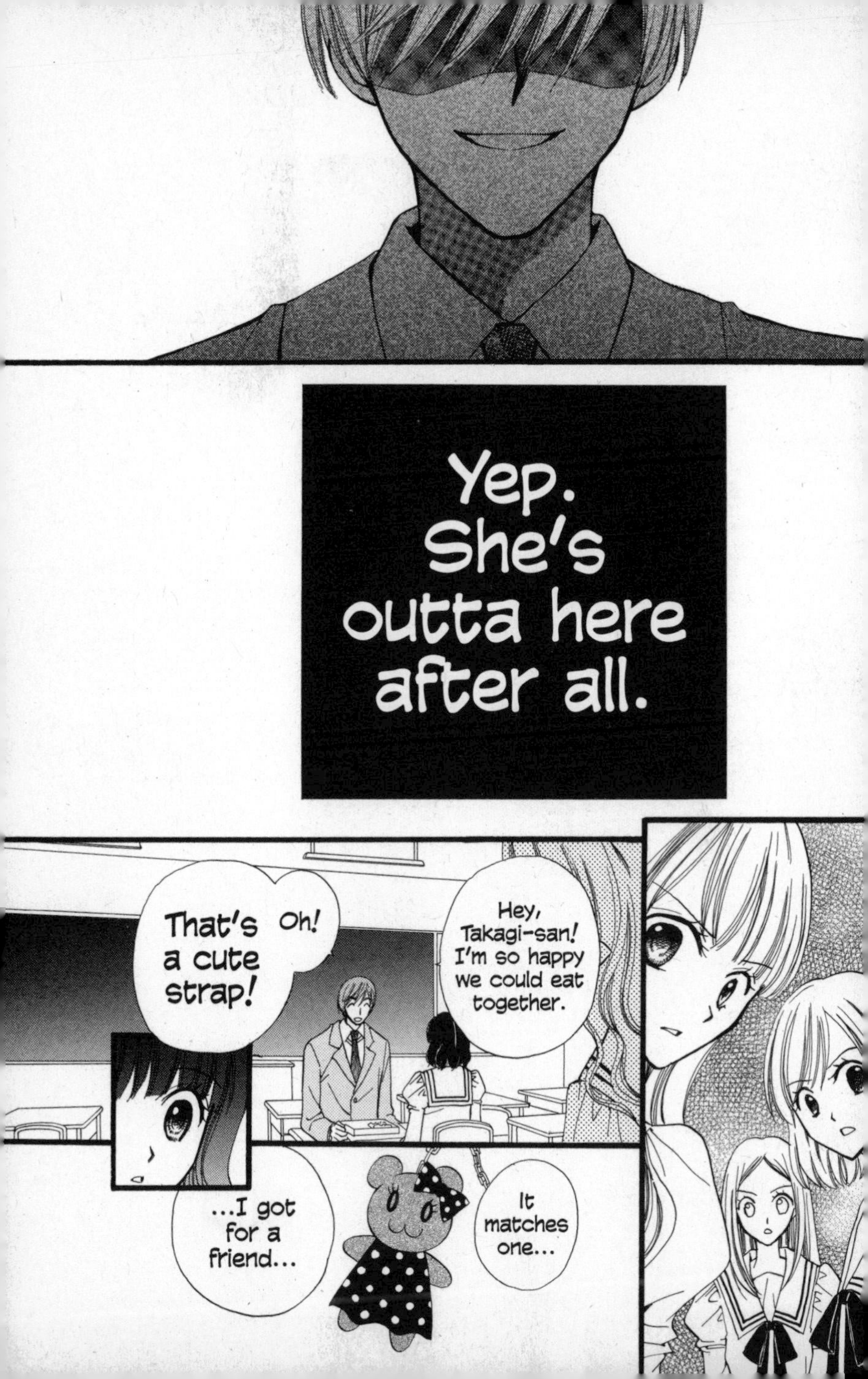
Yep. She's outta here after all.
Hey, Takagi-san! I'm so happy we could eat together.
Oh!
That's a cute strap!
It matches one...
...I got for a friend...

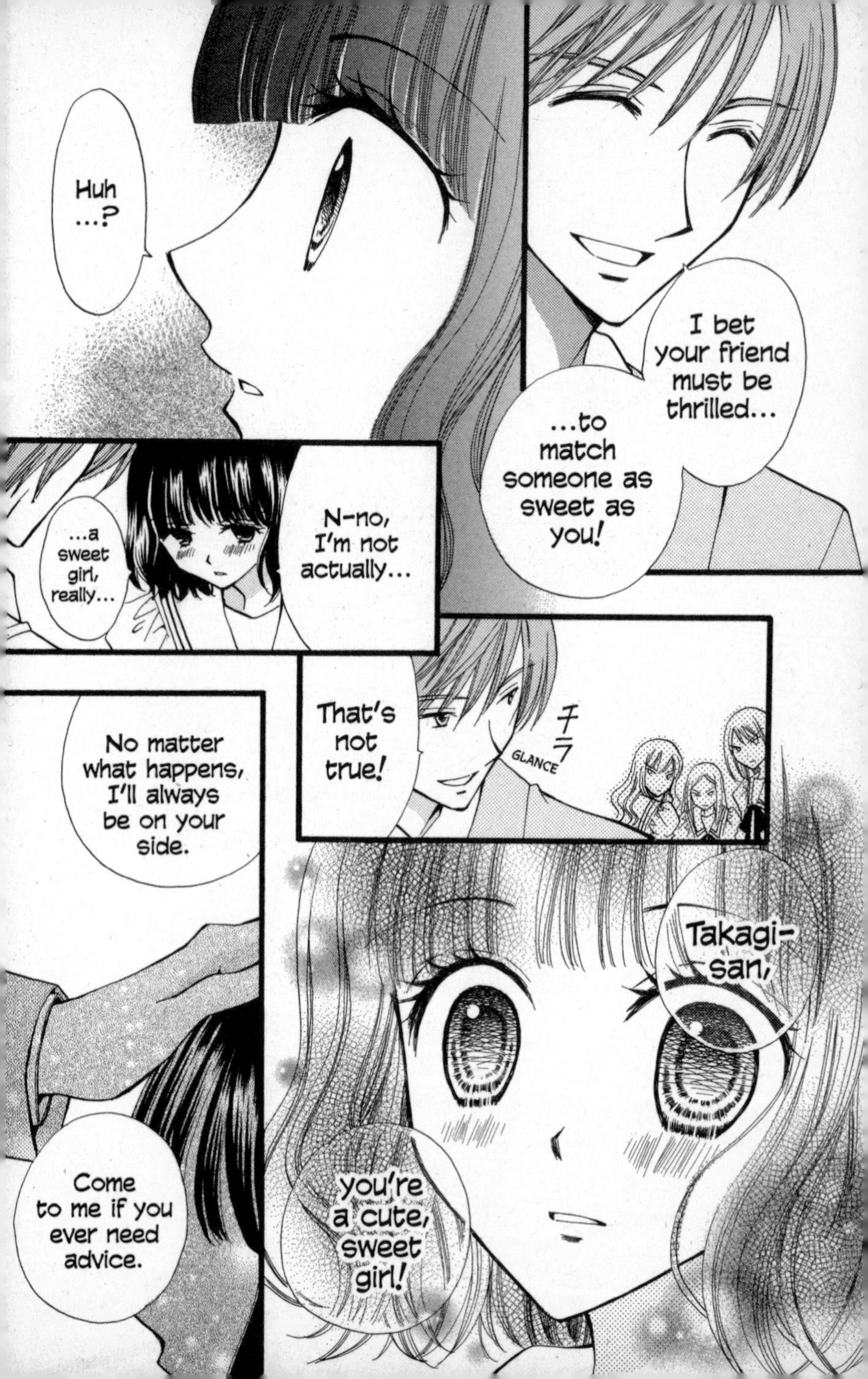
I bet your friend must be thrilled...
...to match someone as sweet as you!
Huh ...?
N-no, I'm not actually...
...a sweet girl, really...
That's not true!
チラ
GLANCE
Takagi-san,
you're a cute, sweet girl!
No matter what happens, I'll always be on your side.
Come to me if you ever need advice.

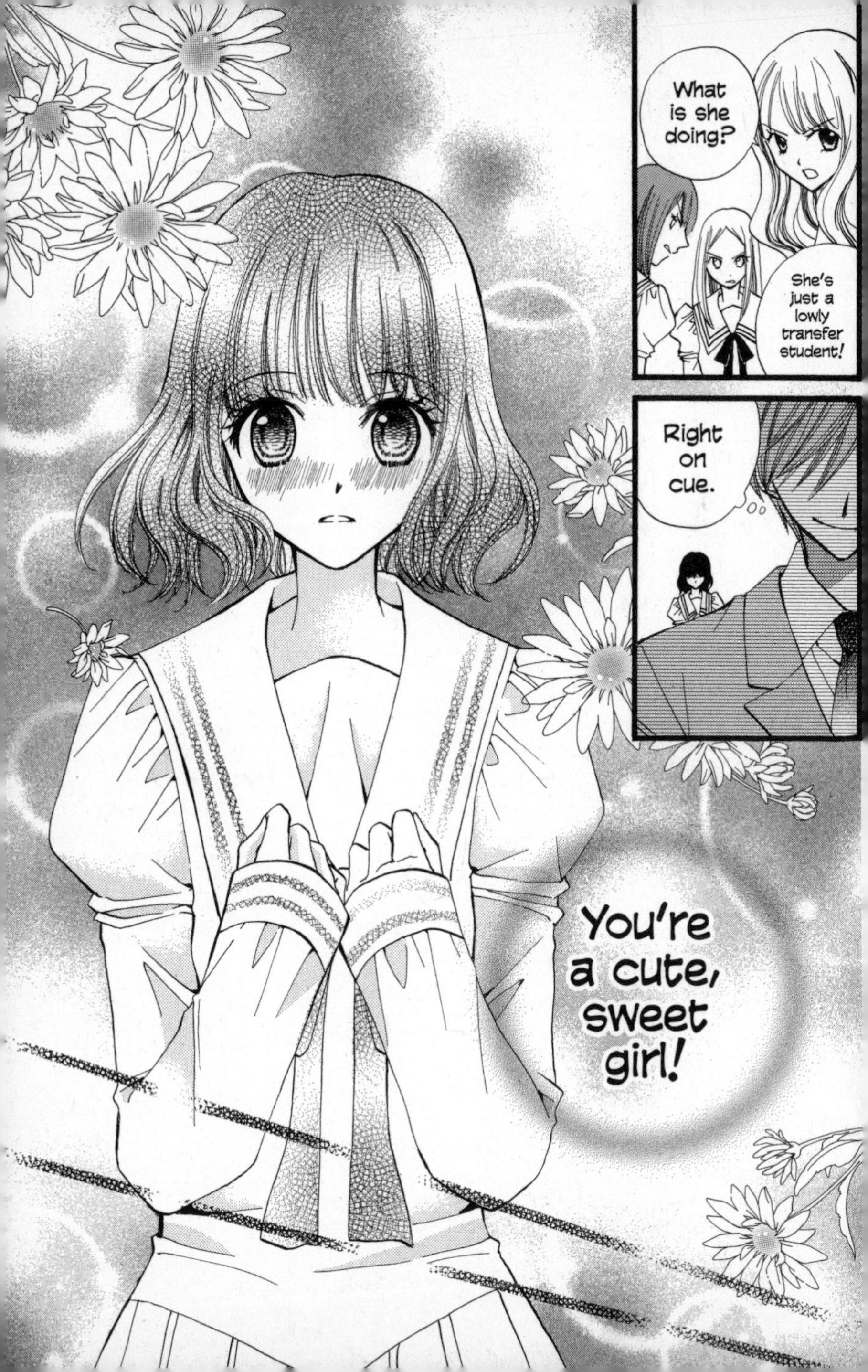
What is she doing?
She's just a lowly transfer student!
Right on cue.
You're a cute, sweet girl!

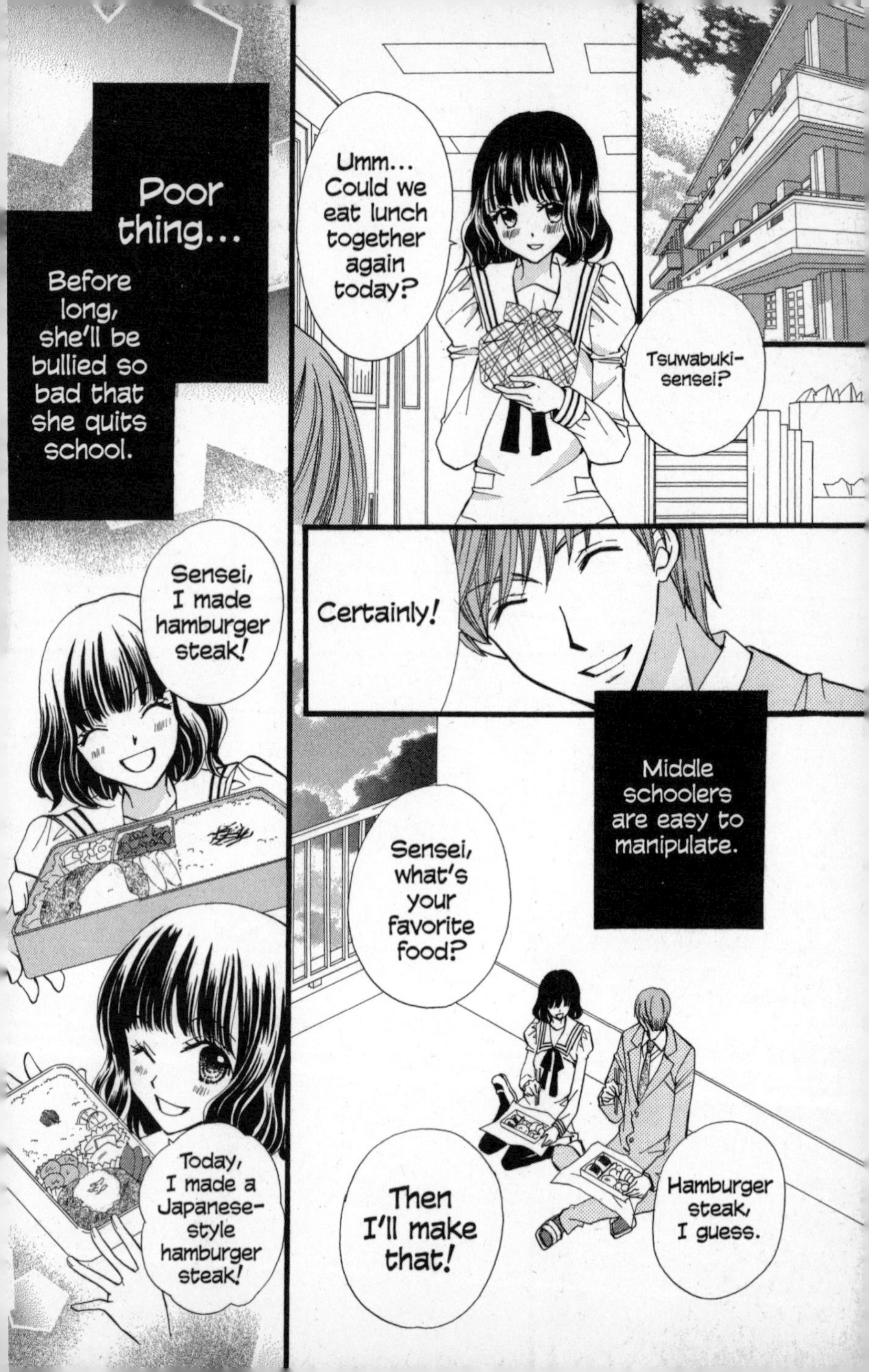

Tsuwabuki-sensei?
Umm... Could we eat lunch together again today?
Certainly!
Middle schoolers are easy to manipulate.
Sensei, what's your favorite food?
Hamburger steak, I guess.
Then I'll make that!
Poor thing...
Before long, she'll be bullied so bad that she quits school.
Sensei, I made hamburger steak!
Today, I made a Japanese-style hamburger steak!

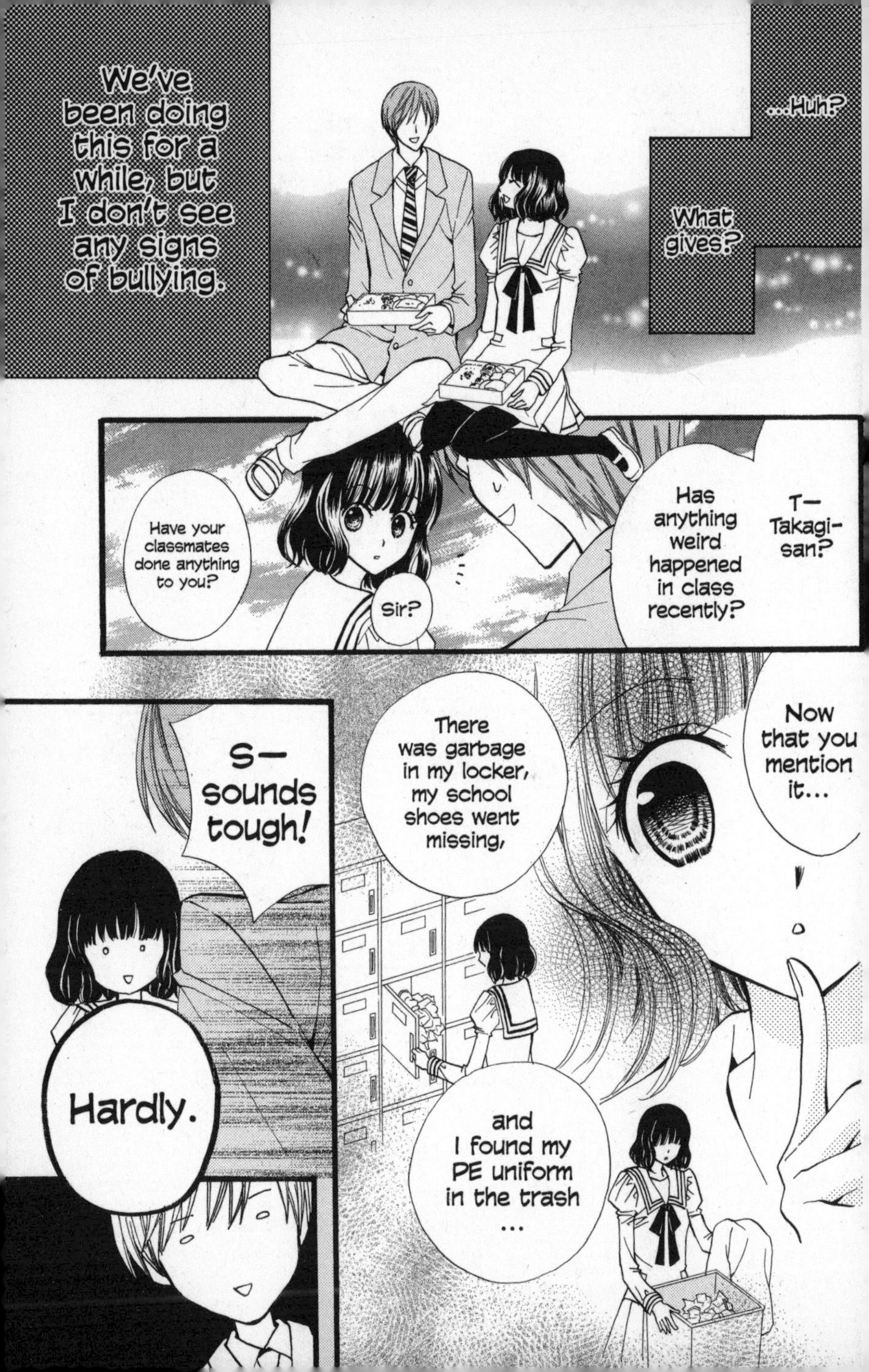
...Huh?
What gives?
We've been doing this for a while, but I don't see any signs of bullying.
T—Takagi-san?
Has anything weird happened in class recently?
Sir?
Have your classmates done anything to you?
Now that you mention it...
There was garbage in my locker, my school shoes went missing,
and I found my PE uniform in the trash ...
S—sounds tough!
Hardly.

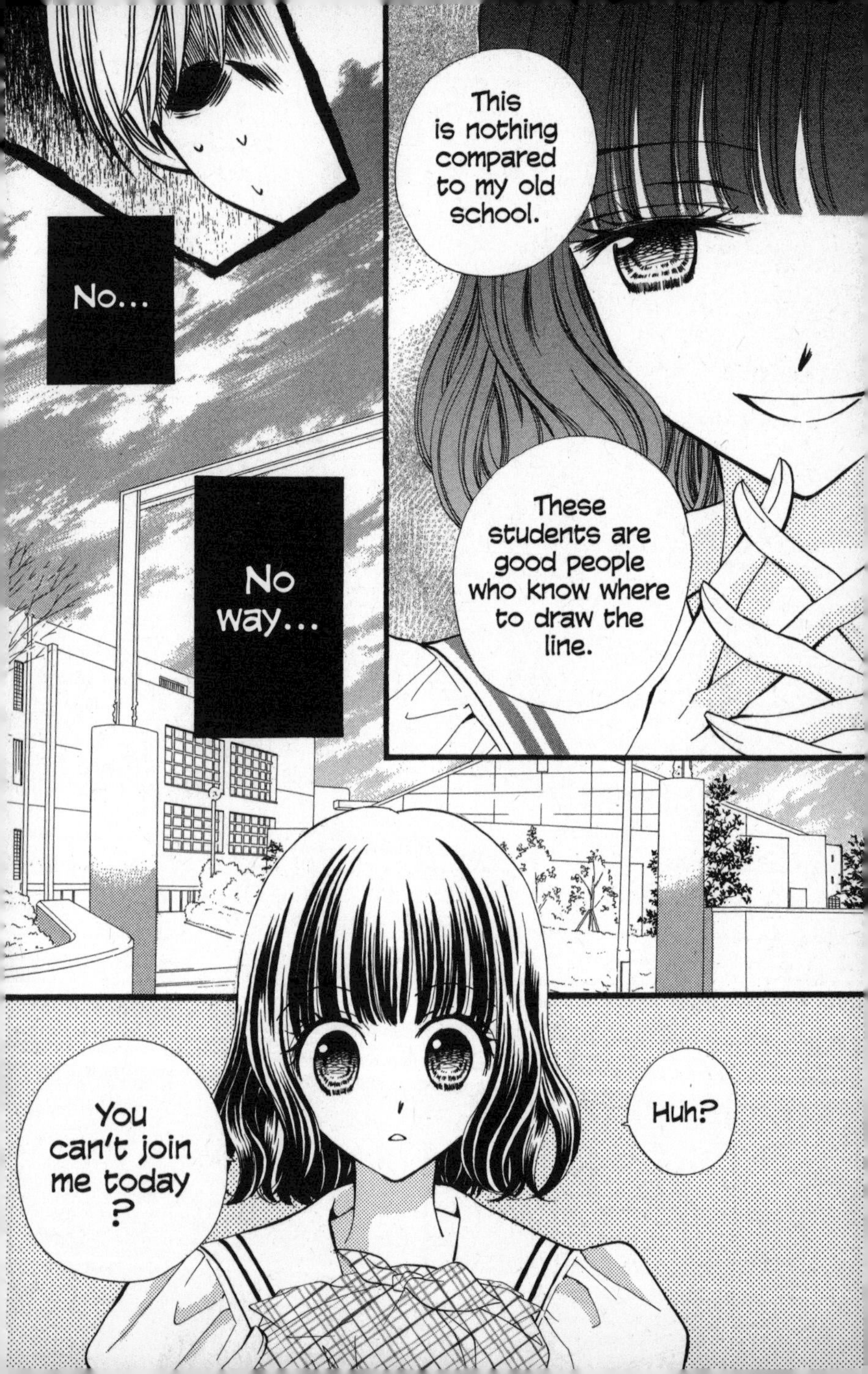
This is nothing compared to my old school.
These students are good people who know where to draw the line.
No...
No way...
Huh?
You can't join me today?

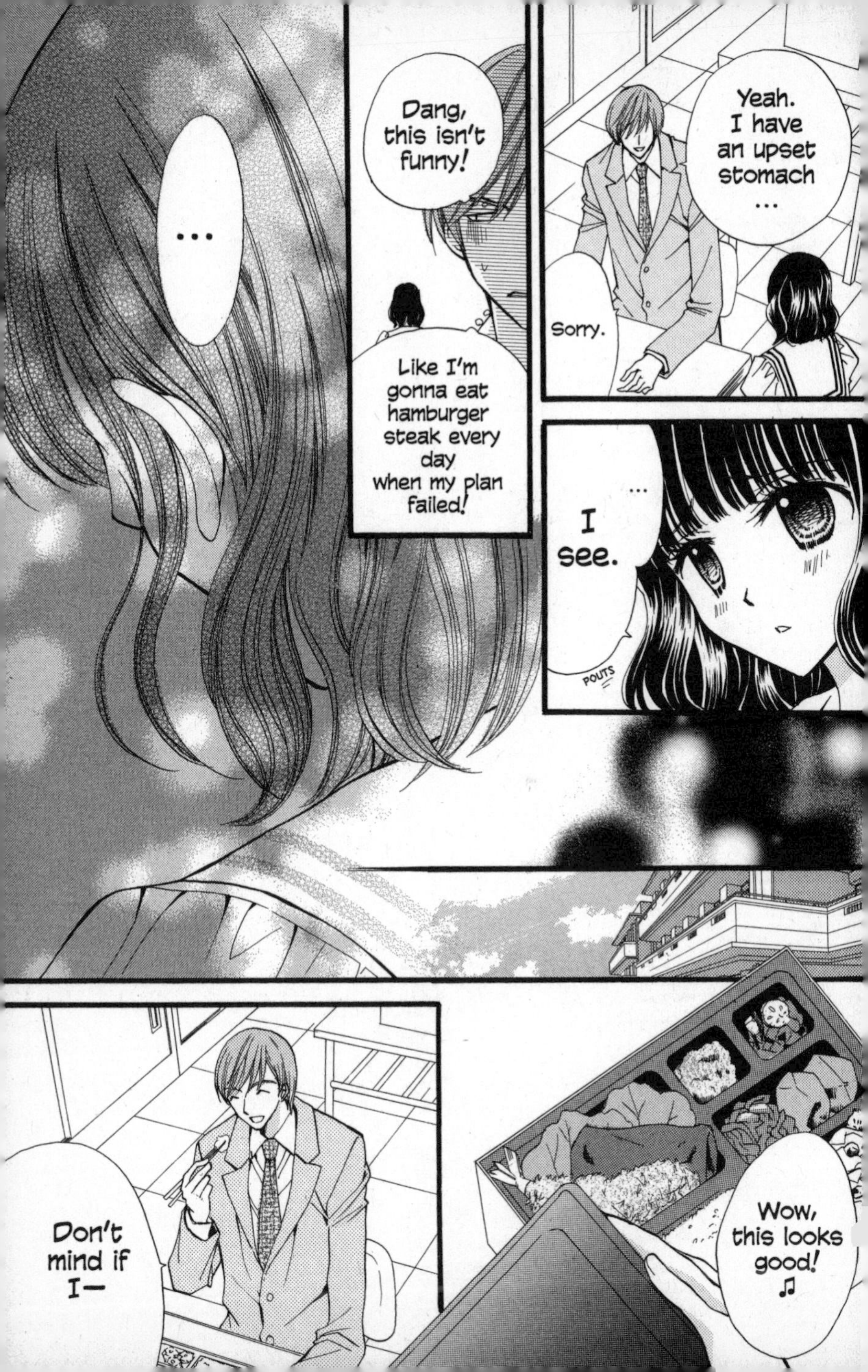
Yeah. I have an upset stomach …
Sorry.
Dang, this isn't funny!
Like I'm gonna eat hamburger steak every day when my plan failed!
… I see.
POUTS
…
Wow, this looks good! ♫
Don't mind if I—

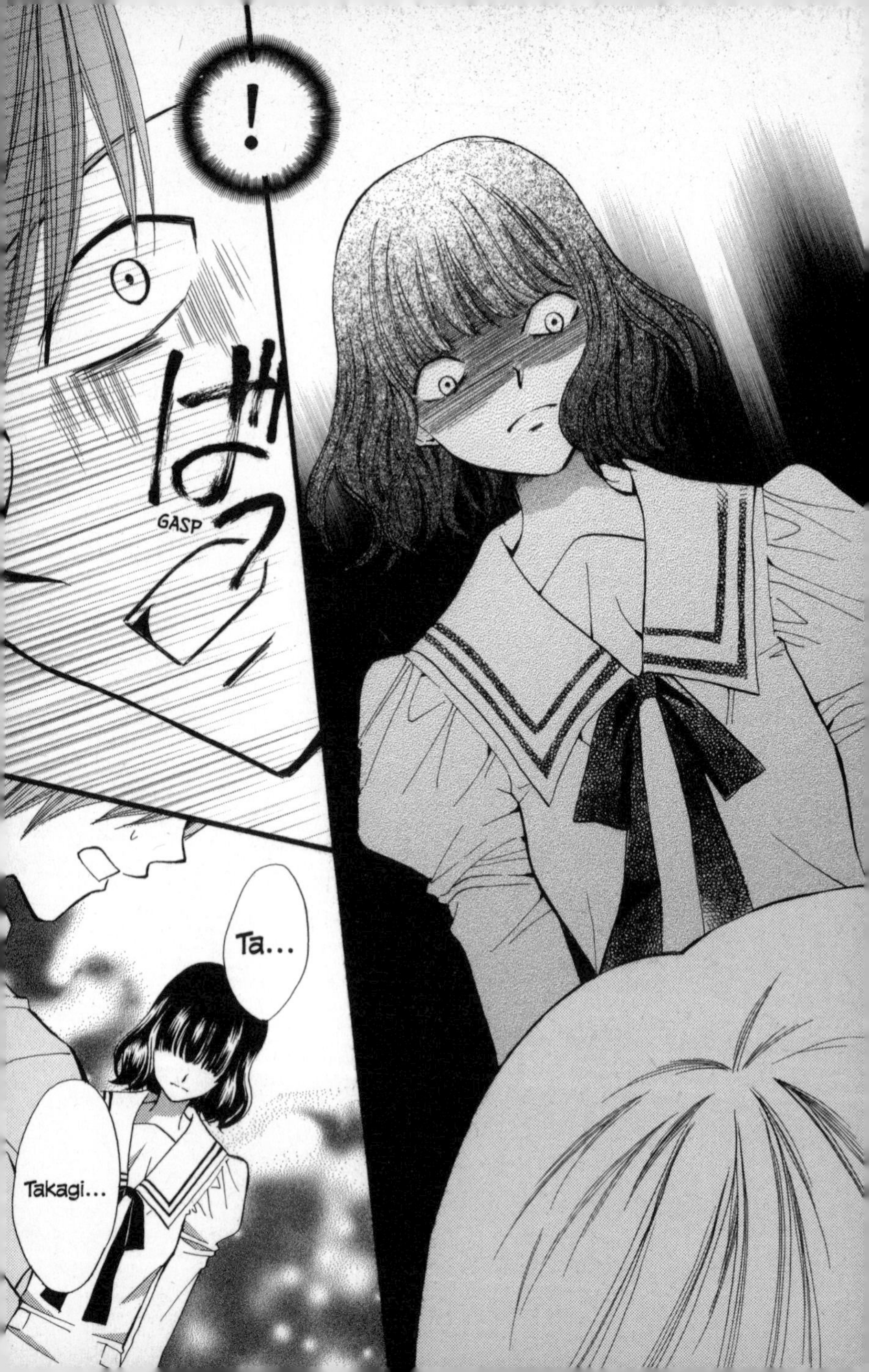
!
GASP
Ta...
Takagi...

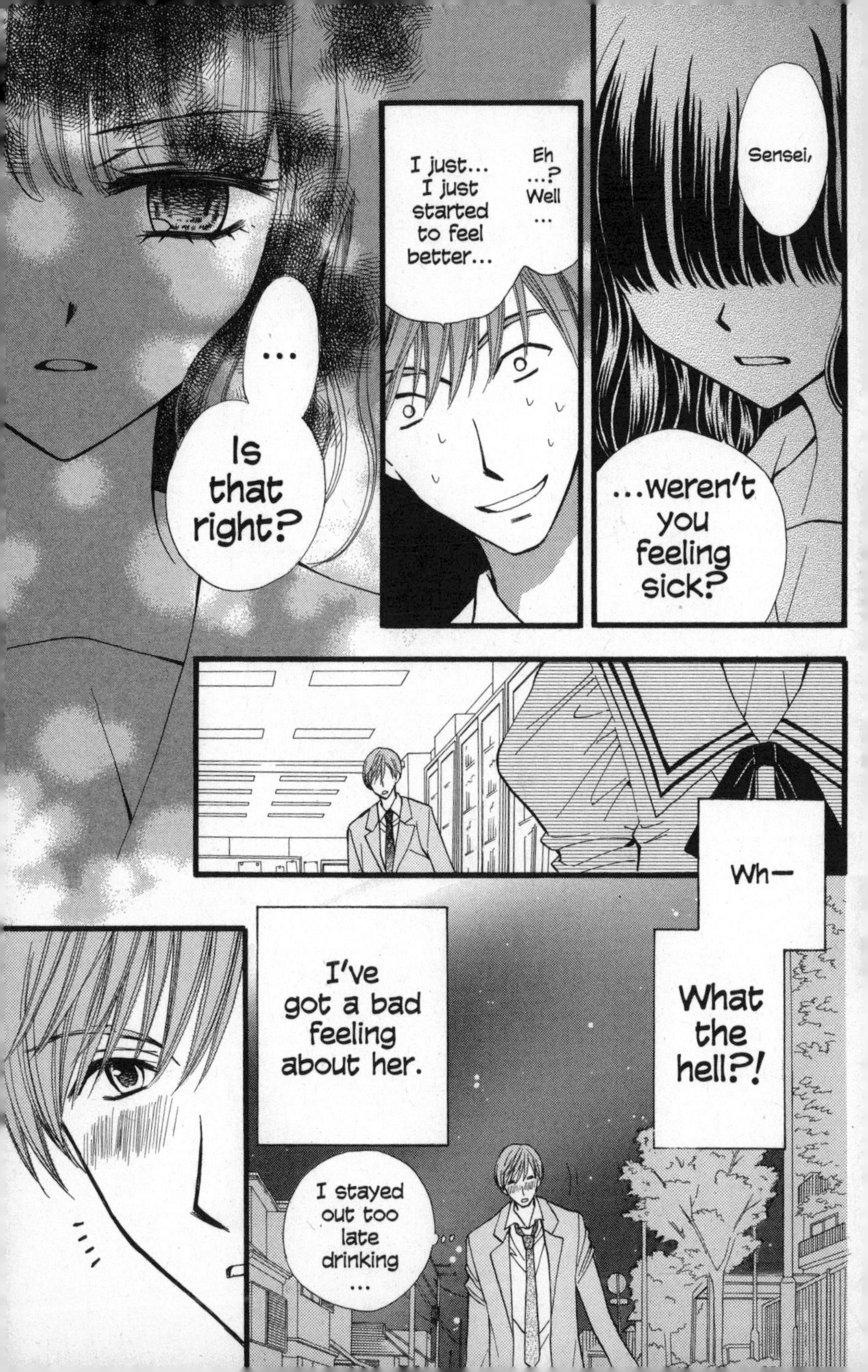
Sensei,
...weren't you feeling sick?
Eh ...? Well ...
I just... I just started to feel better...
...
Is that right?
Wh—
What the hell?!
I've got a bad feeling about her.
I stayed out too late drinking ...

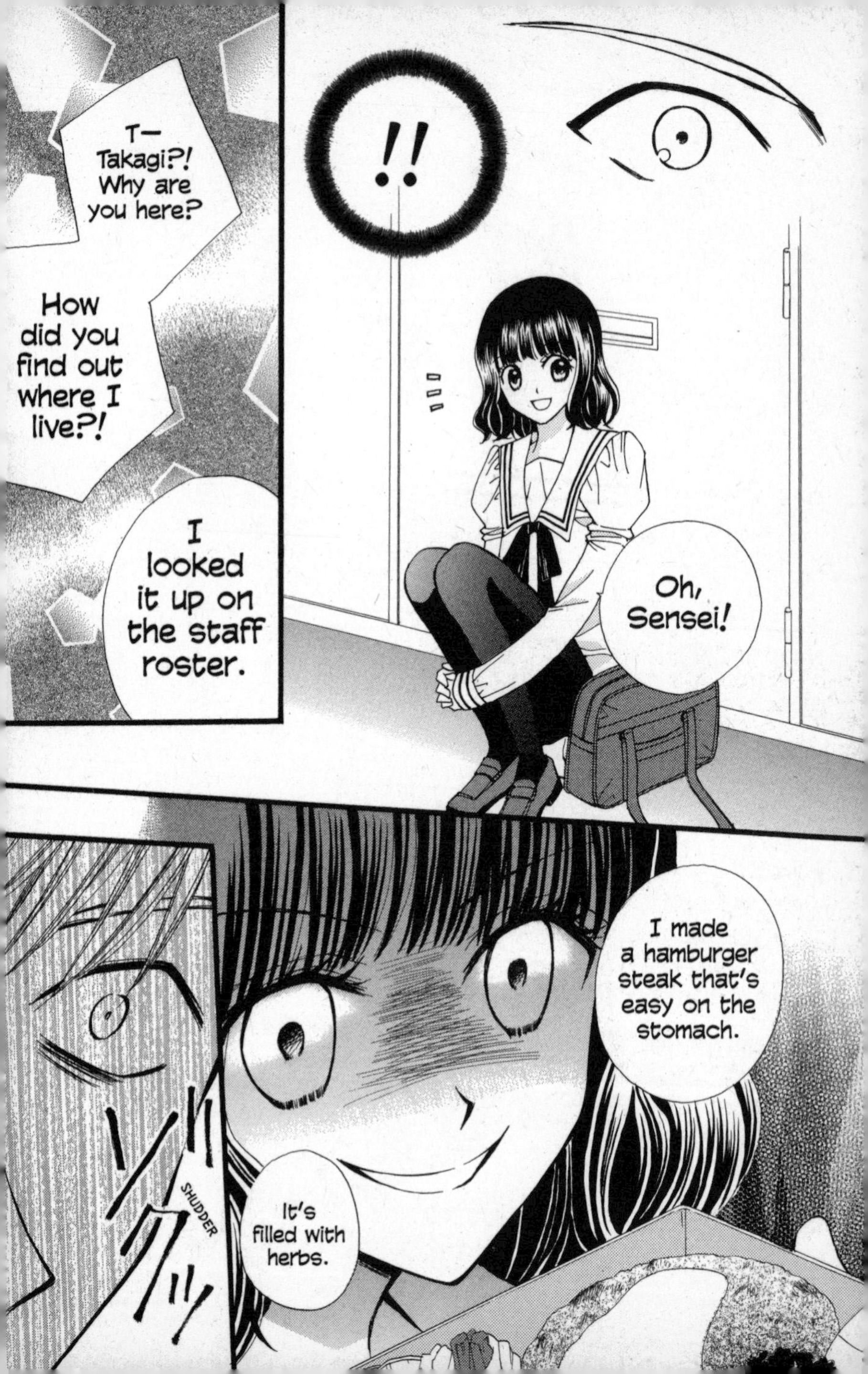
!!
Oh, Sensei!
T— Takagi?! Why are you here?
How did you find out where I live?!
I looked it up on the staff roster.
I made a hamburger steak that's easy on the stomach.
It's filled with herbs.
SHUDDER

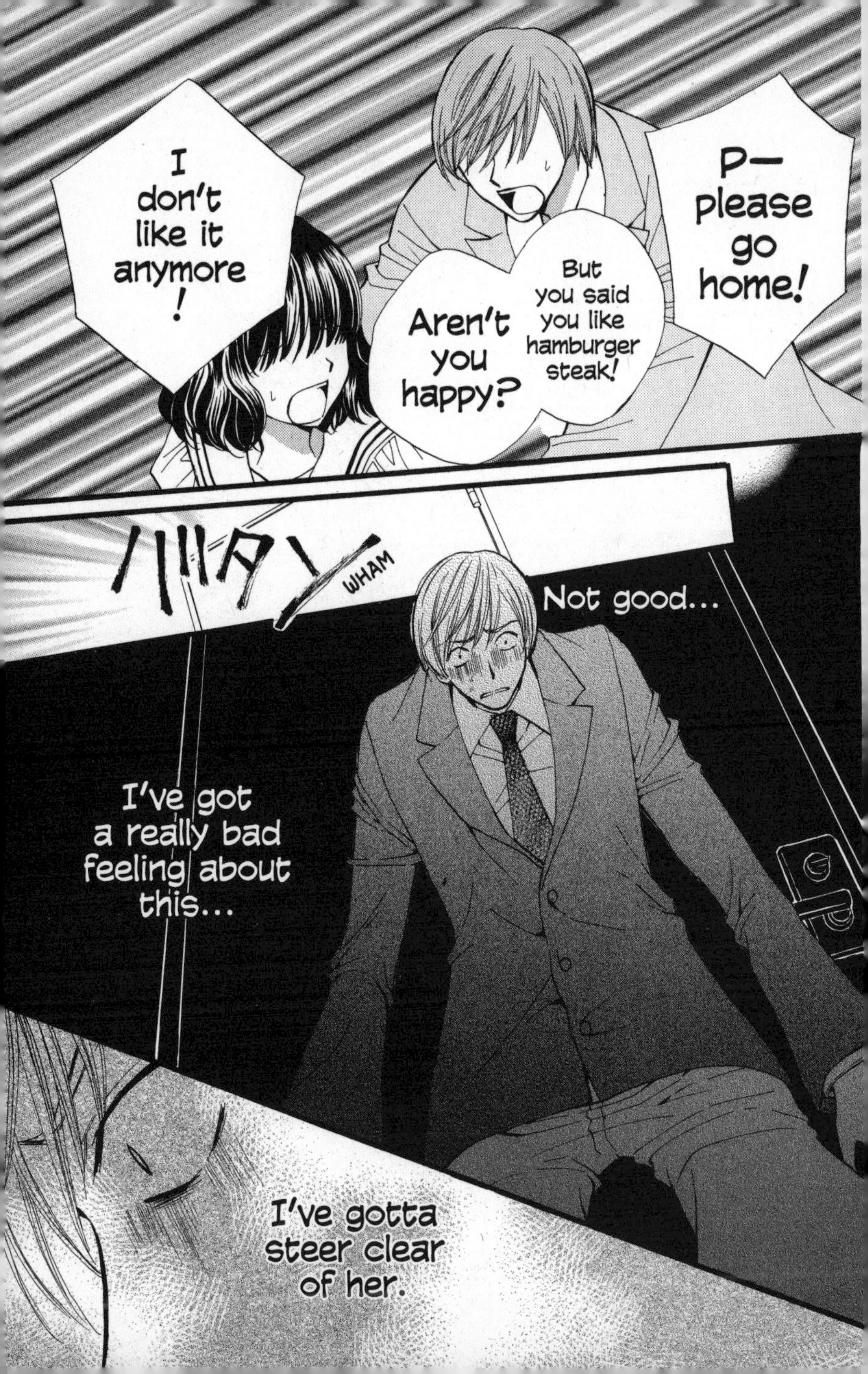
P— please go home!
But you said you like hamburger steak!
Aren't you happy?
I don't like it anymore!
WHAM
Not good...
I've got a really bad feeling about this...
I've gotta steer clear of her.

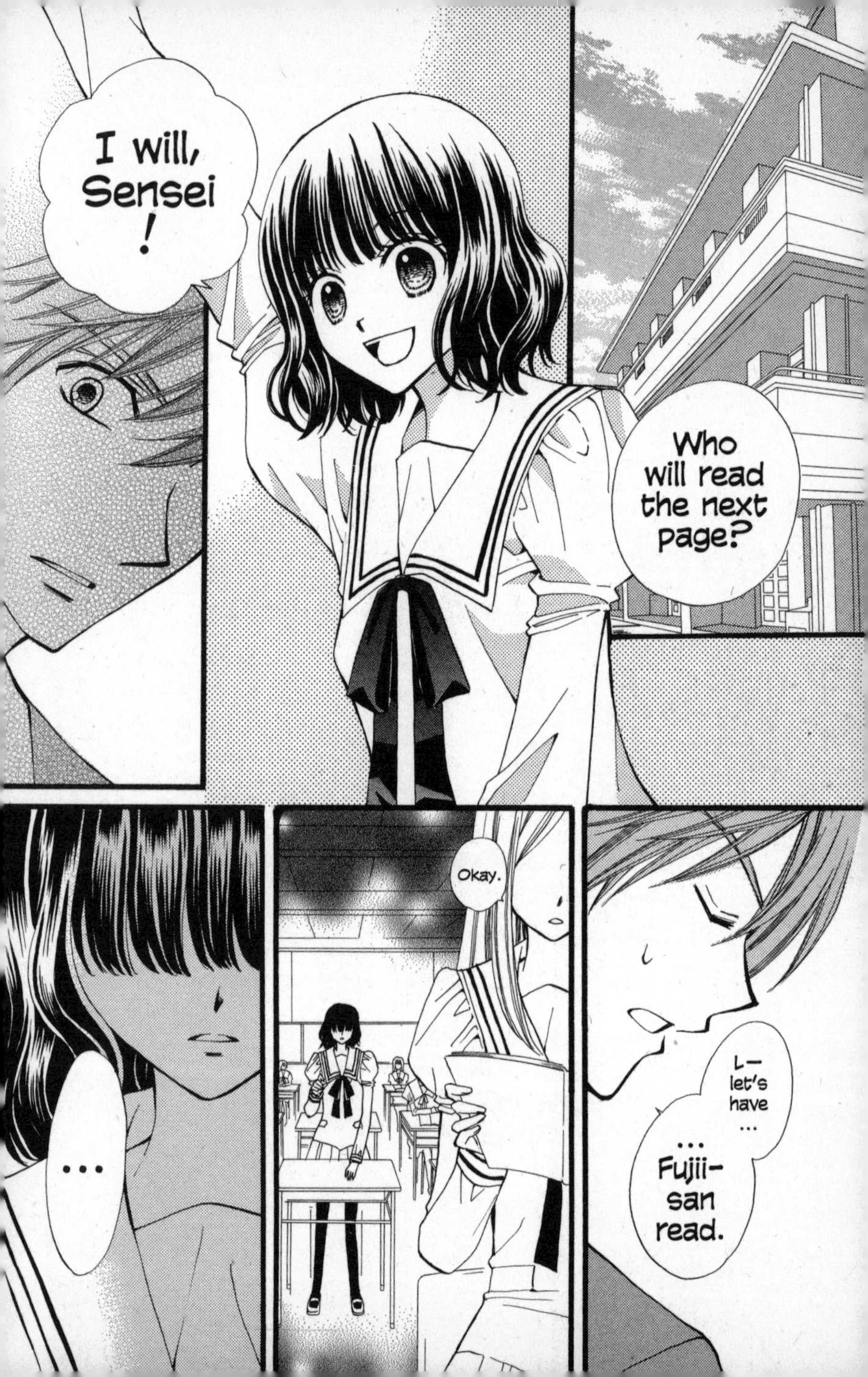
Who will read the next page?
I will, Sensei!
L— let's have … … Fujii-san read.
Okay.
…

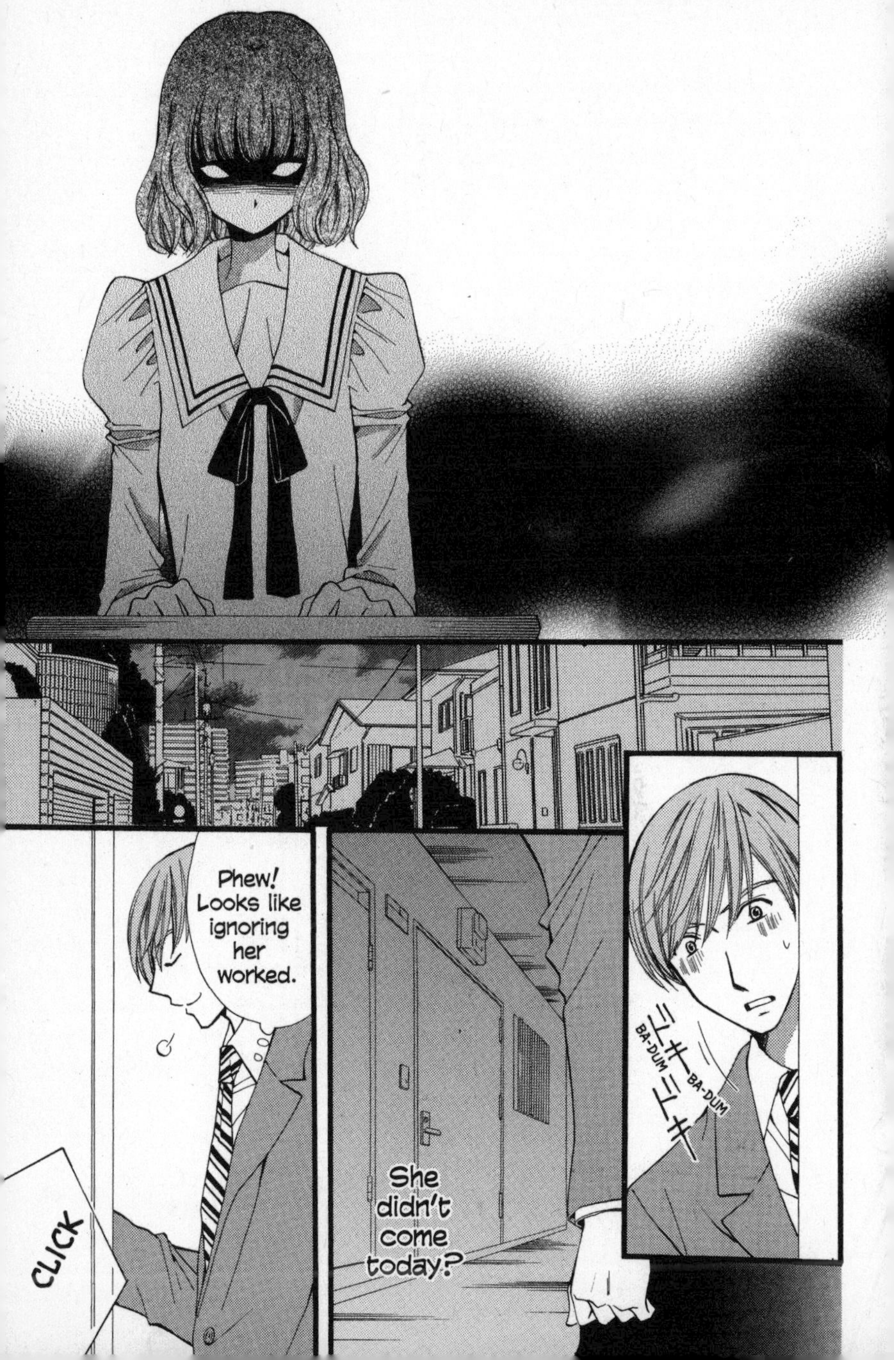
ドキドキ
BA-DUM BA-DUM
She didn't come today?
Phew! Looks like ignoring her worked.
CLICK

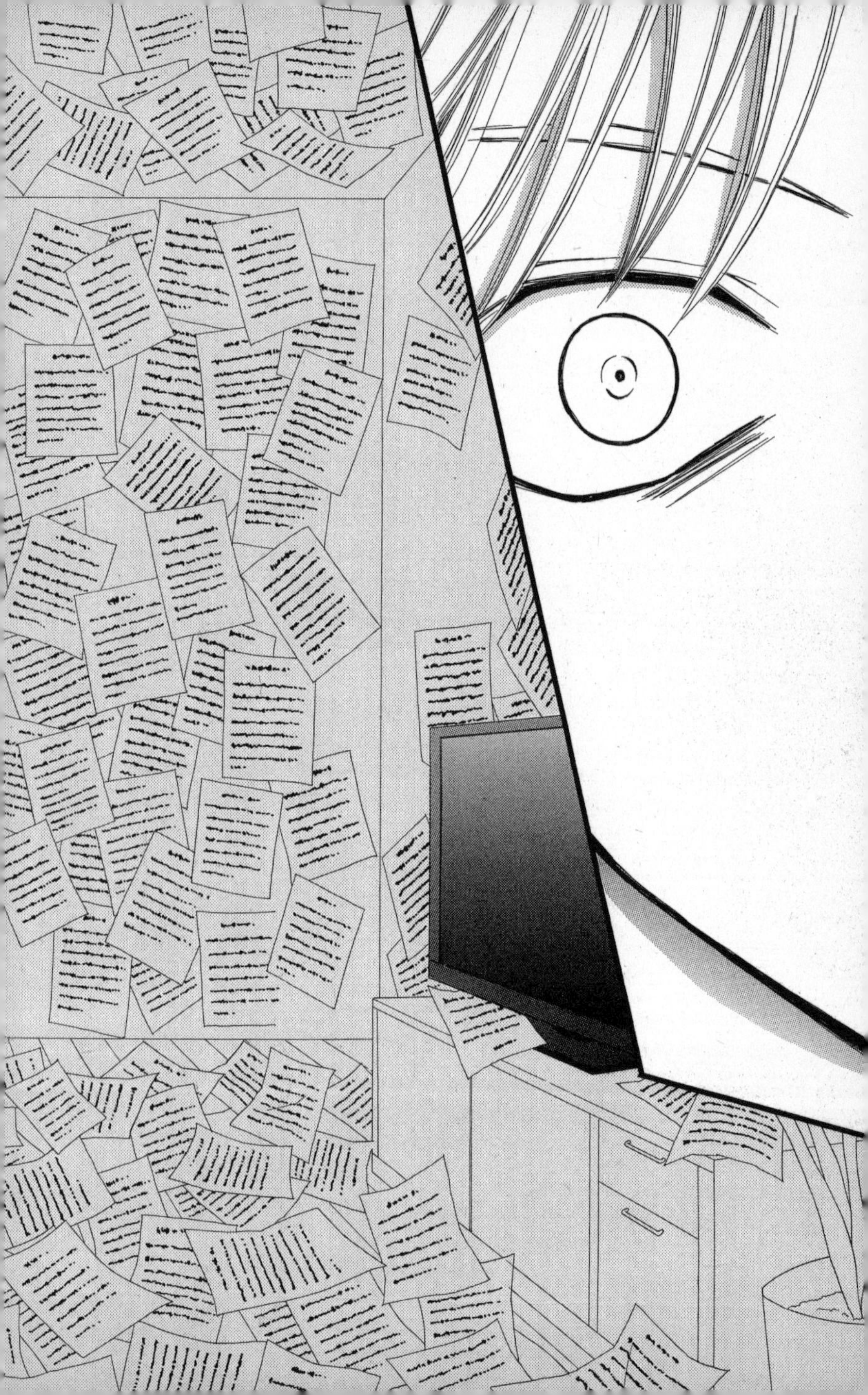

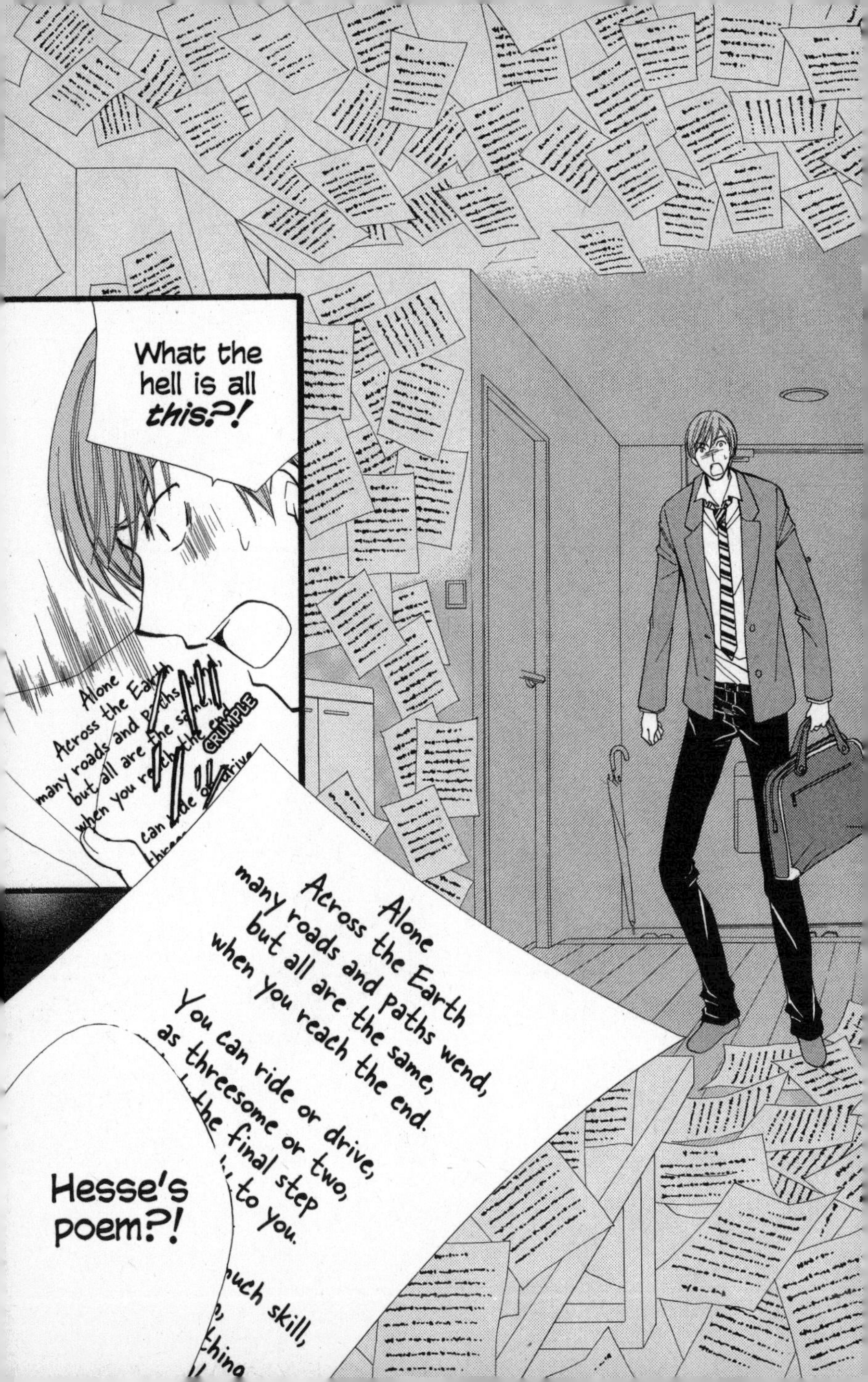

What the hell is all *this?!*
CRUMPLE
Alone
Across the Earth
many roads and paths wend,
but all are the same,
when you reach the end.
You can ride or drive,
as threesome or two,
the final step
to you.
Hesse's poem?!

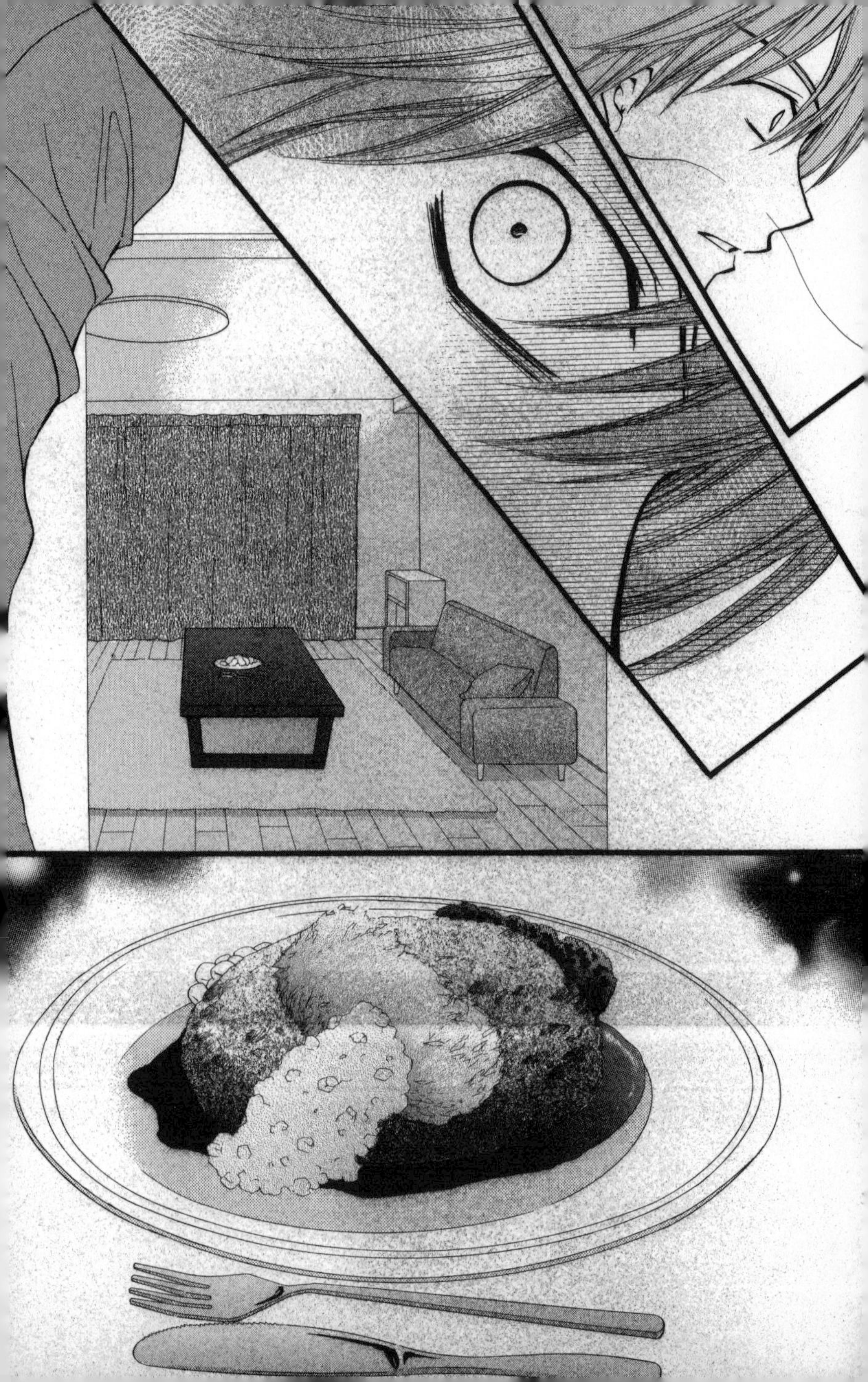

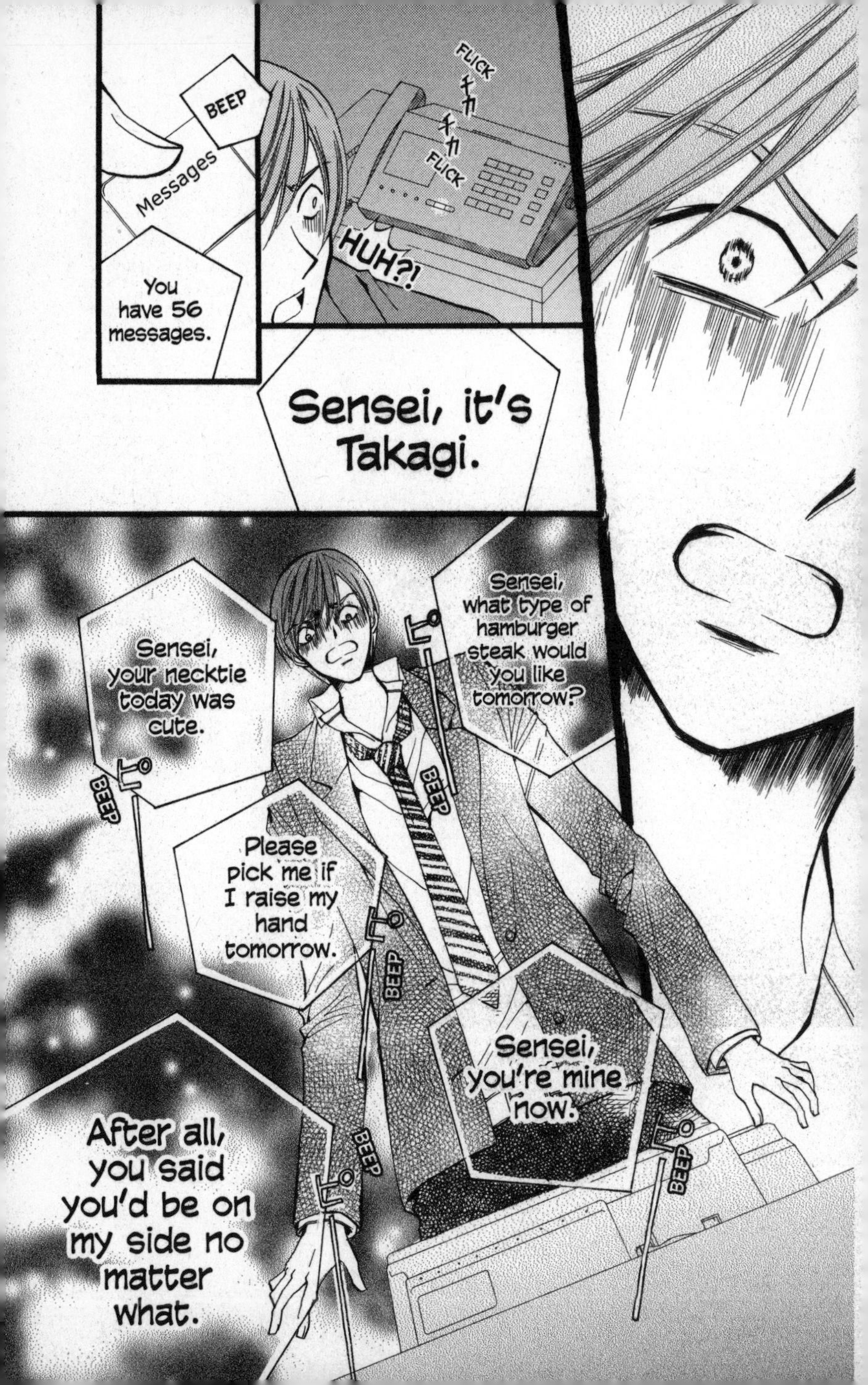
FLICK
チカ
チカ
FLICK
HUH?!
BEEP
Messages
You have 56 messages.
Sensei, it's Takagi.
Sensei, what type of hamburger steak would you like tomorrow?
BEEP
Sensei, your necktie today was cute.
BEEP
Please pick me if I raise my hand tomorrow.
BEEP
Sensei, you're mine now.
BEEP
After all, you said you'd be on my side no matter what.
BEEP

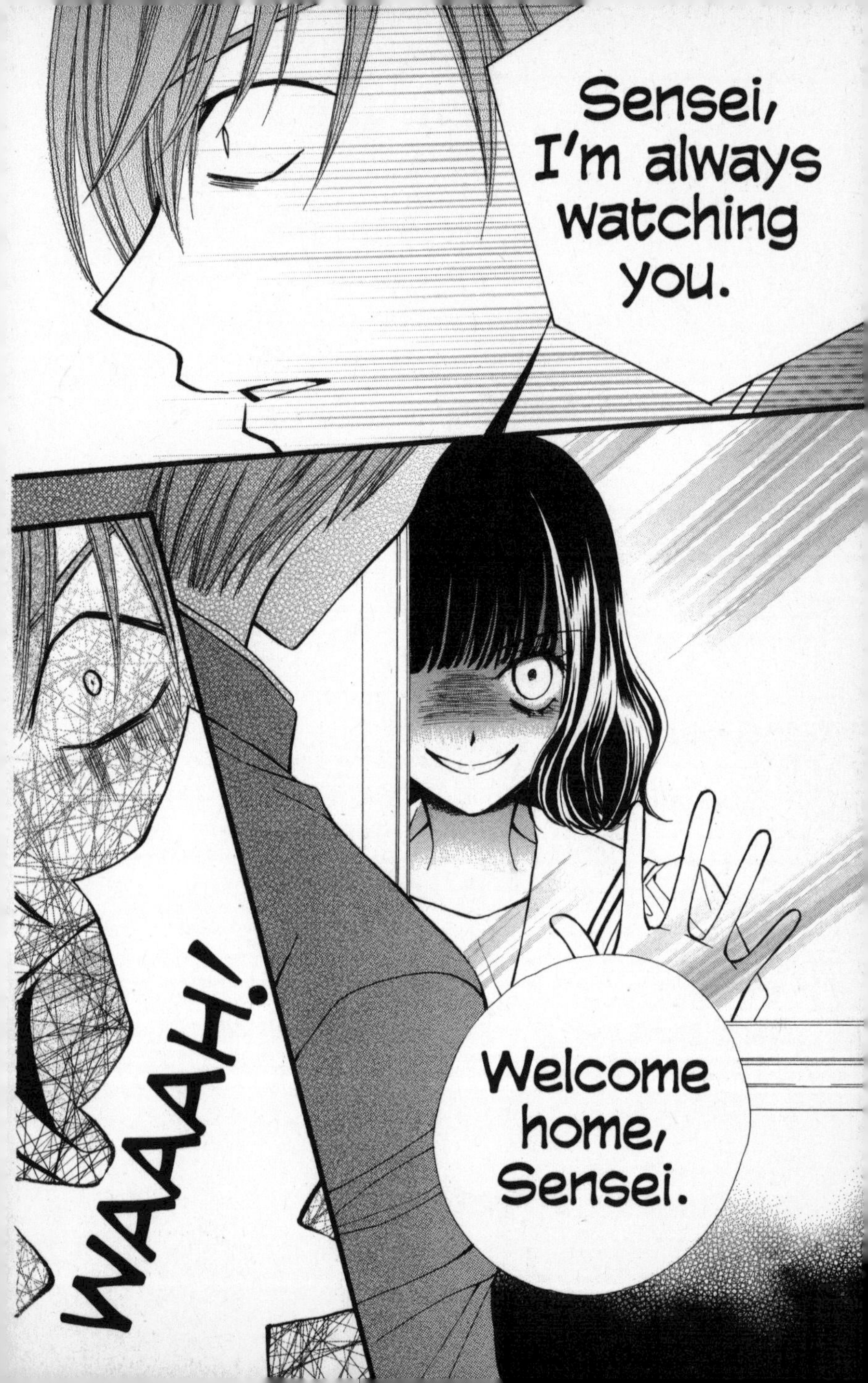
Sensei, I'm always watching you.
Welcome home, Sensei.
WAAAH!

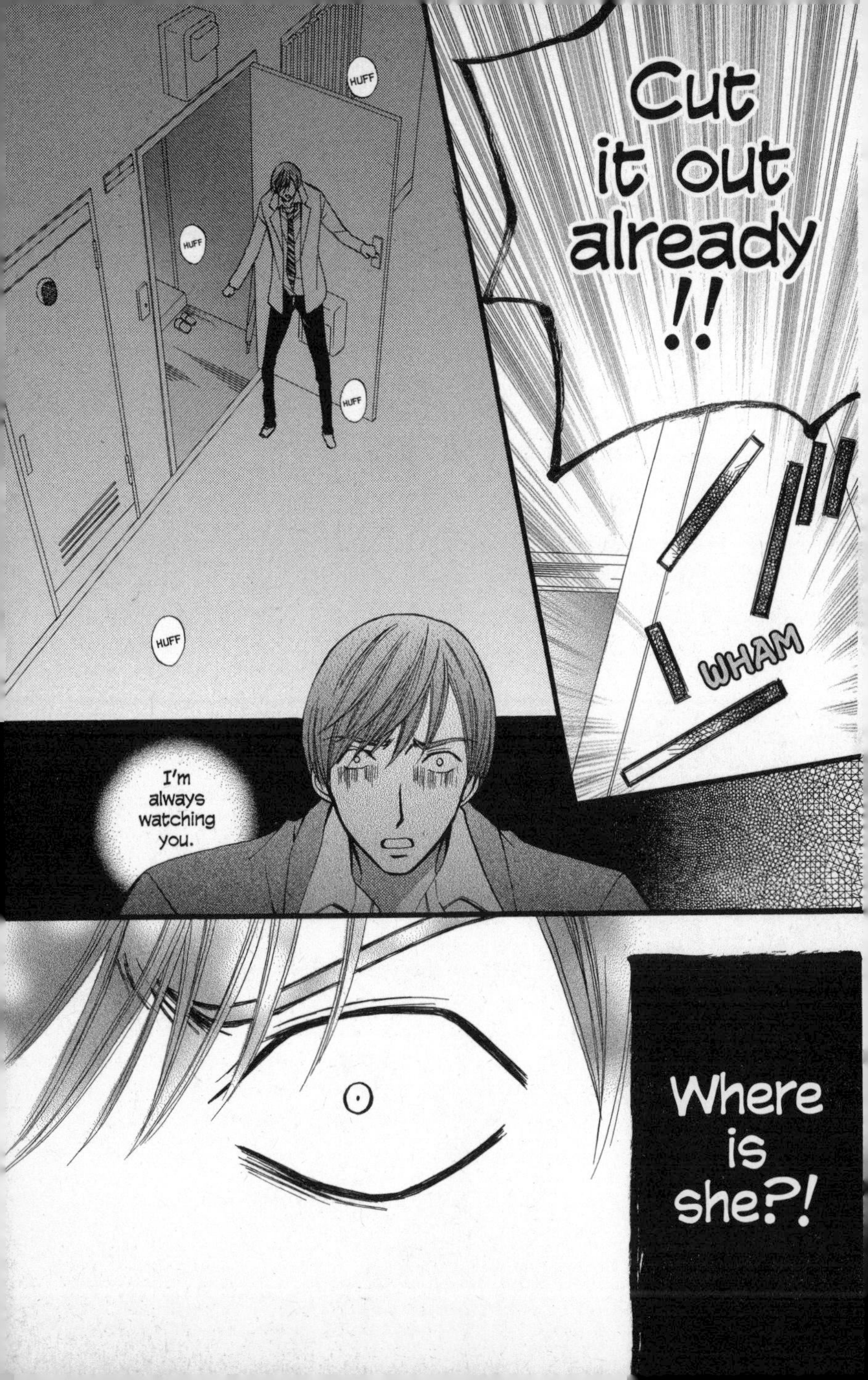
Cut it out already!!
WHAM
HUFF
HUFF
HUFF
HUFF
I'm always watching you.
Where is she?!

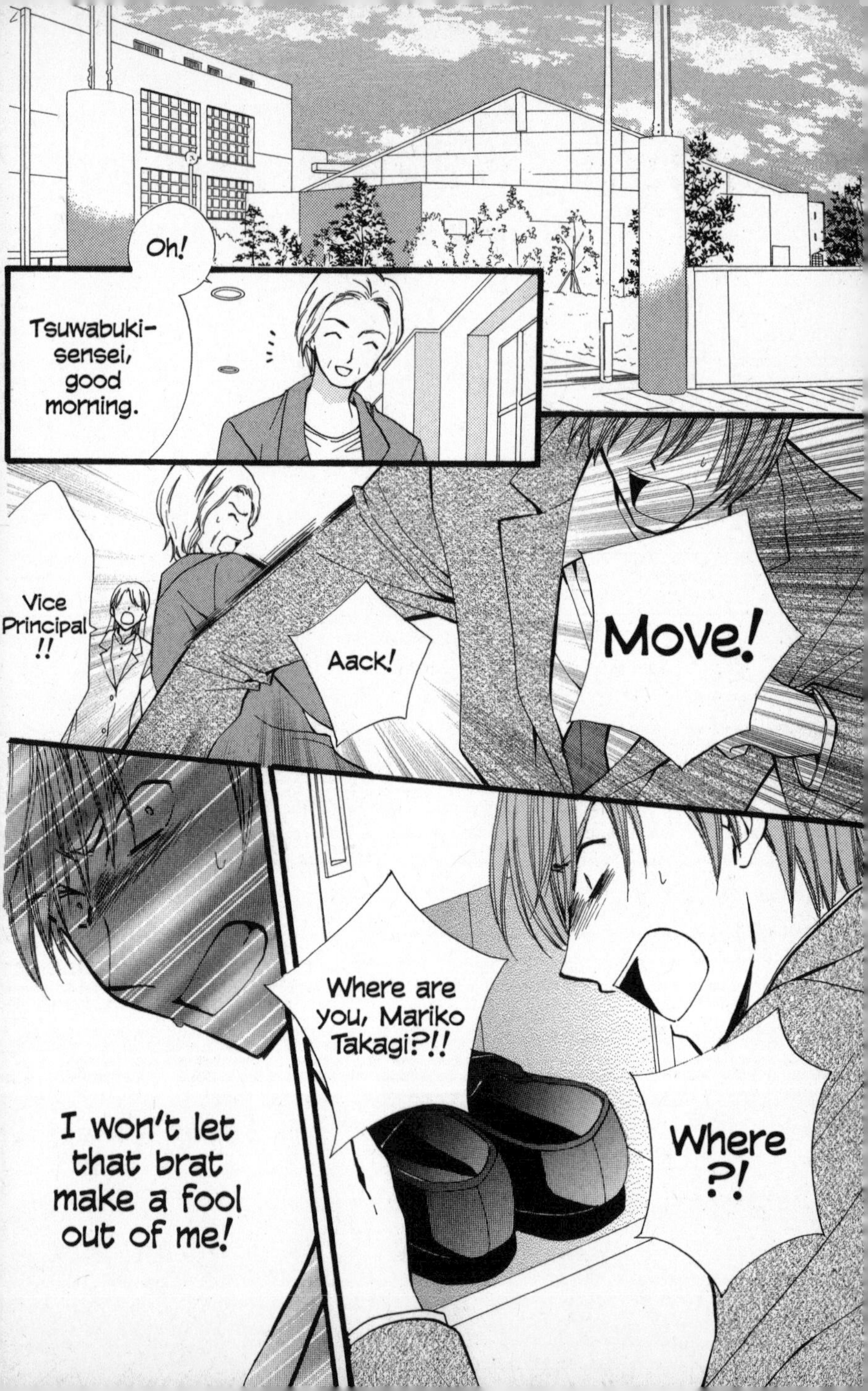
Oh!
Tsuwabuki-sensei, good morning.
Move!
Aack!
Vice Principal!!
Where are you, Mariko Takagi?!!
Where?!
I won't let that brat make a fool out of me!

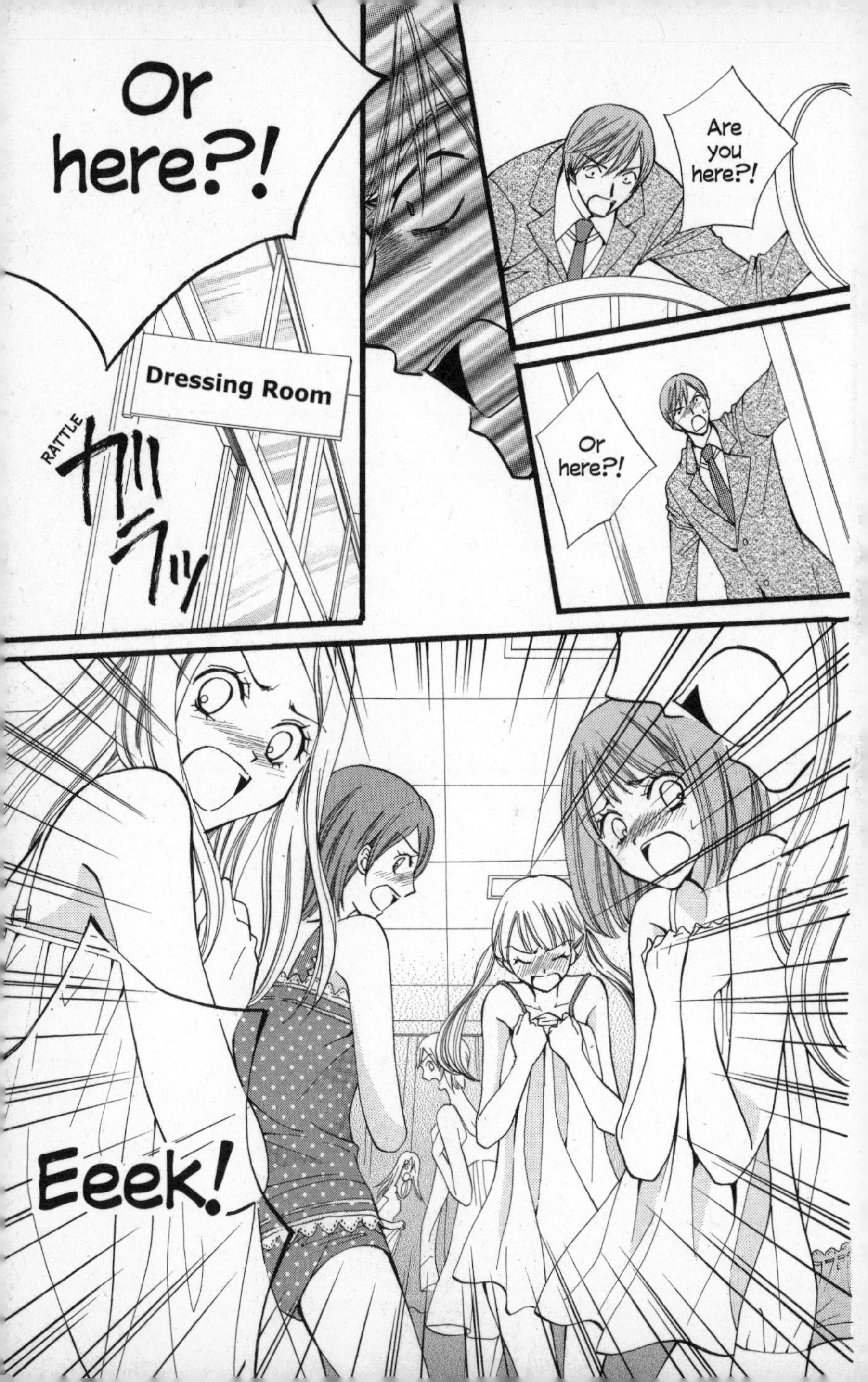

Are you here?!
Or here?!
Or here?!
Dressing Room
RATTLE
ガラッ
Eeek!

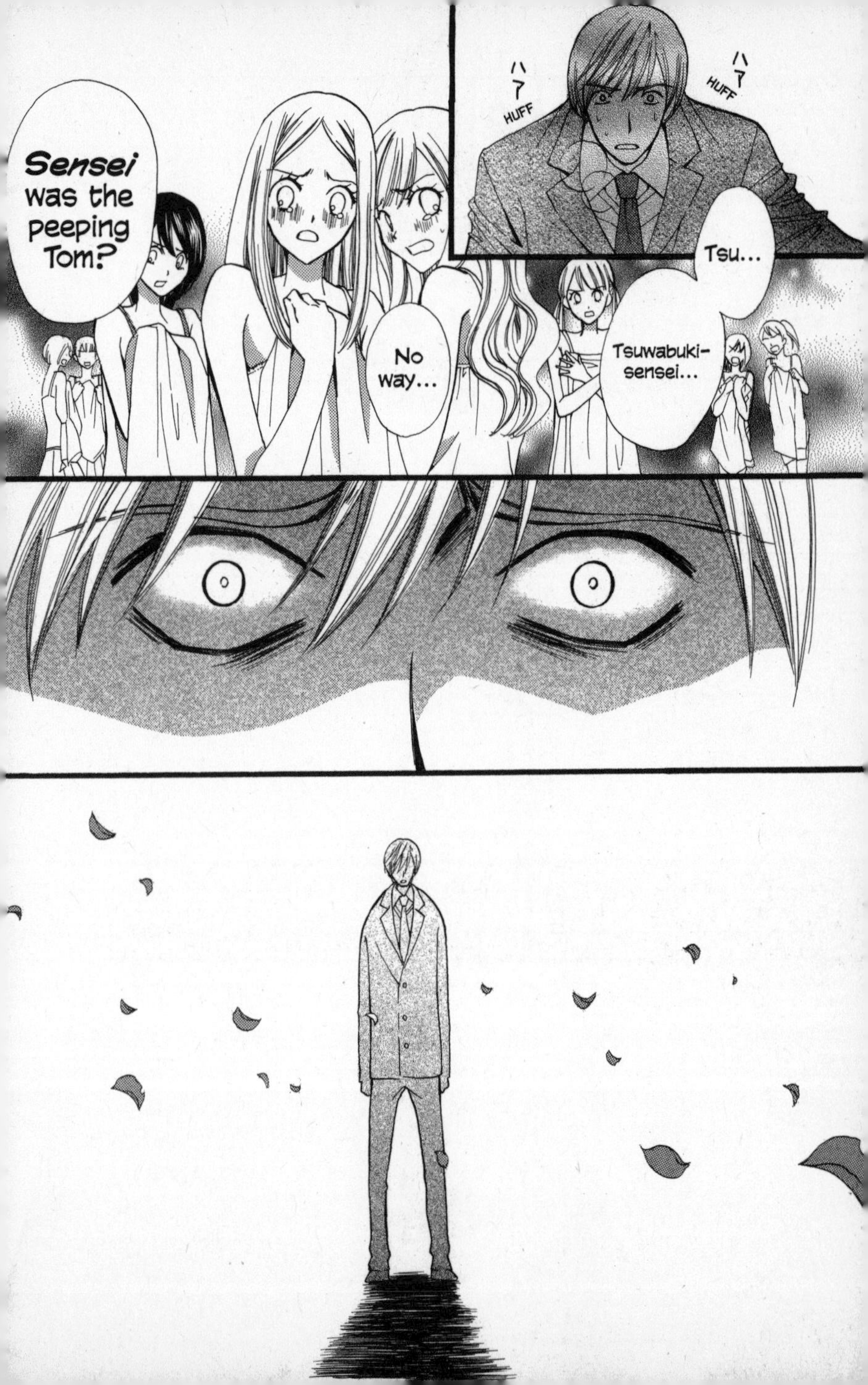
ハア
HUFF
ハア
HUFF
Tsu...
Tsuwabuki-sensei...
No way...
Sensei was the peeping Tom?

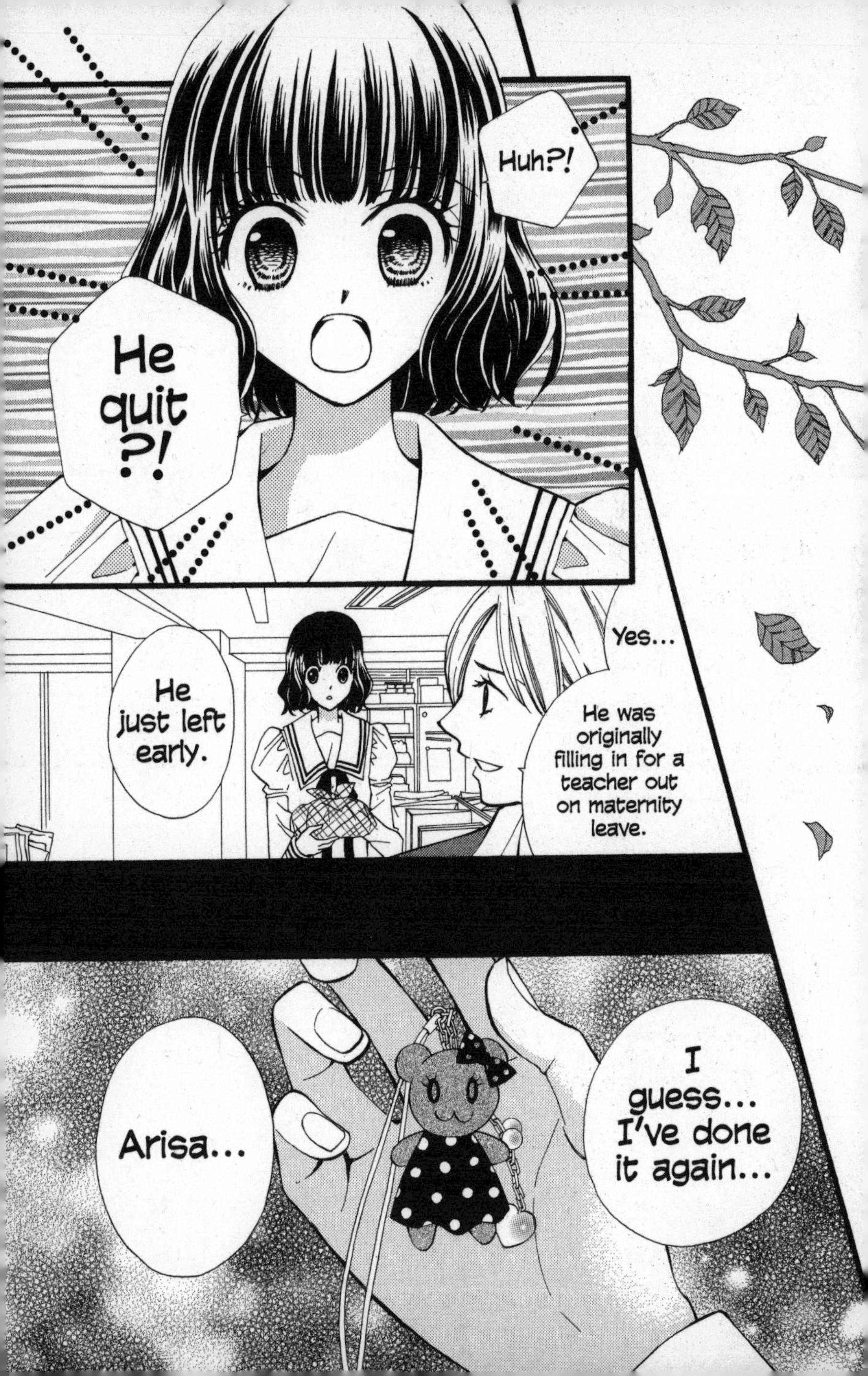
Huh?!
He quit?!
Yes...
He was originally filling in for a teacher out on maternity leave.
He just left early.
I guess... I've done it again...
Arisa...

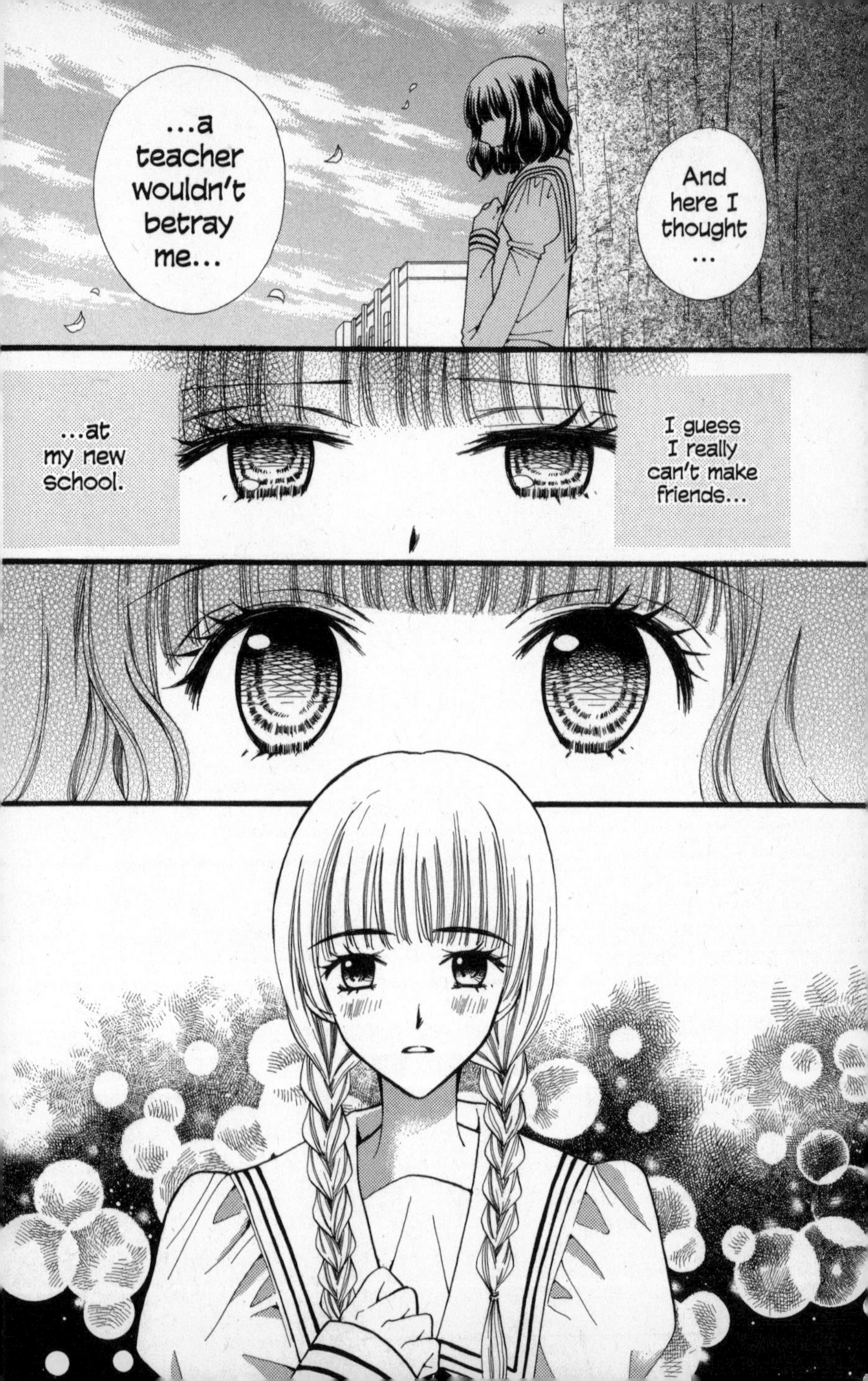
And here I thought ...
...a teacher wouldn't betray me...
I guess I really can't make friends...
...at my new school.

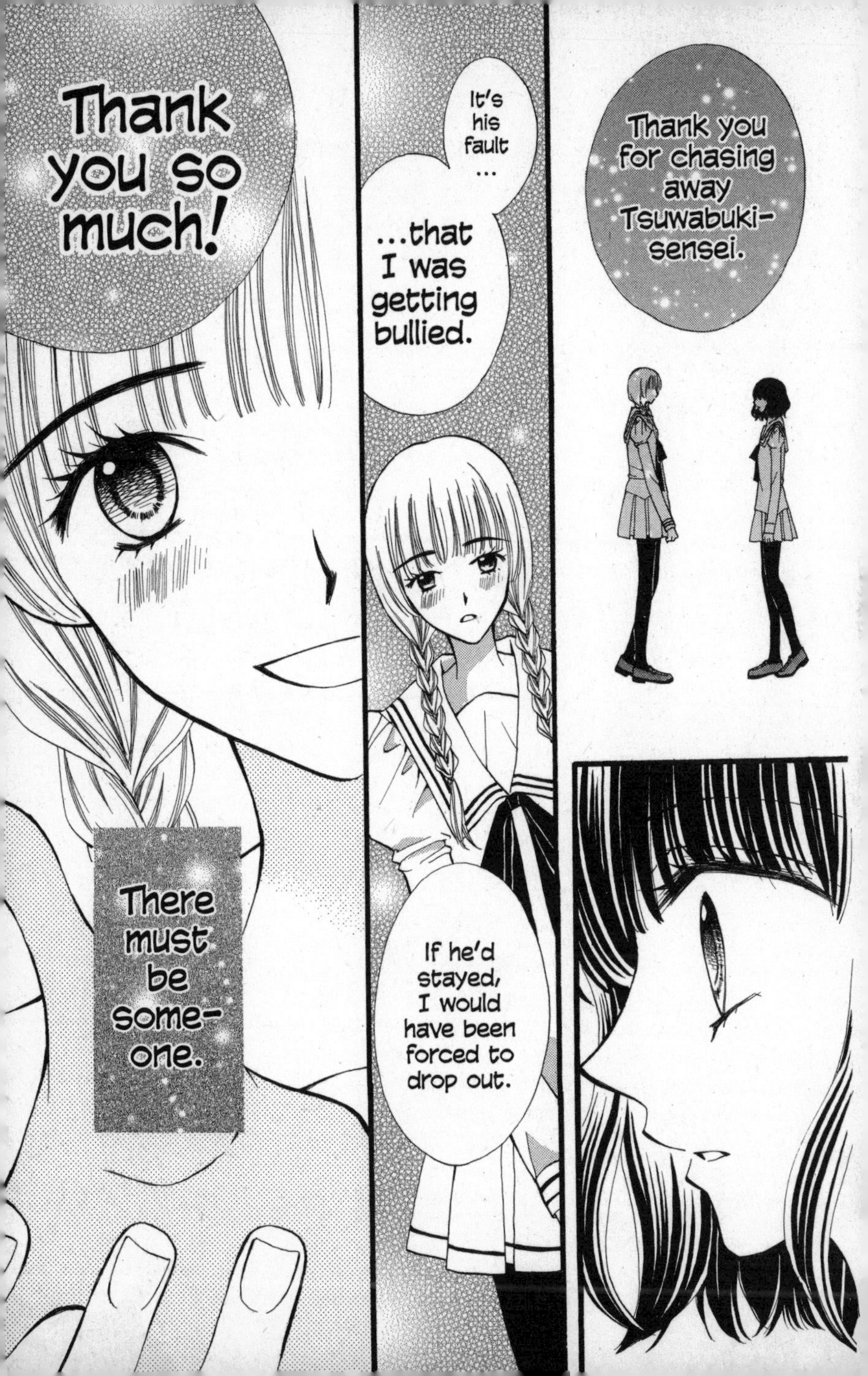
Thank you for chasing away Tsuwabuki-sensei.
It's his fault...
...that I was getting bullied.
If he'd stayed, I would have been forced to drop out.
Thank you so much!
There must be some-one.

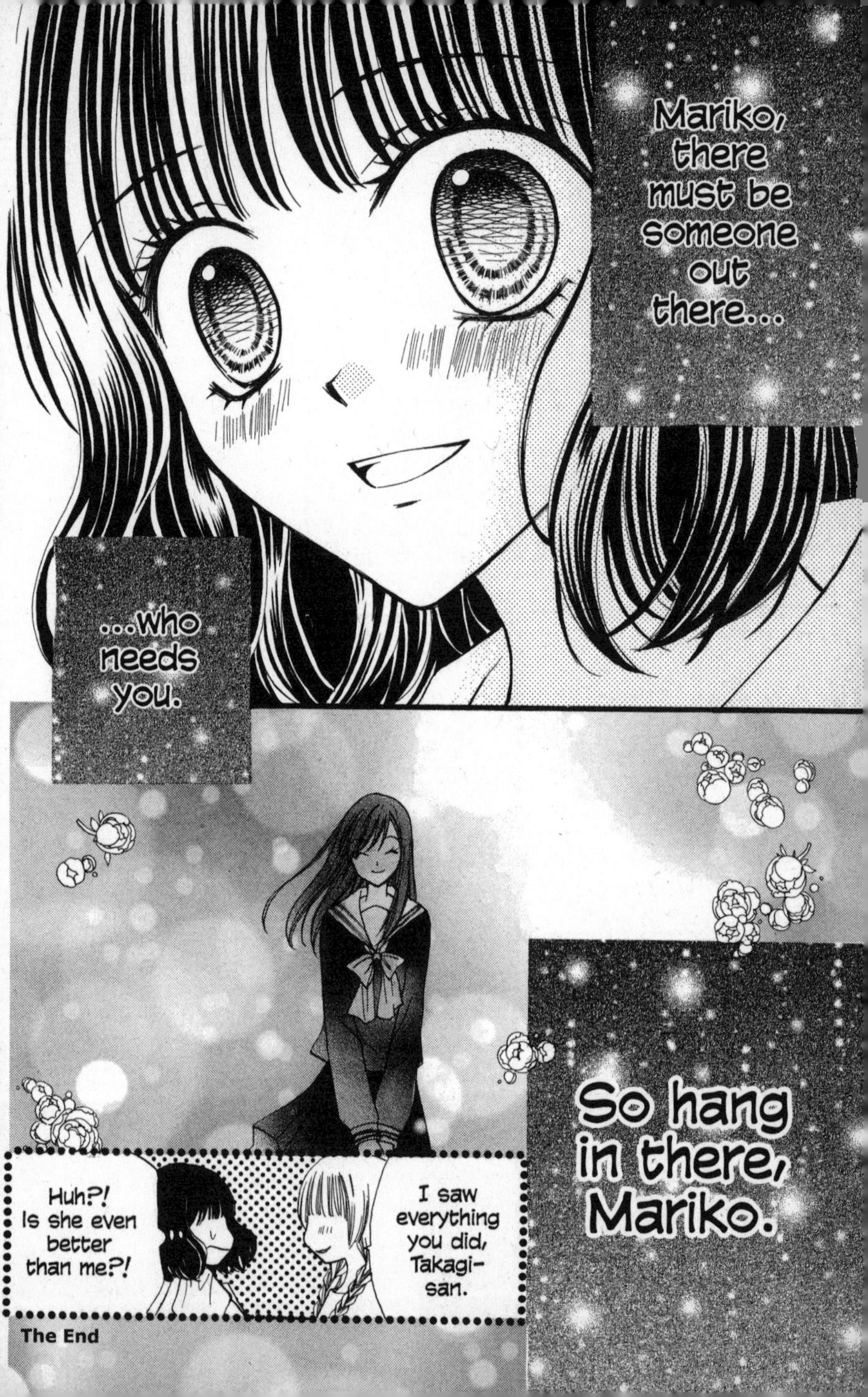
Mariko, there must be someone out there...
...who needs you.
So hang in there, Mariko.
I saw everything you did, Takagi-san.
Huh?! Is she even better than me?!
The End

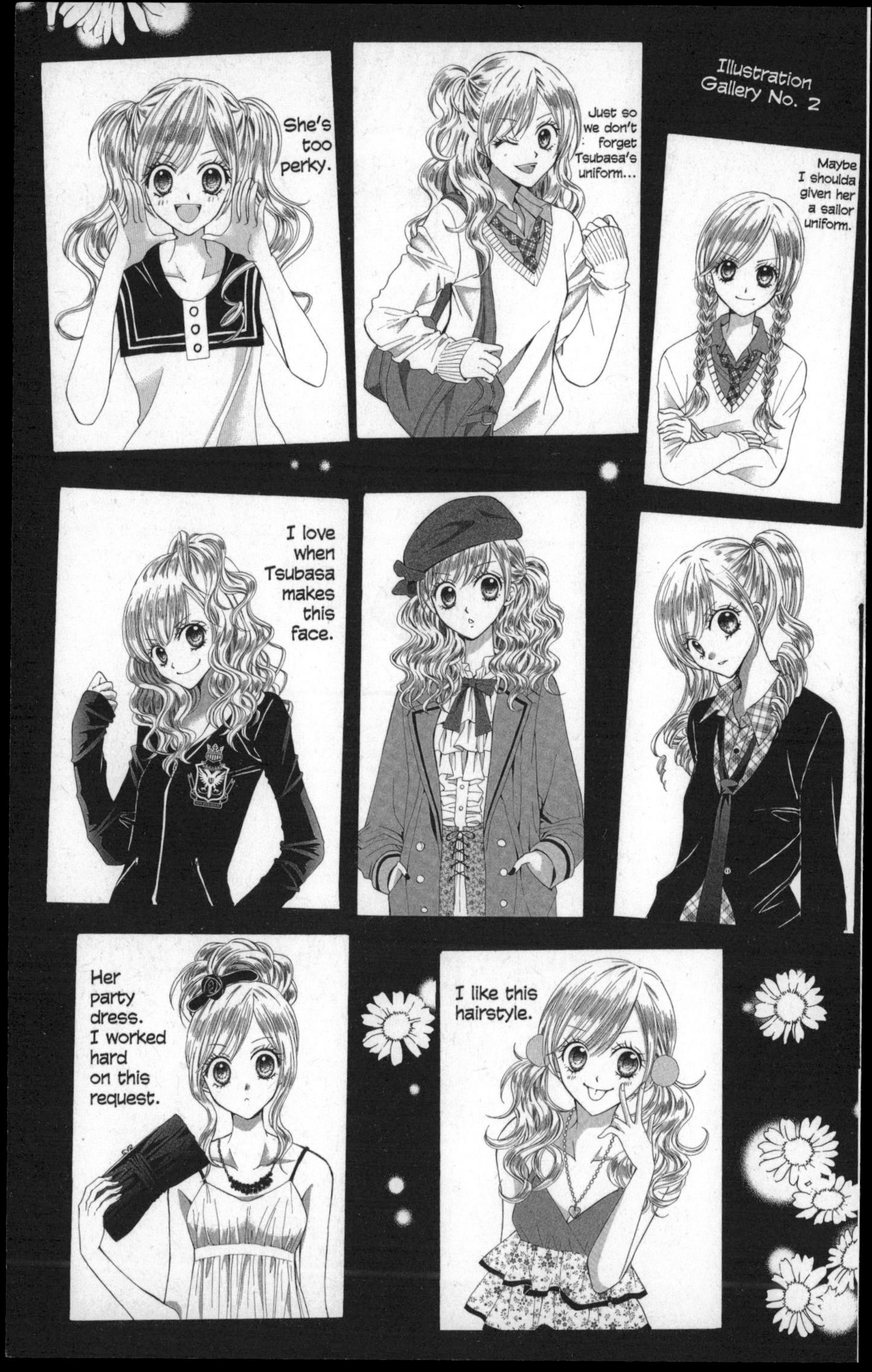
Illustration Gallery No. 2
Maybe I shoulda given her a sailor uniform.
Just so we don't forget Tsubasa's uniform...
She's too perky.
I love when Tsubasa makes this face.
I like this hairstyle.
Her party dress. I worked hard on this request.

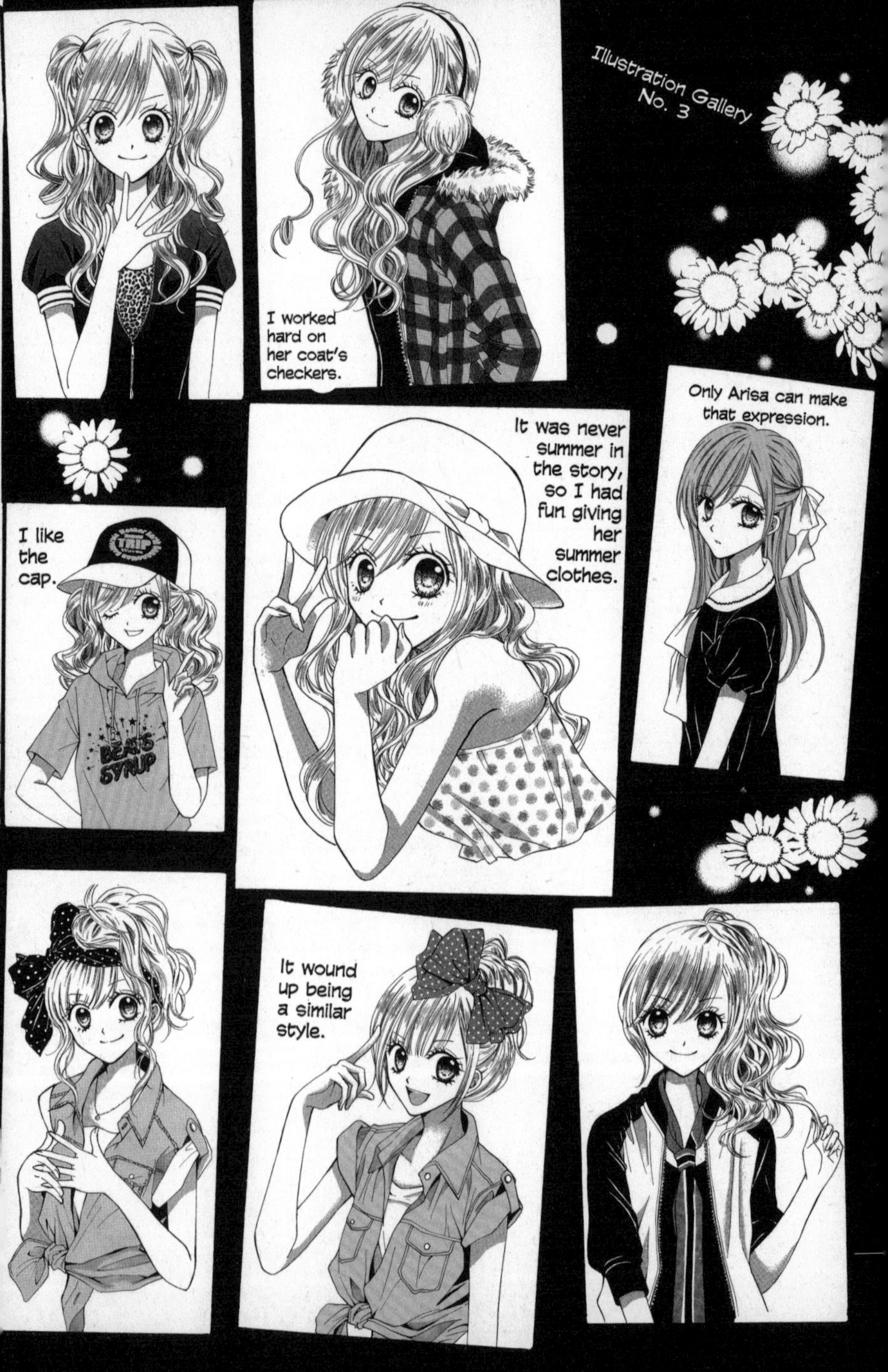
Illustration Gallery No. 3
I worked hard on her coat's checkers.
Only Arisa can make that expression.
It was never summer in the story, so I had fun giving her summer clothes.
I like the cap.
TRIP
BEAT'S SYRUP
It wound up being a similar style.

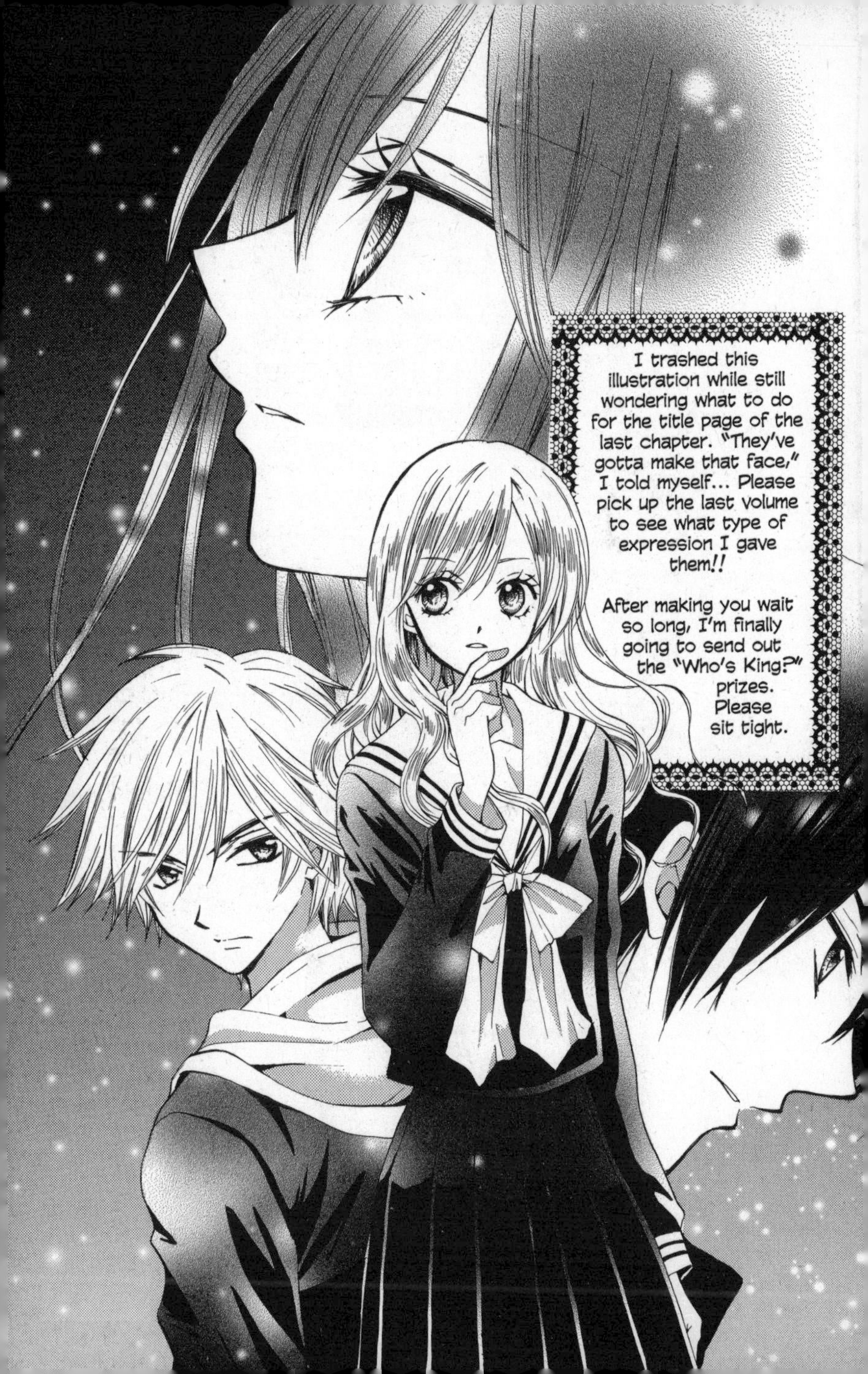
I trashed this illustration while still wondering what to do for the title page of the last chapter. "They've gotta make that face," I told myself... Please pick up the last volume to see what type of expression I gave them!!
After making you wait so long, I'm finally going to send out the "Who's King?" prizes. Please sit tight.

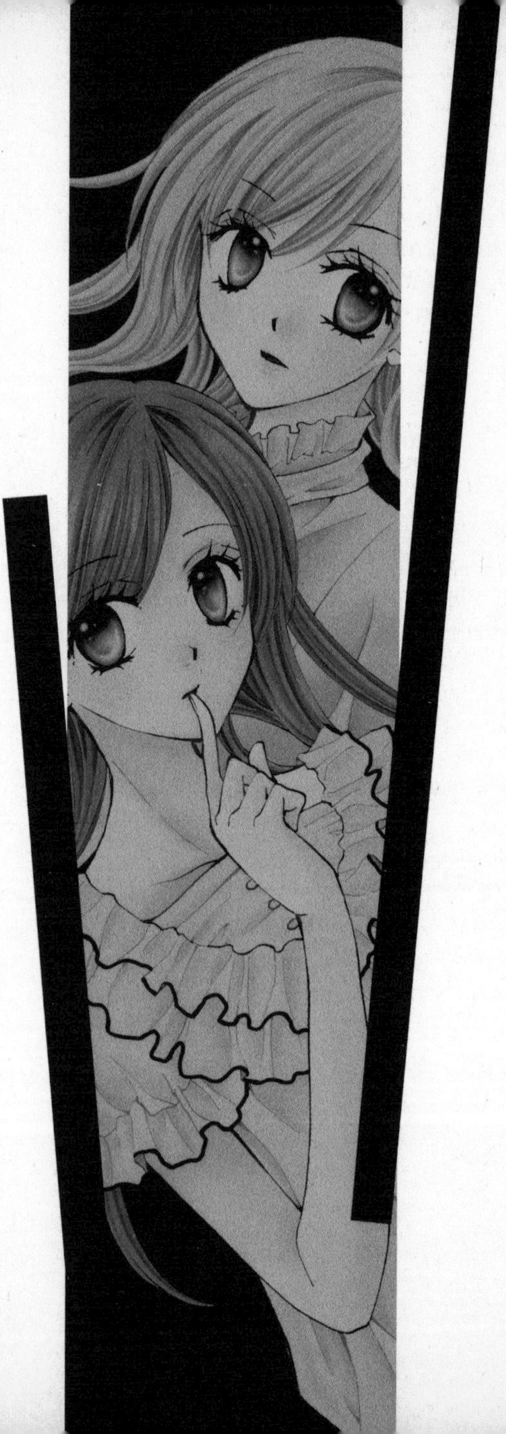

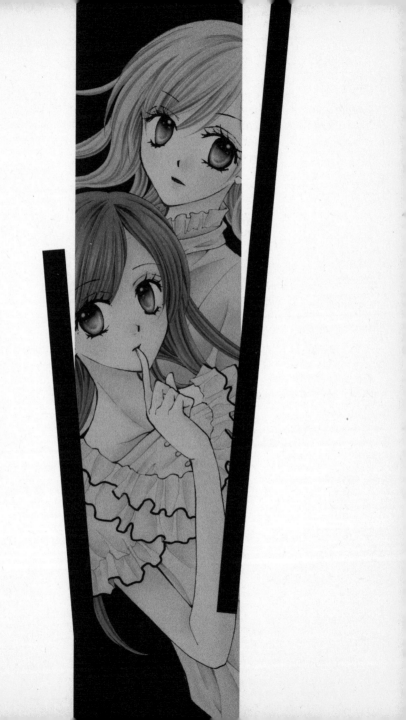

A Kodansha Comics Trade Paperback Original.

Arisa volume 11 copyright © 2012 Natsumi Ando
English translation copyright © 2013 Natsumi Ando

Published in the United States by Kodansha Comics, an imprint of Kodansha USA Publishing, LLC, New York.

Publication rights for this English edition arranged through Kodansha Ltd., Tokyo.

First published in Japan in 2012 by Kodansha Ltd., Tokyo.

ISBN 978-1-61262-252-1

Printed in the United States of America.

www.kodanshacomics.com

9 8 7 6 5 4 3 2 1

Translation: Jackie McClure
Lettering: April Brown
Editing: Ben Applegate

TOMARE!

[STOP!]

You're going the wrong way!

Manga is a completely different
type of reading experience.

To start at the *beginning,*
go to the *end*!

That's right! Authentic manga is read the traditional Japanese way—from right to left. Exactly the *opposite* of how American books are read. It's easy to follow: Just go to the other end of the book, and read each page—and each panel—from the right side to the left side, starting at the top right. Now you're experiencing manga as it was meant to be!